Resolving Environmental Disputes

To Monica
whose questions I value and whose love I cherish

Resolving Environmental Disputes

From Conflict to Consensus

Roger Sidaway

London • Sterling, VA

Learning Resources
Centre

12822833

First published by Earthscan in the UK and USA in 2005

ISBN: 1-84407-013-1 paperback
       1-84407-014-X hardback

Typesetting by MapSet Ltd, Gateshead, UK
Printed and bound in the UK by Cromwell Press Ltd, Trowbridge
Cover design by Andrew Corbett

For a full list of publications please contact:

Earthscan
8–12 Camden High Street
London, NW1 0JH, UK
Tel: +44 (0)20 7387 8558
Fax: +44 (0)20 7387 8998
Email: earthinfo@earthscan.co.uk
Web: **www.earthscan.co.uk**

22883 Quicksilver Drive, Sterling, VA 20166-2012, USA

Earthscan is an imprint of James & James (Science Publishers) Ltd and publishes in
association with the International Institute for Environment and Development

A catalogue record for this book is available from the British Library

Library of Congress Cataloging-in-Publication Data applied for

Printed on elemental chlorine-free paper

Contents

PART 1 UNDERSTANDING ENVIRONMENTAL DISPUTES

PART 2 STRATEGIES FOR COOPERATION

PART 3 THE REALITIES OF POWER

PART 4 THE CASE FOR REFORM

List of Figures and Boxes

FIGURES

BOXES

Preface

ORIGINS AND EVOLUTION OF IDEAS

The principal texts on environmental mediation have been written largely for an American audience and tend to focus on techniques and the advocacy of mediation. Few of the recent texts present detailed case studies and span both theory and practice, nor do they assess the relationship between public participation and mediation. The structure of this book is based on a series of case studies in Britain, the USA and the Netherlands, of which I have a detailed knowledge, interspersed with complementary explanatory and interpretative chapters on theory and practice. It uses examples from contemporary themes in resource management and environmental protection: access to the countryside for recreation, sustainable forestry, pollution and risks to health, and coastal zone management.

The starting point for considering the factors which contribute to conflict and cooperation was a series of empirical observations made in an earlier study, namely that conflicts seemed more likely to arise: when one set of fervently held beliefs clashed with another; from the uncertainty of not fully understanding the underlying issues; from an unwillingness to respond to change; and from poor communication between those involved (Sidaway, 1988). This analysis has been refined over the years but nevertheless is still essentially sound. It epitomizes my approach of the sceptical researcher, searching for general lessons from the particular, and my academic bent for wanting to ground theory in an empirical base, but realizing how difficult both tasks can be.

As an occasional practitioner, I also have sympathy for the arguments put forward by Birkhoff (2002) that mediation practitioners (like the medical and legal professions) learn not from theory but from intuition, skill and experience. She suggests that mediators are 'skilful improvisers' who firstly try trusted recipes and known variations. Being only too well aware of intrinsic difficulties of formal evaluation, I also understand Barach Bush's (1995) assessment that the ideological justifications for using alternative dispute resolution (and public participation) are stronger than those based on science. Nevertheless, my contention is that advancement will come from combining the pragmatic and theoretic approaches, although I know to my cost that this will often not satisfy the most fastidious academic minds.

The alternative perspectives that have been taken by social scientists were analysed by Friedmann (1987) in his investigation of social theories of planning in the public domain. My approach has been eclectic, drawing on several theoretical standpoints to gain insights at different stages of the argument, rather than advocate any particular model. Thus Chapter 3 initially utilizes theories of *social action* in an analysis of the social functions of conflict leading to a deeper understanding of environmental conflicts and their role in the social system. However, this chapter is novel in that it also draws on concepts from the managerial approach of *policy analysis*. This latter approach to problem solving and conflict resolution provides the basis for Chapters 4 and 5 on consensus building and its application in mediation. The ideals of public participation in Chapter 7 are closer to theories of *social learning*, which aim for change 'within the system' by the empowerment of individuals and communities. Finally, the analysis of power and the political process in Chapters 9 and 10 draws on theories of *social mobilization* which assume that changes in political and social systems stem from political struggle at the macro level.

Thus, as the reader's understanding of conflicts is built up, theory is used to unravel and explain apparent contradictions and significant events. The principal aims of this analysis are to identify the preconditions for conflict resolution, to show how consensus building relates to adversarial methods of decision-making, and to demonstrate the potential of participation and mediation techniques. The final chapters consider consensus building in the world of politics, and the overriding issues of organizational power and partnerships to reflect on opportunities for institutional reform and the improvement of practice.

RELEVANCE OF THE CASE STUDIES

The use of case studies stems from my own preference for writing from direct experience of undertaking qualitative research or as a facilitator. In some cases I have had to rely largely on documentary evidence, but most studies are based on documents and semi-structured interviewing, allowing a degree of triangulation between sources. This has not provided a representative sample of situations, but its main merit has been that most are long-term studies which illustrate the successive episodes of conflict and the time it takes to build trust. These cases have proved far more revealing than I had anticipated. For example, I expected that my analysis of the case studies of participation would hinge on the use of techniques involving local communities. In fact, it revealed more about inter-agency partnerships and the need for decision-makers to gain and maintain the trust of the communities they serve. Similarly, my own involvement in developing access policy in England and Wales led to involvement in a major research study and then mediation. So while the access story stemmed from personal interests, delving into its history during the writing of this book revealed much more about an important aspect of English social history and about conflicts over land, its appropriation and ownership, which are universal issues. My own professional experience of the use and conservation of forest resources has been limited to the Northern hemisphere. However, my more recent involvement in working with many students from around the world suggests that the archetypical conflict between indigenous people and the neo-colonial forest services is amenable to the insights of stakeholder analysis and the analysis of power. But it would be facile to assume that Western mechanisms for resolution are as easily transferable as this form of analysis. The other obvious limitation of consensus-based approaches is in dealing with environmental conflicts on the global scale. Political initiatives are hard enough to sustain at this level, let alone interventions to negotiate or mediate. The GM Nation consultation in the UK in 2004 purported to be a national exercise in public participation about genetically modified crops, but proved to be a meaningless exercise when the real decisions were being made by the European Union and the World Trade Organization.

CONCEPTS AND TERMINOLOGY

Environmental disputes[1] are one type of public policy conflict that typically engage many participants with competing interests, so that there is a high level of contention which attracts considerable media attention (Senecah and Sobel, 1998). The definition of environmental disputes used in this book recognizes their politicized nature and distinguishes this level of dispute from inter-personal conflicts between families or within communities. Thus, such disputes are characterized as:

> *an unresolved disagreement between competing interest groups which has reached the public arena, is controversial and may have political consequences: i.e., one interest group is attempting to control the action of another, or its access to a semi-natural resource.* (Based on Sidaway, 1996)

This definition contains most of the features identified in many other definitions of social conflict. What it does not cover is the confusing nature of public policy conflicts, which has been well described by Brown and Marriott (1993, 234):

- *the issues are often complex, many centred ... and involve value judgements;*
- *the nature, boundaries between, costs and participants of a dispute are often unclear;*
- *there is often a variety of participants who each believe that they represent the public interest or a section of it, many of whom act on principle rather than self-interest;*
- *there are many possible outcomes to the dispute;*
- *the standards adopted by society may change as understanding, values or technology develop; and both the*

> *process of efficiently managing the reaction to those changes and the ability to implement the agreement over a period of time is likely to be as important as the agreement itself.*

This latter characteristic highlights the importance of the decision-making structure and its contribution to the outcome of the dispute. Nevertheless, it is worth recognizing that this adversarial type of public dispute is also a feature of Western cultures. Roberts (1979) and Augsburger (1992) are among those who have contrasted these types of public behaviour with those of other cultures:

> *While in one society peace and quiet may be prized above everything, elsewhere people may openly relish a quarrel.* (Roberts, 1979, 33–34)

In short, the definition of conflict and its means of resolution are culturally determined, and this book is largely concerned with conflicts in the setting of Western culture.

The reference to interest groups in the definition above carries with it the assumption that there is a degree of social organization evident in the type of conflict under investigation. Thus the concern is with relationships between groups rather than individuals, although individuals may play prominent roles, and with the fact that conflicts are structured around these relationships. The analysis of environmental conflicts in this book focuses on what McCormick (1991) terms the conflicts of industrial democracies – waste, air and water pollution, commercial energy management, recycling, use and conservation of resources, and spread of urban areas – and many of these tend to be site-specific. Environmental conflicts may occur at the macro level of politics and be 'unstructured': that is, there may be controversy about competing social values which are not formally represented by interest groups (see Clark et al, 1994).

I have preferred to use the term 'conflict resolution' rather than 'conflict management' on the grounds that 'management' suggests a degree of control by an overarching body that rarely, if ever, exists in the confused world of environmental politics. However, 'resolution' may suggest a sense of finality or completion, which is also rare. Given the episodic nature of many conflicts, as one set of events follows and is conditioned by another, outcomes are no more than states of temporary equilibrium. In this context, resolution follows interventions which seek *cooperation* – in which there is agreement on goals between the interested parties, who then take collective action to achieve these goals. Consensus building is one such collaborative approach, when interest groups and stakeholders are brought together to negotiate and thus solve mutual problems.

THE INTENDED AUDIENCE

Much of the line of argument is based on the responses of students and colleagues from whom I have learnt so much. This has influenced my own perspective, which had its early origins in Unitarianism and the tradition of dissent, and saw a period of political activism in the 1970s, which was tempered perhaps by the experience of being an insider in government service before I entered the sceptical discipline of social research. This developing perspective may also help to explain why power becomes a dominant theme in the latter part of this book.

I like to think that what began as an academic text – in that it has been developed from over ten years of research, teaching and leading training courses – will provoke reflection among a wide range of thoughtful people, including students of all ages, academics, practitioners and policy-makers. Indeed, the most crucial readers of this book will be the decision-makers, because of the issues of power and control, and of public involvement (or the lack of it), in decision-making. If anything changes it will be because of a change of heart on the part of decision-makers.

Acknowledgements

Many people have contributed to this endeavour and the doctorate on which it is partly based. Bill Burch at the Yale School of Forestry and Environmental Studies in his seminars, which I attended in 1968–1969, inspired an interest in the application of social theory to environmental issues. Driving on the back roads of Texas in 1991, Bill listened as I described my initial research on conflicts and urged me to register for the doctorate I had postponed 20 years earlier. He kept an avuncular eye on the project and the genesis of this book, and enabled me to return to Yale in recent years for several symposia. Our mutual interest in the forests of Maine has led to many visits together to hike and debate, amongst other things, the survival of the Northern Woods. This led to periods of interviewing people interested in the woods from 1991 onwards. My particular thanks to Tim Glidden, Roger Milliken and Lloyd Irland for their insights and wisdom over the years.

Bill's early interest in the doctorate was matched by Mike Collins, then Principal Research and Planning Officer at the Sports Council, who backed a hunch and commissioned me in 1987 to review a series of case studies of conflicts between the demands of sports and nature conservation in England and Wales. At the end of that study, I drew some initial contrasts between conflict and cooperation. Never an idle man, Mike found time to comment on drafts of the thesis and to encourage me towards completion and publication.

At the University of Edinburgh I found a congenial place of study, thanks initially to Dr Douglas Malcolm and latterly to Guy Hilton and Simon Allen, who have supported my teaching on the MSc courses in resource management and environmental sustainability. This has provided an invaluable means of clarifying and explaining conflicts and conflict resolution to inspiring students from many countries. Equally stimulating has been the work and training courses with Vikki Hilton in Britain, Ireland and Pakistan.

The second academic home of this work has been the Agricultural University at Wageningen. For many years, Han van der Voet was the pillar of strength holding the Werkgroep Recreatie together, and I obtained great intellectual stimulus from him and various members of the group. Han helped me by organizing meetings, obtaining and translating material from the Dutch and acting as co-researcher and co-author of *Getting on Speaking Terms* in 1993 and in my recent study of the Oosterschelde National Park when Thijs Kramer, Paul Post and Chairman Lilipaly generously spared me time to discuss changes in that area over the years. Han and Grietje have provided me with much hospitality and fun at the house of Jan Steen in Rhenen. Above all, Han insisted that I extricated myself from work pressures in Edinburgh to write. Latterly I have worked as closely and convivially with Jan Philipsen, in study visits to Arnhem and the Isle of Texel, aided and abetted by Stu Cottrell, Renske Schulting and René Van der Duim with assistance from the WICE programme.

I have been fortunate to be able to draw on the results of commissioned research from my time as a freelance consultant, and I would like to acknowledge financial sponsorship or assistance at various times from the Countryside Commission, the Countryside Commission for Scotland, the Dutch Ministry of Agriculture, Nature Management and Fisheries, the Economic and Social Research Council (grant R000 23 1792), English Nature, the Nature Conservancy Council, the Peak District Joint Planning Board, the Pentlands Hills Regional Park, the Scottish Executive, Scottish Natural Heritage, the Sports Council, the Upper Deeside Access Trust, the World Wide Fund for Nature and the Universities of Wageningen and Yale. I am grateful to the staff of the organizations involved in these projects and the many other people, too numerous to name, who kindly gave of their time in interviews or who provided information on the case studies during the course of this research. The views expressed do not claim to reflect those of sponsoring agencies nor government ministers. I would also like to acknowledge permission from the *Rights of Way Law Review* to draw on copyright material in my account of the Peak District Access Consultative Group in Chapter 5.

The study of the North Oxford County Coalition (NOCC) was prompted by Pat Field of the Consensus Building Institute of Cambridge, Massachusetts. In addition to being interviewed, Pat provided the initial contacts with the NOCC, and Patty Duguay of River Valleys Healthy Communities Coalition (RVHCC) organized the programme of meetings. Many thanks to Eileen Adams, Jane Aube, Arthur Bordeau, Bruce Bryant, Ellen Doering, Jane DeFrees, Bill Hine, Dieter Kreckel, Richard Lovejoy, Glenn Paulin, Ernie Robichaud, Jeri Weiss and John Welch for agreeing to be interviewed and kindly supplying much valuable information. The field work was supported by a travel grant from the Carnegie Trust for the Universities of Scotland.

In the latter stages of preparing this book, John Mackay, Carol Huston, Andrew Coleman, Susannah Bleakley and Alan Chester kindly commented on draft chapters. I am particularly grateful to Bruce Steadman and Des Thompson for reviewing the final draft constructively and expeditiously, to Ewan Malcolm for acting as a sounding board for some of the conclusions, and to Paul McFerran and Alex Kirby for their work in the final production of text and diagrams. The responsibility for errors and omissions is mine alone. Finally, the real inspiration has come from my wife and best friend, Monica Barry, who has encouraged me while she completed her own doctorate. Many things have been postponed to complete this task; her belief in the endeavour has kept me going. Thank you.

List of Acronyms and Abbreviations

ACAS	Arbitration and Conciliation Advisory Service (UK)
ADR	alternative dispute resolution
BATNA	best alternative to a negotiated agreement
BOD	Breed Overleg Deltawateren (Dutch regional coalition of water sports organizations in the Delta Region)
BOW	Breed Overleg Waterrecreatie (Dutch coalition of water recreation organizations)
BSAC	British Sub-Aqua Club
BWSF	British Workers' Sports Federation
CBI	Consensus Building Institute (Cambridge, Massachusetts, USA)
CCS	Countryside Commission for Scotland
CPRE	Council for the Preservation of Rural England
DEP	Department of Environmental Protection (Maine, USA)
EN	English Nature
EPA	Environment Protection Agency (USA)
EU	European Union
FEN	Forest Ecology Network (USA)
HLF	Heritage Lottery Fund
IAP2	International Association for Public Participation
ICZM	integrated coastal zone management
LAC	limits of acceptable change
LNV	Ministerie van Landbouw, Natuurbeheer en Visserij (Dutch Ministry of Agriculture, Nature Management and Fisheries)
LRC	Lothian Regional Council
MBCG	Morecambe Bay Conservation Group
MCS	Marine Conservation Society
MCofS	Mountaineering Council of Scotland
MNR	marine nature reserve
MOD	Ministry of Defence
NC	Nature Conservancy (UK)
NCC	Nature Conservancy Council (UK)
NFLS	Northern Forest Lands Study (US Forest Service)
NFUS	National Farmers' Union of Scotland
NGO	non-governmental organization
NNR	national nature reserve
NOCC	North Oxford County Coalition (Maine, USA)
NRA	National Rifle Association (USA)

PA	participatory appraisal
PDACG	Peak District Access Consultative Group
PHRP	Pentland Hills Regional Park
PPJPB	Peak Park Joint Planning Board
RA	Ramblers' Association
RIJP	Rijkdienst IJsselmeer Polders (Development Authority for the IJsselmeer Polders, the Netherlands)
RVHCC	River Valleys Healthy Communities Coalition (Maine, USA)
SBB	Staatsbosbeheer (Dutch State Forest and Landscape Service)
SCENES	*Scottish Environment News* (digest)
SLF	Scottish Landowners' Federation
SNH	Scottish Natural Heritage
SPIDR	Society of Professionals in Dispute Resolution
SSSI	site of special scientific interest
UDAT	Upper Deeside Access Trust
VCNP	Voorlopige Commissie Nationale Parken (Dutch standing commission on national parks)
VVV	Vereniging voor Vreemdelingen Verkeer (Tourist Information Association) (the Netherlands)
WICE	World Leisure International Centre of Excellence
WWF	World Wide Fund for Nature
YMCA	Young Men's Christian Association

Glossary

Arbitration – a process of decision-making in which a neutral third party takes evidence and devises a solution to the problem. In binding arbitration, the disputing parties agree in advance to abide by the arbitrator's decision. In non-binding arbitration, the arbitrator makes a recommendation for the parties to consider.

Communities of interest – different groups within a community, each of which has its own set of values and views concerning policy and practice in rural development.

Consensus – a decision reached by mutual agreement.

Consensus building – a negotiation or process of decision-making aimed at recognizing and respecting common interests and working together for mutual benefit.

Consultation – the level of participation at which people are offered some choices on what is to happen, but are not involved in developing additional options.

Effectiveness – the ability of partnerships to implement their objectives and thereby generate positive results through positive action in the community.

Empowerment – a process through which stakeholders influence and share control over development initiatives, and the decisions and resources which affect them.

Evaluation – a process which reviews the effectiveness of a partnership, including its objectives, policies, administration, management and work programmes. Evaluation should review process in a partnership's operation as well as outcomes.

Facilitation – helping others to think through what they want and how to organize themselves to achieve it.

Involvement – a level of participation in which people actively participate in defining the problem and possible solutions, and take part in the final decision.

Mediation – a process of decision-making in which a neutral third party assists the disputing parties to negotiate a mutually acceptable solution.

Participation – a process during which individuals, groups and organizations are consulted about or have the opportunity to become actively involved in a project or programme of activity.

Participatory appraisal – an approach which uses group animation to facilitate information gathering and sharing, analysis and action. Its purpose is to get development practitioners, government officials and local people to work together.

Partners – the individuals who are members of the management boards of a partnership, and, at a broader level, the organizations that are represented in a partnership.

Precautionary principle – the principle that if the consequences of an action, especially the use of technology, are unknown then it is better *not to carry out the action* rather than risk the consequences.

Stakeholders – those who have (or might have) an interest in what happens, because they will be affected by it or may have some influence over it.

Chapter 1

Introduction

The combination of worldwide industrialization and population growth is putting ever more pressure on resources that are unalterably finite. The result is not only the degradation of the planet – including enormous and irreparable damage to other species – but bitter human conflict. (Gray, 2001)

THE DRAMA OF CONFLICT

Conflict is an emotive word implying a struggle between opposing ideas and interests, confrontation, protest and, potentially, violence. The fascination of such language is certainly understood in the world of journalism, as can be seen in the headlines in Box 1.1 on disputes around the world. Immediately we are drawn into the drama of threats to the environment, upon which we all depend, and the injustice of a struggle in which the weak are pitted against the strong.

Study the newspapers in the UK or around the world over a longer period of time and controversies over each of these environmental topics – energy, forest management, waste disposal, mineral working, transport and water supply – recur time and again.

How society's energy needs will be met is one such constant theme. In the 1970s, the concerns in Britain focused on where coal-fired power stations would be sited and the visual impact of transmission lines in areas of natural beauty. Thirty years later, visual impact features in the debate about wind farms, but there are major concerns about how the switch to renewable sources can be made. Meanwhile, nuclear power re-emerges as a possible way of reducing carbon emissions, despite continuing concerns about decommissioning ageing stations and the disposal of radioactive waste.

Some controversies, such as ironstone mining in Oxfordshire, were very much of their time, as they concerned mineral resources for primary industries that have long been exported to other parts of the world. But the bitter battles about the expansion of the UK's airports continue, only varying in the detail of which candidate site might serve London, or to which airports runways will be added (Edinburgh in the 1970s, Manchester in the late 1990s).

BOX 1.1 CONFLICT MAKES THE HEADLINES

'NILE POWER ROW SPLITS UGANDA: Africans want environmentalists out of their backyard so dam project can light their evenings – Charlotte Denny', *The Guardian*, 15 August 2001

'US ENDS BAN ON ROADS THROUGH FORESTS: Pristine woodland at risk as Bush hands states power to open up federally owned areas to commercial logging – Julian Borger in Washington', *The Guardian*, 14 July 2004

'PROTESTERS STEP UP FIGHT TO BURY DUMP PLANS: Fears of pollution, litter and bad smells from landfill sites are driving campaigners to new lengths – Auslan Cramb reports', *The Scotsman*, 15 December 1994

'MISSION TO MOVE MOUNTAINS: A new generation of superquarries is emerging in Scotland, destroying mountains and dividing communities – Rob Edwards investigates', *The Scotsman*, 13 March 1992

'BYPASS SURGERY: Was the decision on Newbury's controversial road scheme bulldozed through? – Oliver Tickell investigates and Jay Griffiths meets the protesters', *The Guardian*, 13 December 1995

'NUCLEAR ROW HITS MELTDOWN: Ian Traylor in Bonn reports on the growing violence over nuclear waste, as a huge force of police protecting a shipment on its slow journey to a storage site faces an explosive combination of organized leftwing militants and anti-nuclear activists', *The Guardian*, 1 March 1997

'SALT IN WOUNDS: Damage to the water flow of the once-mighty Indus is forcing major changes in Pakistan and could lead to conflict – Shahid Husain', *The Guardian*, 15 January 2003

Similarly, the focus on roads and transport in Britain shifts between debates on policies concerning emissions and the costs of congestion to protests on construction sites, but the conflict never goes away. If an issue, such as the construction of new reservoirs, appears to be dormant, it is almost certain that it will re-emerge at some later stage.

The only variation in this pattern of recurring events comes during heightened periods of political activity, such as in the UK one year after the 1997 general election. An article in August 1998 mapped 59 locations of protests about animal welfare, intensive farming, housing and supermarket development, genetically modified crops, quarrying and waste disposal, and nuclear and traffic pollution, as highlighted in the following:

> *A GLORIOUS SUMMER FOR DISCONTENT: Pressure groups all over the country are mobilizing against almost everything.* The modern phenomenon of 'direct action' started with anti-nuclear protests and moved via Greenpeace and Friends of the Earth to environmental, animal welfare and road protesting. Today it is spreading into almost every area of life

and becoming the ultimate obsession of political, environmental
or corporate disquiet. (Vidal, 1998)

Looking back from 2004, a year preoccupied with the aftermath of 9/11
and the consequences of the Iraq war, this may have been a highpoint in
environmental activism, but the short-term issues of domestic politics must
inevitably give way to more profound concerns about climate change.

Look behind the headlines and we begin to detect the clues to
understanding environmental disputes. In the following extract we can read
of passion, nostalgia, lost freedoms, the irreplaceable loss of a living
environment and powerlessness:

> **STANDING GROUND: *Passions run deep over the last patch***
> ***of untouched land in a Lanarkshire village already scarred by***
> ***industry, set to be spoiled for the sake of coal.*** *Maria Donovan*
> *gazes out at the scarred landscape around her Lanarkshire*
> *village and wistfully remembers the days she and her friends*
> *could roam the countryside. Today the view from Greengairs is*
> *mostly taken up by an opencast site and two dumps.*
>
> *The development brings new jobs to the community but many*
> *residents believe too high an environmental price is being paid*
> *for employment. To the north of the village is a small patch of*
> *land untouched by progress but now it too is under threat...*
>
> *Another resident, who has lived in the area all her life, fondly*
> *reminisces about the days her friends played on the land,*
> *known as the glen, and rambled in the fields and woods. 'I'm*
> *afraid Greengairs is finished' she sighs. 'It just isn't the nice wee*
> *place I remember and I can't see them ever getting it back the*
> *way it was.'* (Stewart, 1996)

One further excerpt written from the campaigners' perspective is equally
dramatic and describes the ingredients of their triumph over a hate figure:
the suggested official dereliction of duty, retribution, the end of a long saga
and the value of media attention. But it also raises the question of what
constitutes conflict resolution:

> **STUNNING BREAKTHROUGH ON 'VAN HOOGSTRATEN'**
> **FOOTPATH.** *If it had been a blocked road, traffic jams would*
> *have forced police into action within minutes. As it was a path*
> *used by walkers to cross the country estate of one of the most*
> *notorious millionaire property tycoons in the country, it was*
> *ignored for years by the local highway authority legally*
> *responsible for its upkeep. But on Monday, 10 February, in a*
> *stunning victory for walkers, demolition squads moved in to*
> *remove the obstacles that have blocked the right of way for the*
> *past 13 years. Ramblers campaigner Kate Ashbrook cut*

through barbed wire and a padlock on locked gates. Heavy machinery then moved in and removed concrete pillars and old refrigeration units that had been illegally placed over the path. With a battery of press photographers and TV cameras recording the event, demolition crews used a 21-ton excavator armed with a grapple that seemed to eat its way through the obstructions, picking up the huge concrete pillars as if they were matchsticks. It went on to make an easy meal of the sturdy metal fridges, chewing them up and spitting them out with contempt. (Sparrow, 2003)

PURPOSE AND RATIONALE OF THE BOOK

Even active protagonists locked in political combat concede that there must be some other way of resolving environmental conflicts. This book examines that proposition by examining the following: why conflicts occur, often in a recurring pattern; what role they play in the political process; and how individuals and organizations respond to conflict. It considers the potential contribution of environmental mediation, its limitations and why it is not used more widely. Do decision-makers in the UK have good reasons for saying 'it won't work here' or claiming 'we're doing it already'? Can conflict be prevented by community participation in planning, and what institutional changes would be required to reduce and resolve conflicts?

The twin aims of this book are to analyse the causes of conflict and to assess whether alternative approaches to conflict prevention and resolution could be more widely applied. The basic argument is that one needs to understand conflict and the essentials of conflict resolution and prevention to assess why their applications are limited. Although participation and mediation are often seen as separate professional worlds, they have many commonalities. The arguments for both are based on common democratic values concerning how decisions should be made and the pragmatic benefits to all concerned. My premise is that the approach of consensus building is generic and can be used in different ways in different situations, but principally as mediation in situations of crisis and public participation in planning, processes which aim to achieve the outcomes of conflict resolution and conflict prevention:

> *Opportunities for consensus processes exist at all stages of decision-making involving issues of sustainability – from the establishment of broad policies and regulations, to long range planning, to allocating land and resources, to resolving specific disputes, to licensing, monitoring, and enforcement.* (Canadian Round Tables, 1993, 5)

A detailed examination of both types of processes emphasizes the point that building trust between decision-makers and communities takes considerable time and commitment on both sides.

LAYOUT OF THE BOOK

Part 1, on the nature of environmental disputes, examines how and why such disputes occur. Chapter 2 presents the two principal case studies which will be used to illustrate key points throughout the book. The history of access to the countryside for recreation in England and Wales illustrates the significant history and episodic nature of a continuing dispute of national importance. Recreation and leisure might seem to be an unlikely subject for conflict, and there is a certain irony when 'getting away from it all' causes environmental problems. However, the 'access debate' has two significant elements: competing claims for 'freedom to roam' on privately owned land and, more recently, conservationists' concerns that recreation is damaging and disturbing to wildlife. Such concerns about the pressures on the countryside are part of a long-running cultural debate which goes back at least a century to the relationships between rural landowners and urban populations. Chapter 2 traces the history of conflict over access in the Peak District National Park in England, where the Mass Trespass of 1932 still resonates, and where local attempts to negotiate about reducing the impacts of access on wildlife have been superseded by recent legislation. The second dispute, over the designation of the Pentland Hills Regional Park in Scotland, contains many of the same elements, although it is quite local in nature. It is also ostensibly about countryside access, but on closer examination is more about relationships and the lack of trust between the principal parties over a period of more than 20 years. A number of themes emerge from these case studies and recur throughout the book, notably the choice of strategies to be adopted by campaigning groups (i.e., whether to press for national legislation or to enter local negotiations) and a general distrust of officialdom.

Chapter 3 focuses on conflict analysis and describes how conflicts can be examined at various levels, starting with the analysis of the needs, fears and interests of stakeholders. Conflicts are both multi-dimensional and dynamic. Indeed, in seemingly similar situations, examples can be found of both cooperation and conflict, when the issues are the same but the differences lie in the relationships, or lack of them, between the interest groups. Conflicts are epitomized by the polarized positions of the parties competing within adversarial political debates or public hearings/inquiries. In contrast, cooperative relationships are based on openness and trust.

As in other political struggles, conflicts pass through active and inactive phases as interest groups operate within the political process. They organize and lobby in their attempts to gain legitimacy and the power to use and control the use of natural resources. Sound conflict analysis lays the foundation for conflict resolution by developing an understanding of the dynamic processes of conflict and the importance to participants of historical events within each long-running struggle. The theories underlying this perspective are those of social action and policy analysis. The primary concern of social action theorists is to relate theories of conflict to theories of social change, and to suggest that conflict performs a useful social function. The other broad approach could be termed 'managerial', and is taken by policy analysts whose main aim is to resolve conflicts. A synthesis of these theories is developed to shed light on the function and processes of conflict. Chapter 3 illustrates the value of this approach by further analysing the two case studies described in the previous chapter.

Part 2, on strategies for cooperation, sets out the potential contribution of consensus building to the prevention and resolution of environmental disputes. Chapter 4 firstly describes the various ways in which societies attempt to resolve disputes, from avoiding the issues through to the use of force. Many of the 'novel' alternative methods of dispute resolution currently being advocated are not new, and have their antecedents in earlier systems of decision-making. In essence, conventional systems of conflict resolution depend upon claims being legitimated through the political process, often resulting in legislation. Such processes have strengths (that legal safeguards are provided to protect the rights of the powerless) and weaknesses (that the proceedings become adversarial). The chapter then explores those alternatives which seek consensus rather than compromise, terms which are often confused. Consensus building processes are based on negotiations designed to remove misunderstanding, clarify interests and establish common ground between participants, which in turn leads to a more relaxed non-adversarial approach. The process provides participants with the opportunity to treat others, and to be treated, with respect, and to retain control over the outcome. Consensus depends on trust gained through openness in sharing information, a balanced agenda and representation, early participation and having a genuine influence over decision-making. These principles are set out in an analytical framework depicting the conditions in which voluntary negotiation can lead to a 'principled outcome', where no one party is disadvantaged. This framework is used in subsequent chapters to assess the effectiveness of decision-making and the extent to which it leads to consensus.

Chapter 5 considers the process of mediation, and its use of the principles of consensus building tailored to the local situation. Participation is voluntary and depends on the mediator building conditions of trust, in which the interests of all parties are respected, their legal rights are not prejudiced and confidentiality is maintained. In part, the case for mediation rests on these principles being respected, but also on advancing the values of self-determination, compassion and concern for others. The chapter examines the critiques of mediation and how mediators attempt to address them in designing negotiations. Many of these criticisms concerning access to justice and the use of power could equally be applied to other processes.

During a preparation stage, mediators may spend considerable time making a crucial assessment of whether direct negotiation is feasible or whether it would founder on a fundamental clash of beliefs or imbalances of power. Such differences may be set aside where there is external pressure to settle, the working relationship is important, and stalemate has been reached. This chapter assesses how mediation can meet the consensus building criteria set out in the previous chapter, and presents pointers for good practice. It concludes with an example of environmental mediation: the deliberations of the Access Consultative Group in the Peak District National Park, which negotiated over moorland access and its impact on conservation.

Chapter 6 presents a second and more detailed case study of mediation: the North Oxford County Coalition (NOCC) in Maine. The coalition was formed to bring together members of the local community, government regulators, representatives of local industry and others to consider the potential health effects of emissions from a pulp mill in the town of Rumford. The conflict was precipitated by sensational TV coverage of the apparently high incidence of cancer in mill-workers and their families, which deeply divided the community. During the course of three years of negotiation, most of the initial fears were allayed following an assessment of the medical and scientific evidence by independent experts, and the main outcome of the group's deliberations was a health education initiative: the River Valleys Healthy Communities Coalition (RVHCC). The process was facilitated by the Consensus Building Institute, Cambridge, Massachusetts, and was investigated by the author. Chapter 6 covers the process followed by the mediation team, charts the turning points in the discussions as trust developed within the group, and examines how participants saw the process in retrospect and how the NOCC process met the preconditions for consensus.

Chapter 7 considers the role consensus building can play in the prevention of conflict and the arguments for increasing public participation to resolve conflicts by reaching agreement among stakeholders. These arguments pivot around two main concepts: first, the democratic ideal that people ought to be involved in decisions that affect their lives; and, second, the idea that decision-makers can work more effectively when they have active public engagement and support for their proposals. Both arguments run counter to the 'decide, announce and defend' school of public consultation, an approach that still appears to be endemic despite its failings and the likelihood that it leads to mistrust. It is based on the principle that experts plan for people rather than with them.

The second part of Chapter 7 sets out the principles of 'process design'. Typically, the consultation element of a planning exercise is improvised with no clear objectives, techniques are used because they are in vogue, and it is unclear how the results will be related to decision-making. If public involvement in planning is to prevent conflict, a participation strategy is required that is designed to overcome these failings and is deliberately constructed on consensus building principles. It should consider the purposes that participation can achieve and the critical role of the initiator. A strategy needs clear aims; it needs to assess the timing and level of involvement sought from different stakeholders and the techniques to be used to engage them. The suitability of different participation techniques to encourage different levels of involvement is assessed, as well as their strengths and weaknesses. The chapter concludes by setting out principles of participation on the grounds that clarity of purpose, integrity and commitment to listening to the public on the part of decision-makers are more important than choosing the most appropriate technique.

Chapter 8 examines these principles of participation in the context of partnerships between decision-makers and stakeholders, who may include other organizations or the community in general. Two case studies in this chapter show how trust within partnerships and with local communities can be won and maintained. The long-term commitment of the Morecambe Bay Partnership to community involvement over a ten-year period has enabled national agencies and local government to develop a programme of integrated coastal zone management with community support. Similarly, the Upper Deeside Access Trust (UDAT) has gained credibility from its open style of governance and willingness to explain its proposals to the public. This has enabled the trust to reach consensus on proposals that would have provoked conflict a few years earlier.

Two other case studies in this chapter show the difficulties of building partnerships when such commitment is lacking. An initiative to develop a collaborative vision for the future of the island of Texel on the north-eastern coast of the Netherlands met some local opposition. Although five years later elements of the initial debate continue and several practical projects on sustainability are being developed, the local municipality has failed to secure genuine involvement in its policies, with the result that trust is lacking between politicians and the community that they represent. A recent attempt to develop an integrated management strategy for the Pentland Hills Regional Park (PHRP) engaged local communities in participatory planning. However, since the strategy has been completed there has been limited feedback to the public, and despite agreement between the local authorities the partnership has not realized its full potential.

Part 3, on the realities of power, analyses the relationships between organizational power, decision-making and the resolution of conflict. Chapter 9 firstly reviews the relationships between governments, organizations and people and relates these to the earlier themes of negotiation, conflict resolution, participation and empowerment. It then examines the power relationships within and between organizations. This chapter also traces the contribution of power to triggering conflict and its role in conflict resolution. It elaborates on the proposition presented in earlier chapters, based on social action theory, that the distribution of power determines the outcome of conflict. Thus, changes towards more participatory decision-making do not in themselves produce fair and just outcomes. The relationships in some of the earlier case studies are reviewed before two additional case studies – the designation of the Skomer marine reserve and planning in the Rhine Delta – are presented, illustrating the impact of state intervention and the consequences in terms of the balance of power.

Chapter 10 contrasts the familiar rough and tumble of adversarial politics with the reasonable, rational and ideologically sound alternative of consensus building. Both the theory and the procedures of consensus building differ markedly from the process of voting. While voting can break the log jam of getting nowhere and allow life to move on, it might deliver victory for the majority but leave an aggrieved and resentful minority, which does nothing to resolve conflict. So, to combine the two systems appears to offer the best of both worlds. The advantage should be that, with all the spade-work done, the legislative process will be swift and smooth. But that relies on the supposition that politicians and their advisors will readily endorse broadly based agreements. In reality, marrying consensus and politics may seem like Little Red Riding Hood meeting the Big Bad Wolf. Chapter 10 explores aspects of this fable. The first section outlines the main characteristics of the political process, while the second presents two case studies – one in Maine and the other in Scotland – which illustrate what can happen when consensus building and politics are combined. In both cases, the centre ground developed a consensus, appeared to lose the battle, yet won the war. Both cases lend further support to the argument that consensus building is a long-term process which can take years, rather than an instant solution dependent on applying the latest technique. In the North Maine Woods, the negotiations attempted to devise a long-term solution in the heat of a political debate. That the negotiations were successful in reaching an agreement says a lot for the calibre and commitment of those involved. That they failed to get popular support says as much about the failings of adversarial politics as the minor flaws in their process. Yet over the longer term, most of the elements of the agreement (the Forest Compact) are in the process of implementation. But that has only happened because of the shift in power brought about by environmental activists.

The Scottish case has many parallels. Time has shown that the work of the Access Forum has been far more influential than seemed likely at the height of the political debate on access legislation. In effect, the forum set the agenda with a vital agreement in principle which won the support of the landowning organizations. While their membership may have had misgivings, given the political reality of the changes of power following devolution and the political commitment of the majority parties, access legislation was inevitable. The outcome may have been portrayed as a victory for recreation interests, but the final form of the legislation, which balanced rights and responsibilities, was the brainchild of the forum. These cases suggest that consensus building will never replace the political process, but that it can play a vital complementary role.

Part 4 considers the case for reform and how institutional barriers to the wider application of consensus building could be removed. Chapter 11 returns to the opening questions: why conflicts occur, often in a recurring pattern; what role they play in the political process; and how individuals and organizations respond to conflict. In particular, it considers why environmental mediation has been rarely used in Britain and the circumstances in which it might be applied more widely in future. There are lessons to be learnt both at policy level, by considering institutional reform and re-examining the roles of environmental agencies, and at the practical level, by incorporating the principles of consensus building into decision-making at the planning stage, more soundly established partnerships and the resolution of disputes.

Part 1
Understanding Environmental Disputes

Chapter 2

Introduction to the Principal Case Studies

SYNOPSIS

This chapter traces the history of conflict over access and its recurring themes, its symbolic events and more recent controversies by presenting two case studies which will be used to illustrate key points throughout the book.

The first dispute – the conflict over access to the countryside for recreation in England and Wales – is part of a cultural debate between rural landowners and the urban population which goes back at least a century. This is also a political struggle in which the main players are represented by the landowners' organizations and the Ramblers' Association (RA), both well versed in political infighting and with well established political connections. Underlying their competing claims is a clash of values: landowners protecting their territory and privacy, and ramblers seeking the freedom to roam over predominantly privately owned land. There is also a complex philosophical and legal argument over whether public rights of access for recreation need to be established in law or whether they have long existed, but have been usurped by the power of landowners over the centuries and should be restored to the people. Time and again history is preyed in aid, historical precedent is cited and tales of famous battles are recited to rally and maintain support. The main setting for the first case study is the Peak District National Park in England, where the mass trespass of 1932 still resonates in debates about freedom to roam, and where local negotiations have been superseded by recent legislation.

The second dispute, over the designation of the Pentland Hills Regional Park (PHRP) in Scotland, contains many of the same elements, although it is quite local in nature. It is also ostensibly about countryside access, but on closer examination is more about relationships and lack of trust between the principal parties – local government and the farming community – over a period of more than 20 years.

Following this initial presentation of these cases, we shall return to them several times: in Chapter 3, where social theory is used to gain deeper insights into them; in Chapter 5, where the establishment of the Peak District Access Consultative Group (PDACG) is examined as an example of a mediated negotiation between the conflicting parties; in Chapter 8, where more recent attempts to seek public participation in planning for the PHRP are examined; and in Chapter 11, where the mismatch between consensus building and the political process is explored in the context of latest access legislation in Scotland.

ACCESS TO THE COUNTRYSIDE IN ENGLAND AND WALES

Historical Context

> *'The long march of the footpaths revolutionaries'*; The Times, 21 April 1982
>
> *'Warning of clashes by frustrated walkers'*; Daily Telegraph, 22 April 1982
>
> *'Escalating the footpath war'*; Sunday Times, 18 September 1988
>
> *'Ramblers pledge fight for access'*; The Guardian, 8 May 1989
>
> *'Battle for countryside turns ugly: conflict heats up between irate duke and ramblers'*; The Guardian, 28 April 1998
>
> *'War flares over Wall walk'*; Observer, 1 August 1993

Newspaper headlines are written to catch the eye, but they also tap into the underlying strength of feelings over the particular issue. In this respect, sub-editors of the major English newspapers have long recognized that the 'access debate', with its elements of conflict and class war, will attract the attention of their readers. The debate itself started long before 1982 and continued well beyond the two decades from which these headlines are taken. As will be seen later, it reached a climax, if not resolution, with the legislation of 2000 in England and Wales. History has played a prominent role in this debate, particularly in the writing of the campaigners for access when celebrating their 'victory' in achieving the long awaited legislation (Ramblers' Association, 2001b).

The history of access to the countryside in England and Wales has to be seen in the context of the development of the outdoor movement, which in turn has reflected the social changes of the times. The pattern of 18th-century reform, the working class and liberal movements of the 1920s and 1930s, the period of social reconstruction of the 1940s, and increased mobility and relative affluence since the 1960s are all reflected in the evolution of the open air movement. The origins of this political struggle can be traced back several centuries to disputes over the respective rights of

1826	Society for the Preservation of Ancient Footpaths founded in Manchester
1880	Manchester YMCA Rambling Club founded
1884	First attempt by James Bryce to introduce Access to Mountains (Scotland) Bill in Parliament
1900	Sheffield Clarion Ramblers founded
1931	National Council of Ramblers' Federations founded
	First Winnats Pass rally campaigns for access in the Peak District
1932	Mass trespass of Kinder Scout
1935	National Council of Ramblers' Federations becomes the Ramblers' Association (RA)
1939	Access to Mountains Act allows local authorities to apply for access orders but also made trespass a criminal offence (repealed by 1949 Act)
1947	Special Committee on Footpaths and Access to the Countryside recommended need for access orders to all suitable land in national parks but not where this would seriously conflict with other users
1949	National Parks and Access to the Countryside Act gives powers to local authorities to enter into formal access agreements and to prepare maps of open country. Where access could not be agreed with landowners, application could be made for compulsory access orders
1951	Peak District National Park designated
1952	Peak Park Joint Planning Board (PPJPB) publishes open country map
1953–1970	19 access agreements made within the Peak District covering 76 square miles
1970s	First concerns by naturalists and moorland owners that 'wander-at–will' access might harm wildlife
1978	National Park Plan (NPP) suggests that access might be limited in areas of high conservation value
1981	PPJPB acquires Roaches Estate
1984	PPJPB acquires Eastern Moors (Stanage). Peak Park Wildlife Advisory Group prepares report on access and wildlife
1985	RA launch 'Forbidden Britain' campaign to identify areas from which the public are 'unreasonably barred'
	PPJPB identifies six moorland areas for new agreements
1989	Review of NPP promotes concept of access corridors and research on effects of access on wildlife
1990	Anderson's report for PPJPB suggests evidence of wildlife disturbance from access. RA responds by publishing harsh critique by Watson. Chatsworth Estate enters into access agreement with PPJPB which contains access corridors and sanctuary areas
1991	Review of National Parks promotes access management. RA stages mass trespass campaign which continues throughout the 1990s
1992	Government response to Review of National Parks reaffirms voluntary access agreements. PPJPB circulates draft Access Strategy advocating 'limits of acceptable change'
1993	Dark Peak site of special scientific interest (SSSI) re-notified, consultation on Special Protection Area for wild birds. Renegotiations begin on terms for renewal of existing access agreements. Access consultative group established which recommends collaborative procedure for preparing access management plans
1999–2000	Renewed campaign for access legislation following election of Labour government in 1997 Parliamentary debate of access legislation
2001	Countryside and Rights of Way Act receives royal assent
2004	New right of access to open country comes into force in South East and parts of North West England

Sources: Peak Park Joint Planning Board (1995); Stephenson (1989); Sidaway (1979); Ramblers' Association (2004).

Figure 2.1 *Historical Summary of Access to the Countryside in the Peak District and England and Wales*

landowner and peasant, landlord and tenant, gamekeeper and poacher, and rich and poor, which have been well documented by Hill (1980), Hopkins (1986), Stephenson (1989), Shoard (1999) and others. It is a struggle tinged with bitterness, reflecting, among other things, attitudes of town and country, class and social status which change little over the years.

> *The attitude of the countryside to the invaders from the towns has varied between rapacity – the townsman is rich and one can make money out of him – and resentment – one does not want a lot of 'townees' trampling over one's fields and breaking down one's hedges – but in the main has been suspicious and hostile.* (Joad, 1946 in Holt, 1995)

> *The ramblers are just a bunch of the dirty mac brigade. The great unwashed. They're disgusting creatures. Would you have a lot of herberts in your garden?* (Van Hoogstraten, 1998)

A detailed chronology of events is set out in Figure 2.1.

Walking and the Footpath Movement in England and Wales

The first strand in this story is the long tradition of walking that has been established in England and Wales. The literary traveller is a well known figure, and many such journeys are well documented. Among these travellers were such notables as Samuel Johnson, Arthur Young, William Cobbett, George Borrow and Daniel Defoe, to name but a few. Many of them were social commentators; others, such as William Wordsworth, walked or travelled for pure enjoyment. Many of these travellers went on horseback, but others walked, for this was frequently the only means to get around. At much the same time, walking began to be appreciated as a form of recreation in the writings of Elizabeth Grant of Rothiemurchus, Elizabeth Gaskell and Beatrice Webb (Holt, 1995). There are also accounts by the less affluent but equally adventurous, such as Thomas Bewick (Weekly, 1961), then an apprentice but later a celebrated engraver, who walked considerable distances in Northern England as a means of visiting relatives and seeing the world, but who clearly found walking enjoyable in its own right. The distances he and others covered in those times might be the envy of the backpackers of today.

It was from the everyday travels of working folk that a rights of way system developed, and this is probably peculiar to Britain. Its origins are ancient and functional, from the days when paths and tracks served as the prime means of communication. Hippisley Cox (1973) and others have researched the prehistoric tracks of Southern England which linked settlement, fort and burial place along the dry ridges of the limestone and chalk. Theories have been advanced in archaeological circles that the famous system of straight Roman roads that traverses Britain followed much more ancient 'ley lines', and part of this system has passed into the modern road network. The roads continued to be commonly used by walkers, riders and cyclists until the speed and volume of traffic made them unsafe.

If the ancient tracks were the arterial routes, there is also a considerable network of footpaths, bridleways and green lanes which were once the everyday routes to the workplace, the shop, the pub or the family in the next village. The legal status and maintenance of this system has been much in dispute over the years. Footpath case law built up, but was so complex that it has necessitated several attempts at codification. The result is a network that may be well defined and well managed locally, but more often it is little used or even untraceable. However, it forms a good starting point for an account of the recent history of the struggle for public access to the countryside in Britain. This account starts in 1826 with the formation of the Manchester Society for the Preservation of Ancient Footpaths. It was not the first footpath preservation society in Britain, but it is one of the better documented. It came into being to fight a notable battle, that of keeping open the local paths at Flixton, a village near Manchester. Concerted action by a determined group won the day against the self-interest of a landowner. If this had been an isolated incident it would not be particularly memorable, but the Manchester Society was one of many groups formed in Northern England to fight for rights of way. Not all the fledgling groups survived, but many federated and eventually formed the basis for the Ramblers' Association and the lobby for the Pennine Way, the first long-distance route to be established in Britain. It was a radical and probably largely working-class movement, which sought access to the hills as a right for the people to escape from the squalor of the Northern industrial towns.

The footpath movement grew with the industrialization of Britain, which, among other things, segregated most people's work and leisure in a distinct way and increasingly drew the population away from its natural contacts with the countryside. The path network which had been functional in some areas now came to be valued for recreation, and became the focus for many disputes between landowners and walkers. The aggrieved organized themselves into clubs and associations which flourished or languished, amalgamated and reformed over the years. The political value of groups joining together into wider federations was recognized, and links with the early socialist movement and the Northern Nonconformist tradition of religious dissent were strong. For example, the Sheffield Clarion Ramblers was an offshoot of Robert Blatchford's socialist journal, *The Clarion*, while other clubs were allied with the Methodist church (Holt, 1995). The Liverpool, Manchester and Sheffield federations of clubs instigated the formation of the National Council of Ramblers' Federations in 1931, which became the Ramblers' Association in 1935. By 1950, the Association had a membership of nearly 9000, which grew to 30,000 by 1980, 50,000 by 1985 and then doubled by 1994 and is now 142,000. Its interests are wider than its name suggests, one of its concerns being the conservation of the countryside. Since its inception it has been a very effective element in the broader amenity movement in Britain.

There is another major strand of this movement that also starts in the middle of the 19th century. In contrast to the Northern footpath movement, it was probably more aristocratic or middle class in its membership and mainly Southern in location. It was a part of the 'establishment', which furthers its ends by traditional means: personal connection, influence and, if need be, litigation. The Commons Preservation Society, formed in 1865, was concerned to stop the closure of commons by lords of the manor and to secure the preservation of open space for public exercise and recreation. In 1899 the Society amalgamated with the Footpaths Preservation Society to form the Commons, Open Spaces and Footpaths Preservation Society (subsequently referred to as the Commons Society), which still exists as the Open Spaces Society.

The political pressure exerted by the footpath movement in the 1930s and 1940s resulted in a succession of government reports which included recommendations on rights of way surveys, signposting and clearer legal status for footpaths. Eventually these recommendations found their way into the National Parks and Access to the Countryside Act of 1949. But the voluntary movement of ramblers has never covered the country comprehensively; in most rural counties landowners held and still hold political and magisterial sway, so that the 1949 Act was implemented only in part by most local authorities. As a result, the rambling and farming organizations take opposed political stances, with farmers pressing for the 'rationalization' of rights of way which, in the eyes of the ramblers, would set the precedent for wholesale closure of the system.

Access to the Mountains and the Battle for Legislation

The campaign for access to the mountains also had its origins in the 19th century. Initially concerned with specific rights of way, it sought to reaffirm people's freedom to roam at will across the large open areas of upland England. Although these upland areas rarely reach an elevation of 3000 feet, tree cover is scarce. The hilltops and mountains of England and Wales are largely open, rough grazing land attractive all year round to the long-distance walker and the seeker of solitude. These uplands are mainly in private ownership, and rights of access have been bitterly disputed, with the landowning interests arguing that the creation of such rights would be an infringement of their territorial rights and an invasion of their privacy, and the ramblers arguing that ancient rights had been removed by the inclosure of land and that these rights should be restored.

The last 20 years of the 19th century heralded successive legislative attempts to re-establish general rights of access with gathering public support. In 1884, James Bryce introduced an Access to Mountains (Scotland) Bill in the House of Commons. Its purpose was stated in Clause 2 of the Bill:

> *No owner or occupier of uncultivated mountain or moor lands in Scotland shall be entitled to exclude any person from walking or being on such land for the purpose of recreation or scientific or artistic study, or to molest him in so walking or being.* (Stephenson, 1989, 40)

The social context to Bryce's Bill was the (then) recent memory of the Highland Clearances, when much common grazing land was lost to 'improvement' in the form of sheep grazing and deer forests for the benefit of the landowners. Although the 1884 Bill failed to get parliamentary time and a second attempt by Bryce in 1884 also failed, a full debate took place in 1892, when Bryce re-introduced his Bill. Two aspects of that debate are of particular interest: Bryce's challenge to the prevailing concept of landownership, and his justification for a legislative solution. A lawyer and something of a polymath, he saw private ownership as an expropriation of common rights, including access, and dismissed ideas of compensation to landowners:

> *There is no such thing in the old customs of this country as the right of exclusion for purposes of the mere pleasure of the individual and there is no ground in law or reason for excluding persons from a mountain ... we must not be asked to pay compensation for what we have never given away.* (Stephenson, 1989, 136)

On the efficacy of voluntary negotiation in the face of superior power:

> *Bryce pointed out that talking to landowners and sporting tenants, explaining to them the need for access, and asking them to oblige, simply did not produce results. 'It used to be said – "All that is wanted is to make this subject known and good feeling will do the rest." But, Sir, we have waited a good many years for this good feeling on the part of landowners, and we discern no sign of its appearance.'* (Shoard, 1999, 171)

Although backed by petitions from several Scottish towns and learned societies, and accepted by the Conservative government of the day, the Bill failed to reach the statue book (Stephenson, 1989, 135). It was re-introduced by himself and other MPs in 1898, 1900, 1906 and 1908, and was always resisted by the parliamentary strength of the landowners. Charles Trevelyan's Bill of 1908 differed from Bryce's only by omitting the phrase 'this Act shall not apply to England and Wales' (Stephenson, 1989, 138). There were, in all, 17 attempts to introduce an access bill in the 55 years between 1884 and 1939.

This public debate was closely followed in the press, with the *Times* taking one side, claiming in a leader on 14 May 1924 that there was no need for access legislation, only to be countered the following day by an editorial in the *Manchester Guardian*:

> *...The* Times *writer goes on to say that ... 'as a general rule the man or woman or child who wishes to explore the waste places of this island can do so without let or hindrance from anyone.'*
> *... Of the English Pennine Moorlands it was almost true some fifty years ago, and it has definitely ceased to be so since. The case of the higher parts of the Derbyshire Peak, over which anyone could ramble at will in 1890, and are now strictly preserved, to the exclusion of walkers and climbers, is only typical of what has been taken at almost every part of the Pennine range.* (Stephenson, 1989, 141)

Meanwhile, the Northern ramblers did not rely on parliamentary endeavour but steadily built public support by rallies and demonstrations, notably at Winnats Pass in the Peak District. There were those who saw deliberate trespass as an individual philosophical statement:

> *You need have no qualms of conscience about it; for there is no sin in a question of this kind; and if the owner of the field should come to you, as he once came to me, with a great hedgestake in his hand, and hard words in his mouth, there is a kind of 'blarney' which he cannot withstand ... indeed, the journey I am now taking you on is a perpetual trespass; so that you can either make up your mind to the iniquity of the thing or go back.* (Phillips in Stephenson, 1989, 45)

Indeed, many such incidents, some politically motivated, between keepers or farmers and ramblers ended in court, usually to the disadvantage of the ramblers (Stephenson, 1989). There was certainly resentment that Kinder Scout, a dozen square miles of moorland at the southern end of the Pennine Chain, was uncrossed by any right of way. This and adjacent moors were strictly preserved for grouse shooting. On 24 April 1932, 400 or more people gathered at Hayfield for a mass trespass on Kinder Scout, instigated by the British Workers' Sports Federation (BWSF), notably Benny Rothman, and impatient with what they saw as the futility of earlier protests. There were scuffles with the police and gamekeepers, in which one keeper was injured, as the marchers made their way to the top of Williams Clough to hold a celebratory meeting (Stephenson, 1989). On the way back five demonstrators, including Rothman, were arrested and charged with riotous assembly and assault. They were tried the following July, and BWSF held another rally in Winnats Pass just before the trial. All five received prison sentences of up to six months. Whether the mass trespass actually held back the cause for access is contested (Stephenson, 1989), but over the years it gained symbolic significance, with many commemoratory events attended by Rothman until his death in 2002. Significantly, one of those who doubted the wisdom of mass trespass was Sir Lawrence Chubb, Secretary of the Commons Society, who was to play a key role in subsequent events.

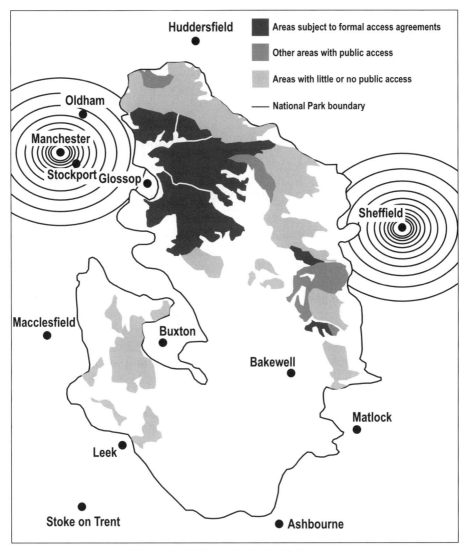

Figure 2.2 *Map of the Peak District*

However, the alternative legislative approach was to prove just as unsuccessful. In 1938, Arthur Creech Jones (later to become a minister in the 1945 Labour Government) introduced a simple Access to the Mountains Bill that was little different in content from Bryce's. Indeed, he used similar arguments during the Bill's second reading, while his Conservative opponents argued that it was a direct attack on private property (Stephenson, 1989). During the committee stages, Chubb privately negotiated to find an alternative measure that would be acceptable to the Land Union and the Central Landowners Association. This divided the access movement, and the eventual outcome was certainly a compromise weighted in favour of the landowners. The Act of 1939 only allowed for access orders to be made for specific areas, rather than providing a general right of access, and the onus and costs of obtaining such orders fell largely on rambling organizations. The Act excluded Scotland. Even more inflammatory, as far as the ramblers were concerned, was the introduction of a criminal offence of trespass. The Act was never implemented, and was eventually repealed and replaced by the National Parks and Access to the Countryside Act of 1949. Yet, ironically, it established the principle of limiting open access to specific areas, which has consistently remained in all subsequent legislation in England and Wales.

The National Parks and Access to the Countryside Act

The next opportunity for legislation came with the Labour landslide in the 1945 general election, following increasing political pressure for national parks. In 1926, the annual report of the Ministry of Health had stressed the need for the preservation of the countryside against development and recommended the reservation of green belts around towns. That year also saw the founding of the Council for the Preservation of Rural England (CPRE). In 1929, the CPRE sent a memorandum proposing that national parks be established to the then Prime Minister, Ramsay MacDonald, who had earlier supported the access to the mountains bills. MacDonald appointed a committee of inquiry to consider whether land should be reserved for national parks as had been done in the USA and Canada. This committee found in favour of nature reserves and measures to protect the countryside rather than publicly owned national parks, which had been established in many other countries. This was the first of many committees established with increasing frequency as the national parks lobby drew together the main elements of the open air movement and thereby grew in strength.

It is striking how, in the midst of the Second World War, attention focused so clearly on the social reconstruction which should follow the cessation of hostilities. The Scott Committee of 1942, with very wide-ranging terms of reference, recommended the designation of national parks, better access to the countryside and green belts. John Dower was appointed to conduct a survey of possible national park areas and, when he reported in 1945, he defined a national park as:

> *an extensive area of beautiful and relatively wild country in which, for the nation's benefit and by appropriate national decisions and action:*
>
> *(a) the characteristic landscape beauty is strictly preserved;*
>
> *(b) access and facilities for public open-air enjoyment are amply provided;*
>
> *(c) wildlife and buildings and places of architectural and historic interest are suitably protected, while;*

(d) established farming use is effectively maintained. (Dower, 1945)

By the time of the Labour landslide in the 1945 general election, agitation for countryside legislation was so strong that the Hobhouse Report of 1947 concentrated on the mechanisms of how national parks should be established, not on the case for their establishment. While the outdoor movement of this time was broadly based, the links with the labour movement were very strong indeed. Many prominent members of the 1945 Labour government were equally active in the RA, yet this did not automatically guarantee the swift passage of access legislation. As with Chubb's negotiations on the 1939 Act, there were moves for compromise behind the scenes. Stephenson recounts how a 'temporary' official in the Ministry of Town and Country Planning, working on the national parks legislation, noted the public support for the Dower and Hobhouse reports, but also recognized that 'the agricultural interest is, by common consent, a first priority today' (Stephenson, 1989, 50). The same author records how the Minister, Lewis Silkin, had spoken at a rally condemning the 1939 Act and was therefore thought to be sympathetic to the principle of open access. Yet, under the influence of his civil servants and after consultation with the Ministry of Agriculture, he came to favour limiting any new public rights of access to specified areas of uncultivated land in national parks. This was the provision that found its way into the 1949 Act, although Silkin himself admitted that the powers given to local authorities were much the same as those provided by the 1939 Act (Stephenson, 1989). Holt, in her introduction to Stephenson's book, comments:

> *The processes of policy formulation within Whitehall and the government thus resulted in the Hobhouse proposals being watered down, even in the most favourable political climate for a root and branch change which had so far come about.* (Stephenson, 1989, 52)

Nevertheless, Section V of the 1949 Act did provide mechanisms enabling county councils to negotiate access agreements, and where agreement could not be reached the Act empowered the council to make a compulsory access order. However, this latter power was seldom, if ever, used and the use of the (voluntary) access agreements has also been limited. But the scene had already been set by the Town and Country Planning Act of 1947, which established the principle of agricultural exemption, whereby the use of any land for the purposes of agriculture or forestry was excluded from its provisions, a freedom from planning restrictions on land use enjoyed by no other industry. This freedom, combined with the farmers' reluctance to concede any other 'proprietary interest' in their land holding, had obvious implications for access to open country (Centre for Leisure Research, 1986).

The 1949 Act also required county councils to survey and complete 'definitive maps' of rights of way. The intention was that, after objections had been heard, such maps would provide an accurate picture of existing rights of way but could be altered to reflect future needs. It appears that the complexity of these procedures, the differing priorities of county councils (often reflecting the strength of local political interests), and the preoccupation of highway authorities with vehicular traffic, meant that the process of securing an accessible system has been arduous and, despite subsequent changes in legislation in 1981 and 2001, is still the focus of a continuing campaign by the RA (Ramblers' Association, 2001a).

Given the history of conflict over access and its proximity to the major Northern conurbations of Manchester and Sheffield, it was no coincidence that in 1951 the Peak District was the first national park to be designated in England and Wales. Indeed, it is still one of the few areas that is both within easy access of major urban centres and meets Dower's definition of a national park as 'relatively wild country'.

Although the intention of the National Parks and Access to the Countryside Act of 1949 was essentially conservationist – 'to preserve those rural landscapes considered to be of national importance from the prospect of development' – the administrators of national parks were required to balance a number of interests. These are encompassed in Dower's definition of a national park and the recommendation of the Hobhouse Committee that park management would be needed 'to ensure that the peace and beauty of the countryside and the rightful interests of the resident population, are not menaced by an excessive concentration of visitors, or disturbed by incongruous pursuits' (Hobhouse, 1947). This echoes the fear of the 'menace' of urban hordes and of 'uncontrolled access' which appeared at the beginning of this chapter.

Key Points

In this account of a long-running conflict, we can identify most of the themes which will be explored throughout this book:

- the conflict between ideologies: in this case, between the rights and freedoms of the people ('we can only learn liberty from the use of liberty', Symonds, 1933, vii) and respect for private property and the status gained by the ownership of (large areas of) land;
- the value of political organization and the risk of compromise when confronted by superior power; leading to
- a continuing debate within a campaigning group (the RA) about tactics and strategy: whether to negotiate or to use the techniques of public protest to sway public opinion and thereby gain influence and power;
- the role of influential individuals; and
- the closed processes of policy formulation within government, which may negate the wishes of the majority.

THE DESIGNATION OF THE PENTLAND HILLS REGIONAL PARK

The Pentland Hills: 'A Lung for the City'

The literary references of writers such as Sir Walter Scott and Robert Louis Stevenson illustrate the inspiration that is provided by the spectacular backdrop that the Pentland Hills give to Edinburgh. Their scenic importance is perhaps derived more from their dominance and isolation in the coastal plain, and their proximity to Edinburgh, than their own particular character. (Lothian Regional Council, 1995)

The 500-m peaks of Allermuir and Caerketton at the northern end of a 27-km range face the city of Edinburgh, while the open landscape of the hills and the enclosed valleys provide an oasis of wildness and isolation so near to the city. However, the wildlife interest of the land has been impoverished by repeated grazing and burning. There has been a long tradition of public access to the privately owned land, with use of the hills probably as high in the 1930s, when access was by rail, as now, when most people travel by car and use a different range of access points. Not only have patterns of recreational use changed, but activities such as mountain biking now add to the pressures on hill paths. For many people, there is still some uncertainty about where they can go and this has added to the latent conflict between the ramblers' organizations, which have long advocated a right of freedom to roam in the Scottish hills, and the farming community.

A detailed chronology of events is set out in Figure 2.4 and the proximity of the hills to Edinburgh is shown in Figure 2.3.

The introduction to this case study, which features several times throughout this book, concentrates on the controversy over the designation of the regional park in 1983–1986. This continued during the formal consultation process leading up to the approval of the subject local plan in 1988. Despite the plan's approval, four years later the local newspaper featured an article headed 'The Open War':

Farmers' Fury: Pentlands access brings problems to the people who make their living on the slopes. Pentland Hills Regional Park was created four years ago to preserve the scenic splendour of the slopes for generations to enjoy. But the thunder clouds are gathering. (McGhee, 1993, 10)

The article quotes several of the protagonists, such as a farmer who recalled:

When the park was set up we decided to co-operate and make the most of it. But at the moment we are at a serious disadvantage and a farmer going bankrupt is not going to be able to maintain this landscape which everyone values so highly.

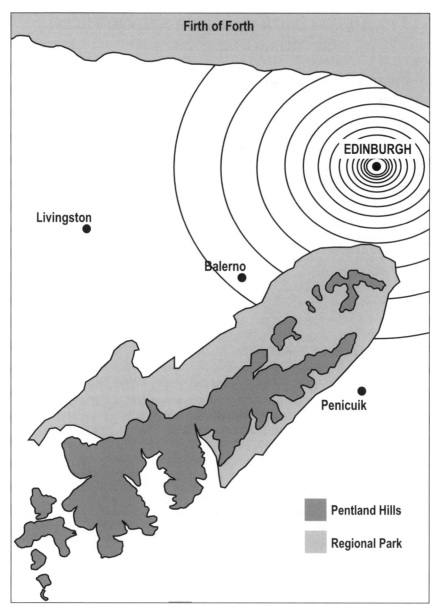

Figure 2.3 *Map of the Pentland Hills*

1967	Countryside (Scotland) Act conferred powers on local authorities to conserve the countryside and to make provision for recreation
1968	Local amenity groups concerned about threat of encroachment onto the Pentland Hills by residential development on the outskirts of Edinburgh
1969	The army decided to modernize their ranges at Castlelaw and Dreghorn amidst public objection
1970	Establishment of Pentland Hills Technical Group by local authorities and Countryside Commission for Scotland (CCS) to consider countryside recreational needs
1972	Publication of the report of the Technical Group: Pentland Hills, Conservation and Recreation (the Blue Book)
1973	Establishment of consultative committee with wide-ranging membership to discuss the Blue Book
1974	Publication of Park System for Scotland by CCS
1975	Creation of Lothian Regional Council's (LRC) Leisure and Recreation Department. Director-designate appointed to co-ordinate the project and supervise the ranger service. Formation of advisory committee with local authority and local organization membership to implement the Blue Book and to prepare a series of locality schemes over the next three years
1978	Advisory committee replaced by smaller Rural Land Management Group to offer advice to planning team from owners, farmers and other land users
1981	Countryside (Scotland) Act conferred powers on regional councils to designate regional parks and to manage land under the control of the council as a single administrative unit. Initial recreation developments at Flotterstone
1982	LRC's Leisure and Recreation Department dissolved. Discussions between the three regional councils culminated in the exclusion of areas in Borders and Strathclyde from the proposed park
1983	Publication of a Policy for Regional Parks by CCS. Meeting with Scottish Landowners' Federation resulted in one-third of the area being removed from the proposals
1984	Consultation on LRC's proposals, including public hearing, followed by decision by LRC to designate, which confirmed the principles of the Blue Book and the making of the designation order
1985	Public inquiry considered objections to designation order
1986	Confirmation of order by Secretary of State with recommendation that Subject Local Plan be prepared
1987	Appointment of consultative committee
1988	Draft plan issued for consultation
1989	Appointment of regional park manager and advisory committee. Adoption of Pentland Hills Regional Park Plan. Withdrawal of Ministry of Defence (MOD) proposal to extend training areas. First management agreements and farm plans under new authority.
1990	Park authority publishes Farming and the Regional Park – Cultivating a Partnership.
1993	National Farmers Union sends letter of complaint to chairman of the advisory committee. Farmers sub-group to advisory committee formed. Evening News article writes of 'open war' between farmers and park authority
1996	Abolition of LRC

Source: Sidaway (1996).

Figure 2.4 *Historical Summary of the Designation of the Pentland Hills Regional Park*

> *Because it is called a regional park, visitors think it belongs to the taxpayer and that they are free to roam anywhere – a real problem at lambing and during nesting times.*

A member of a walking organization expressed other frustrations:

> *In some people's mind, the park is a means of decreasing access. No public rights of way have been hindered but this fencing is offensive to the Scottish tradition of freedom to roam. To be denied that freedom makes me angry. It spoils the feeling of being in the wild. Some method has to be found where landowners can be happier in welcoming people to the countryside. If this happens there will be less trouble. Two hundred years of progress meant that many townies had lost touch with the countryside. We have to find some way of repairing that so that the divide between town and country is not so stark.*

Meanwhile, the park's Chief Ranger thought that the main problem could be communication. 'We're all after the same thing. It's just a matter of how you get there' (McGhee, 1993, 10). This proved to be true, for this was not so much a conflict between farmers and ramblers as a case of poor communication, particularly on the part of local authorities.

The Origins of the Regional Park

Concerns about the Pentland Hills go back to the middle of the 19th century with, for example, the formation of the Scottish Rights of Way and Recreation Society in 1845 and Robert Louis Stevenson's fears of encroaching development. 'It seems as if it must come to an open fight at last to preserve a corner of green country unbedevilled' (quoted in Crumley, 1991). The pressures of development and extensions to military use prompted the establishment of the Pentland Hills Technical Group in 1970, and the Group's report (1972) contained the first proposals to designate the Hills as a regional park. The title of the report (known at the time as the 'Blue Book') hinted at striking a balance between conservation and recreation, and if this concept had been carried consistently through the subsequent debates, designation should have been a formality attracting little opposition, but this was far from the case. How then did the proposals appear on paper, and did the park vary in concept from the earliest proposals to the policies of the subject local plan?

In fact, the concept of the proposed regional park varied very little from study to plan. The Blue Book proposed a set of six principles 'against which future demands for recreation development can be considered'. These were as follows:

1   The proximity of the Pentlands to Edinburgh gives their scenery an amenity value greater than the intrinsic quality of the landscape might suggest. Stringent controls should be exercised over forms of land use which are potentially damaging to the appearance of the hills and, where necessary, funds made available for the positive conservation of those intimate features of the landscape (such as hardwood plantings) on which the attractiveness of the scenery so much depends.

2   Planning for increased use of land for recreational purposes must aim at co-existence in harmony with the older traditional uses and their modern counterparts.

3   To maintain the present variety of recreational opportunities in the Pentlands and to ensure a proper balance in the development of facilities (particularly between the east and west sides), we recommend that, in so far as the study area should be managed for recreation, such management should be co-ordinated.

4   In providing for recreation in the Pentlands, the emphasis should be on passive enjoyment of the countryside and on those informal recreation activities ... as being appropriate.

5   The Pentlands should be regarded as a day visitor area for recreation.

6   Finally, the supplementary and complementary role of the Pentlands to that of the coast and other countryside in providing for day visitors should be recognized and the present local authorities should, in advance of the proposed reorganization of local government, cooperate in planning comprehensively for the management of day visitor resources in the coast and countryside around Edinburgh (Pentland Hills Technical Group, 1972, 48).

Thus the growing needs of recreation near the city were to be met, but the emphasis was on conserving the resource by only allowing 'appropriate activities' and seeking co-existence between recreation and existing land uses. The study advocates a 'general policy for recreation management' based on the aim of integrated resource management. Indeed, regional park status is proposed 'to give recognition to the importance of integrated resource management' (Pentland Hills Technical Group, 1972, 48, 50 and 61).

Conservation of both the visual and natural resource and the preservation of solitude are seen as necessary constraints placing limits on recreation provision to a limited number of major access points, whilst the remainder of the area is to remain undeveloped to preserve its 'remoteness'. Thus on a close reading it is clear that the authors of the Blue Book were primarily motivated by a concern to conserve the Pentland Hills, with the conservation of the natural and human resources, with agriculture as well as wildlife. The detailed proposals (locality studies) in the Blue Book concentrate on how these aims were to be achieved. However, they are all concerned with recreation developments, and the concept of integrated resource management is not further developed. This apparent emphasis on recreation may not have been intended but it is how many interested parties interpreted subsequent events.

Although the Lothian Regional Council (LRC) worked steadily to implement the recommendations of the Blue Book and establish a regional park, it lacked the statutory authority to formalize the arrangements until 1981, when the proponents of designation (the Regional Council and the Countryside Commission for Scotland (CCS)) were keen to see their new legislative powers implemented.

LRC established committees to consider the proposals and concentrated its developments on land already in its ownership at Hillend, Bonaly and the regional reservoirs. It held a public hearing in 1984 and subsequently gave assurances that it would safeguard the character of the hills when the council formally resolved to designate the park in October 1984.

The Response to the Designation Proposals

During the period of consultation on the Designation Order in November 1984, 82 representations were received, of which only eight could be classified as support for the proposals. Even in those cases the support given was so qualified that it could almost be classified as opposition. The objectors fell into four main groups:

- 26 landowning and farming interests;
- seven conservation organizations;
- 21 representatives and members of the local community (that is, residents within the proposed park or the adjoining settlements); and
- ten residents of Edinburgh and farther afield.[1]

In essence, the objections of the farming community were:

- the perceived threats to its livelihood from increased recreational use;
- the use of the title 'park', which might give the impression that land was now publicly owned and freely accessible;
- the costs of the proposal and their lack of justification;
- the lack of evident public support for the proposals; and
- boundary considerations.

Conservation organizations were more likely to give heavily qualified support for the proposals, but their main misgivings centred on:

- the lack of clear aims and a management plan; and
- the need for a consultative committee on which their interests were represented.

Local community councils and individuals living in neighbouring settlements expressed a wide range of misgivings, with the cost of the proposals being perhaps their main concern. Edinburgh residents, on the other hand, were rather more concerned about the use of the title 'park', the development they thought that implied (including increased and inappropriate forms of recreation provision), and the potential disruption to their enjoyment of the hills and to wildlife.

Thus, to the opponents of the scheme the park was still perceived purely as a large recreational scheme, not least because the committees charged with developing the proposals concentrated on the locality schemes, while the department initially charged with promoting the park was the Leisure and Recreation Department of the LRC. Although various advisory committees were established, there was little direct contact between the Regional Council staff, local inhabitants and recreational users. The lack of clear proposals in the form of a management plan created uncertainty, and was a major feature of opposition by the conservation interests.

Debate became increasingly confrontational, particularly after a public meeting at Currie High School in September 1984 when only nine out of approximately 250 people supported designation. This was partly because of the arrogant way in which LRC officials presented their case as a foregone conclusion. The controversy gained considerable coverage in the local press, which was influential in turning public opinion against the proposal. Representations on the designation order were formally considered within a public inquiry held in 1985, and there was no attempt to negotiate on the proposals. The Reporter to the inquiry concluded that the Pentland Hills merited designation. 'Indeed, there can be few areas in Scotland which are more suitable for such designation, in terms of landscape, traditional and recently developed recreational uses, existing rights of way and proximity to a large population' (Bell, 1985, 64). Although he could not impose conditions on the Designation Order, the Reporter also concluded that the successful operation of the regional park depended on the preparation of a five-year plan aimed at 'consolidation of the existing de facto features of a regional park' (ibid, 66). This quasi-condition offered the clarification of intentions that had hitherto been lacking, and contributed to the general acceptance of the Secretary of State's decision confirming the Designation Order, made in 1986.

Attitudes to Designation

The representations made to the public inquiry held before designation in 1985 and the written representations made during consultation on the subject local plan during 1988 show how support for the park increased.[2] Of the 82 representations made at the time of designation, 66 were of outright objection, but this changed markedly by the time of the consultations on the subject local plan, when only nine objections were received. Many former objectors were taking neutral positions (17 out of 54 representations) or even joining the supporters of the plan, who were now slightly in the majority (28 out of 54 representations).

By the time of consultations on the subject local plan, the argument had changed from whether the park should be established to how it should be managed. Objections of principle were still valid, and basic beliefs on the rights of landowners or 'freedom to roam' were unchanged, but they had become less material to the debate. Hence consultation responses concentrated on detailed proposals. This apparent shift in opinion is even more marked when one considers the interest groups concerned. The 1991 interview survey revealed that the park was now accepted by landowners and farmers as a political reality. Their response to designation was pragmatic, although they were still opposed to the park in principle, and often made sweeping criticisms; half the farming respondents made some statement of acceptance, however resigned. For example:

> *I had been opposed to the regional park, totally, now we are stuck with it and we have to get something out of it.*
>
> *We are all for working together as long as they don't tell us what to do.* (Sidaway, 1991a, 16)

However, the farming community actively cooperated with the park management, as was evident from either their positive attitudes to the ranger service (nine respondents) and/or their participation in management agreements or projects (six respondents).

The position of the conservation and recreation organizations and local community groups changed from one of generally highly qualified support to one of firm support with only occasional misgivings. For example, it appeared that several organizations had made formal objections to designation for tactical reasons, either to obtain modifications to the proposals, to ensure representation on any consultative committee or to ensure that they could cross-examine other objectors. It also appeared that none of these organizations were opposed to the park in principle, but they were concerned with how it might be organized or managed. The history of what was seen as poor consultation and indifferent management by the Regional Council, the lack of clarity of its intentions and the absence of a plan had brought about their initial 'opposition'. One honorary officer of a local community organization described how being presented with a 'fait accompli' by the Regional Council at a public meeting 'whipped people [who had hitherto favoured the park] into a frenzy'. It was small things like this that produced an end-result in the weight of initial objections from community organizations.

Most of the same elements in the Blue Book were to appear in the subject local plan and in much the same order, but the conservation emphasis of the plan set out in the 'Aims of the Regional Park' was quite explicit:

1 *To retain the essential character of the hills as a place for the peaceful enjoyment of the countryside.*

2 *Caring for the hills, so that the landscape and the habitat is protected and enhanced.*

3 *Within this caring framework, to encourage responsible public enjoyment of the hills.*

4 *Co-ordination of these aims so that they co-exist with farming and other land uses within the park.* (Lothian Regional Council, 1989, 2)

Nevertheless, although the two documents were similar in intention, supporters of the park needed considerable reassurance before they would accept that recreation and conservation were to be kept in balance. Many of the attitudes of the opponents of the park have persisted, and their residual hostility to its designation flairs up from time to time. This may come from landowners arguing (as late as 1997) that the park should be abolished, or from those keen to conserve the Pentland Hills:

The [people defending the hills] need an organization dedicated to the wellbeing of the hills ... which can be as effective as the Pentland Hills Regional Park is ineffective. The park is an aberration. It was unwanted. It is unloved. It is also expensive and wasteful. (Crumley, 1991)

Conclusions

The recent history of the Pentland Hills Regional Park appears to have passed through two distinct phases. The long-drawn-out exploratory phase, which aroused much local opposition, was followed by a period of (perhaps resigned) acceptance following the confirmation of the Designation Order.

That the park was so long in gestation was perhaps inevitable given the lack of an enabling legislative framework. However, the LRC's involvement over that period did not, for a variety of reasons, lead to a gradual acceptance by the public of the benefits that designation might bring. On the contrary, it was a period of constant and apparently consistent objection which only ended with the Secretary of State's decision.

During that initial phase, issues of principle featured strongly in the debate, although it seems likely that many fears were exaggerated and some of the grounds of objection used at the time of the public inquiry were based on suppositions which probably had little basis in fact, e.g., the loss of capital value of the land. With hindsight, it appears that the LRC did not communicate its purposes effectively and spell out clearly what the implications and potential benefits of designation might be. It may also be that such information might have fallen on deaf ears. In phase two, the consultations on the subject local plan were certainly marked by better communications once the battle of principles was over.

Yet the concerns of the farming and landowning communities were unchanged and they considered that most of their fears had been justified. They grudgingly accepted the reality of the park, that designation went through the full political process, and that while, in the main, they did not agree with the Secretary of State's decision, they learnt to live with it. The various remedial actions undertaken by the LRC dealt only with administrative details as far as the farming community were concerned, e.g., consultation on a plan and the operation of the advisory committee. 'We talk to them and have our say and they do what they like' (farmer interviewed in 1993). Nothing substantial was done to improve their livelihood and this is a fundamental weakness of the regional park designation. The only remedy that had widespread support among the farming community was the extension and redirection of the ranger service, but in their eyes its effectiveness was severely limited by the lack of funding for practical work that might mitigate the disturbance to their enterprises or the damage to their properties.

For the public interest groups the balance sheet looked rather different. Remedies were applied which met their initial concerns and many uncertainties were removed by the subject local plan, its consultations and the operation of the advisory committee. But the public interest groups were concerned that a park authority, which should be able to operate in their interest, was under-funded, so that the worst aspects of wear and tear could not be restored or, as far as the most radical critics are concerned, major improvements could not be contemplated.

The very different perspectives on the park title, the ranger service and the park authority epitomize the distinctions between landowning and public interests. To the former, use of the title 'park' provided a fundamental problem. They considered that it was misleading, suggesting that the public had rights on private land which did not exist, and it acted as an insidious form of publicity encouraging people to visit the hills. To the public interest groups it was an irrelevance. It was not an issue, or made no difference.

If it was hoped that attitudes to the regional park would significantly change once designation had taken effect and that people would be won over by management, limited comfort can be gained from the findings of the 1991 study (Sidaway, 1991a). The farming community accepted the reality of political power, and it was prepared to make the best of a situation with which it did not agree. However, to alleviate more of its concerns required a long, sustained, well resourced effort. Local people have long memories while officials and politicians come and go.

Key Points

Although the same issue as in the previous case study – public access to private land for recreation – lies at the heart of this local conflict, ideology did not play such a prominent part because the dispute was largely between the farming community and the local authority. Nevertheless, this case illustrates several important themes which will be explored later:

- The failure of official decision-makers both to communicate their intentions and to address the needs of the affected farming community. In this respect, the local authority was not aided by a basic flaw in the regional park mechanism: it provides a cachet but is not accompanied by compensatory resources.
- The local authorities did not build trust in the initial stages of this dispute and, as will be seen in the accounts of later stages in following chapters, has been struggling to gain trust ever since.
- The failure of formal consultation exercises to engage with local communities, as in the case of the 1989 subject local plan.

Chapter 3

Using Social Theory to Explain Conflicts

Conflict is the means to change, the means by which social values of welfare, scarcity, justice and opportunities for personal development can be achieved ... the only guarantee that the aspirations of society will be achieved. (Burton, 1972, 137)

SYNOPSIS

This chapter describes how conflicts can be examined at various levels, starting with the analysis of the positions, interests, needs and fears of stakeholders. Conflicts are both multi-dimensional and dynamic. Indeed, in seemingly similar situations, examples can be found of both cooperation and conflict, when the issues are the same but the differences lie in the relationships, or lack of them, between the interest groups. Conflicts are epitomized by the polarized positions of the parties competing within adversarial political debates or public hearings/inquiries. In contrast, cooperative relationships are based on openness and trust. As in other political struggles, conflicts pass through active and inactive phases as interest groups operate within or outside the political process. They organize and lobby in their attempts to gain legitimacy and the power to use and control the use of natural resources. Sound conflict analysis lays the foundation for conflict resolution by developing an understanding of the dynamic processes of conflict and the importance to participants of historical events within each long-running struggle. The theories underlying this perspective are those of social action and policy analysis. The primary concern of social action theorists is to relate theories of conflict to theories of social change and to suggest that conflict performs a useful social function. The other broad approach, which could be termed 'managerial', is taken by policy analysts, whose main aim is to develop models of decision-making. A synthesis of these theories is developed to shed light on the 'function' and 'processes' of conflict. This chapter illustrates the value of this approach by further analysing the two case studies described in Chapter 2: the controversy over the designation of the Pentland Hills Regional Park (PHRP) in Scotland, and the struggle for public access to open countryside in England and Wales, exemplified by access to the moors of the Peak District National Park.

CONFLICT ANALYSIS

Positions, Interests and Beliefs

The confused nature of public policy conflicts was briefly described in the Preface, particularly the complexity of the issues, the lack of clarity over the numbers of participants, and confusion over which of them truly represent the public interest, although many claim to be acting on grounds of principle rather than their own self-interest (Brown and Marriott, 1993). Implicit in this description is a concern about the relationships between groups rather than individuals, although individuals may play a prominent role. It is somewhat typical of these situations that the proponents do not always say what they want; indeed, they may make exaggerated claims of their needs. They are seemingly setting out their stalls and bargaining, yet many elements are not open to negotiation and the underlying rationale of these claims is obscure. A number of attempts has been made to define a series of basic concepts which allow these situations to be analysed; these principally include positions, interests, needs, fears and beliefs. The dominant paradigm is that of negotiation.

Advocates of the negotiation approach to resolving conflict place great emphasis on 'interest-based bargaining' and the need to differentiate between 'positions' and 'interests' (e.g., Fisher et al, 1997; Susskind et al, 2000). In their terminology, positions are indeed negotiating stances, whilst interests are the underlying motivations, needs, desires and concerns of the negotiators. The distinction between position and interest was illustrated when the National Rifle Association (NRA) demanded the right to use firearms within Los Angeles National Forest, California. By recognizing but not challenging the NRA's ideologically-based position, the mediator involved was able to identify a negotiable goal that would satisfy its primary interest, in this case the use of a safe isolated gully as a target practice site, and thus work towards a feasible solution in a suitable location (Tice, 1990).

People tend to organize around a 'cause', which might be based on their material interests, their principles or their political agenda (Mack and Snyder, 1957). Many other authors emphasize the role of ideology and principles in environmental conflicts and that fundamental differences in values, beliefs or ideology are not open to negotiation (Van Doorn, 1966; Deutsch, 1973; Baumgartner et al, 1978; Amy, 1987). The main distinctions they make are between beliefs (i.e., values or concerns about future goals and the way the world should be) and interests (typically economic concerns) which may be threatened or advanced by conflict. Yet while conflicting ideologies are a common feature of such disputes, ideological differences are often suppressed in the bid for consensus, allowing interest groups with differing ideologies to reach settlements. This would suggest that the ideologies or underlying beliefs of interest groups remain unchanged, while their interest in a resource may be negotiable.

Equally, negotiation over bargaining positions appears to be somewhat futile, but there is often scope to negotiate at the level of interests, as these can be expressed or achieved in different ways (Acland, 1995). Acland suggested that while values are not negotiable, an individual's relative priorities may change – for example, placing greater emphasis on family welfare over personal pride in a given situation. He advocated building agreement around the common ground of shared interests, values, needs and fears, which is consistent with the move from positional to interest-based bargaining. 'One of the unfortunate effects of an adversarial process is to exacerbate fears while doing little to reassure people their needs will be satisfied' (Acland, 1995, 51). In practice, the subtle distinction between interests and needs may be difficult to sustain. Indeed, some authors prefer to simplify the analysis to examine the basis of a dispute in terms of positions, needs and fears, recognizing that fears are often no more than negative expressions of needs (Cornelius and Faire, 1989).

The synthesis of these ideas recognizes that negotiating over positions is indeed futile, and obscures what people are really seeking: the satisfaction of interests that can probably be met in a numbers of ways. The clues to identifying interests come from questioning people's concerns, usually expressed as fears and needs. Understanding personal or group beliefs and values provides motives, helps to explain interests and may provide the common ground to build trust. The relationships are set out in Figure 3.1.

This form of analysis is illustrated in two examples: the designation of the PHRP and moorland access in the Peak District. In the Pentlands case, many concerns over the proposed designation of the regional park were subsequently alleviated. These are set out in Box 3.1. The underlying interests have been deduced from this evidence, and demonstrate that there was a common interest in effective conservation of the hills, and fears that this would not be delivered on the part of the different stakeholders (see Figure 3.2).

Thus the first level of conflict analysis is stakeholder analysis, in which the interested parties are identified. Various definitions of 'stakeholder' have been suggested that emphasize the interests or concerns which people or organizations may have with the outcome of a decision. For example, Wilcox (1994) considers stakeholders to 'have an interest in what happens because they will be affected by the outcome or can have some influence over it'. He suggests a set of questions which help to identify legitimate claims to stakeholder status, namely:

- Who will benefit or be adversely affected by proposals?
- Who might help, delay or hinder the initiative?
- Who has skills, money or resources they can contribute?
- Who ultimately is in a position to decide if this goes ahead or not?

These relationships are further explored in an analysis of the perspectives of the principal stakeholders concerned with moorland access in the Peak District National Park in the early 1990s (see Figure 3.3). By this time the dispute had developed from a bilateral conflict between the farming community and ramblers to include nature conservation interests. The standpoint of the national park authority is also explored in its promotion of moorland management as part of the national park plan.

While there are common elements in the two case studies, as countryside access is a common theme and the beliefs of the farming community and the recreation interests are consistently the same, differences in needs and fears illustrate the differences between what was essentially a local conflict in the Pentlands and the more politicized situation of the Peak District as an element of a national campaign for access. It may be that interest groups tend to move towards more principled arguments as a conflict escalates, while different factions within an interest group may argue from different standpoints. Typically, the national headquarters of an organization will argue from a position of principle, which may help to legitimize the advancement of its interests in the eyes of the general public while reassuring the group's membership that its leaders remain faithful to the cause.

POSITIONS
Negotiating stance expressed as claims, demands or solutions
which are *Non-negotiable* and hinder negotiation

CONCERNS
May be expressed as needs and fears and which help to identify interests
Non-negotiable but may be increased or decreased
NEEDS – basic, underlying, can be met in a number of ways
FEARS – perceived risks to the satisfaction of needs

INTERESTS
Often obscured/hard to detect
Can be met in a variety of ways and are Negotiable

VALUES AND BELIEFS
Views on what is right or wrong and how the world should be, which reflect personal or group identity. The priority given to different values may change in given situation
Non-negotiable

Source: derived from Acland, 1995; Fisher et al, 1997; Cornelius and Faire, 1989.

Figure 3.1 *Assessment of Positions, Interests and Beliefs*

Box 3.1 Needs, Fears and Interests in the Pentland Hills

The conflict concerning the designation of the Pentland Hills Regional Park (PHRP) was described in Chapter 2. The survey on which this account was based (Sidaway, 1991a) gathered data on the responses of each interest group towards the proposed designation, their concerns (the representations they made at each stage) and the extent to which these changed as the Designation Order was confirmed and the subsequent plan began to be implemented.

By tabulating the representations made when designation was first proposed, it is possible to classify them as the needs and fears of organizations or individuals, and to deduce their underlying values and interests in the area (see Figure 3.2). This shows that the needs of the landowners and farmers were largely economic, and their major concerns were expressed as fears that increased recreational use of the hills might affect their livelihoods or those of their tenants, or that additional planning restrictions would depress land values. They were united in considering the title 'park' to be misleading and an incitement to trespass by the public. Those landowners with sporting interests rated the potential disturbance to shooting as highly as, or more highly than, disruption to farming. Landowners and farmers were also concerned about the cost of managing the regional park, which they saw as extravagant and unnecessary. The interview survey showed that their grounds of opposition to designation remained unchanged as the process unfolded.

However, the concerns of the farming community did change in two important respects. Firstly, the ranger service, which was earlier criticized as being inadequate to serve the needs of farmers, was later supported by the vast majority of the farming community. Secondly, objections about the lack of precision in the Lothian Regional Council (LRC)'s early proposals and the need for a management plan appeared to be satisfied as the plan developed. Perhaps more significantly, they were willing to cooperate with the park once designation had taken effect.

The 'public interest' organizations representing conservation, recreation and local community shared many of the farming community's concerns about designation, and considered that these were alleviated by the preparation of the subject local plan and subsequent changes in management. For example, fears about the urbanization of the hills by major recreation developments and a high public profile for the area generated by over-publicity were allayed. Nor were the conservation professionals' fears of disturbance to wildlife realized. But while most of these organizations were satisfied with the plan, they were not satisfied with the evident lack of resources to implement its proposals. Most of these organizations were concerned about their lack of representation on the advisory committee, particularly the sport and recreation interests. None of the public interest groups thought the use of the title 'park' would make any practical difference to levels of recreational use or visitor behaviour.

Most of the non-economic concerns of the conservation, recreation and community organizations were alleviated at the second stage because their interests had been met. However, as the regional park designation did not carry with it any economic benefits to the farmers and landowners, these interests were not satisfied and their concerns remained.

Basic beliefs can also be inferred, i.e., statements of values held by the individual which change rarely, if at all. For example, landowners are likely to believe in the sanctity of private property, while ramblers may believe that there should be public rights to roam over privately owned open land. Others may be deduced from telling phrases in the interviews: for example, 'we are all for working together as long as they don't tell us what to do' illustrates the conviction that lives and livelihoods on farms depend on autonomy to respond to the vicissitudes of the seasons, and this must not be hamstrung by the demands of bureaucracy.

Source: Sidaway, 1991a.

POSITIONS

Landowners and farmers – oppose park as unnecessary
Conservation and recreation organizations – qualified support for park in principle
Local communities – object to park being 'urbanized'

CONCERNS

Expressed as representations to the draft Designation Order

FEARS

Shared by all groups – ineffectiveness of park management, i.e., inadequate ranger service; disturbance to wildlife from water sports; inadequate budget; inability of Lothian Regional Council (LRC) to manage park; uncertainty of aims from lack of park plan; excessive publicity leading to overuse of park
Landowners and farmers – loss in land values; additional planning restrictions; effects of increased recreation on livelihoods; misleading park title
Conservation groups and local communities – impact of recreation on wildlife.
Conservation/recreation groups and local communities – 'urbanization' of recreation

NEEDS

Recreation groups – safeguards for access
Conservation/recreation groups and local communities – representation on advisory committee

INTERESTS

Landowners and farmers – maintenance of capital value of the land, income and privacy; minimal interruption to farming and sporting activities
Conservation groups and local communities – survival of wildlife, improvement of habitats
Recreation groups – improvements to existing access, e.g., agreed path network
Recreation groups and local communities – quiet enjoyment of the hills

VALUES & BELIEFS

Landowners – sanctity of private property
Farmers – autonomy of decision-making
Recreation groups – freedom to roam at will
Conservation groups – primacy of nature
All groups support the conservation of the hills

Figure 3.2 *Assessment of Positions, Interests and Beliefs during the Designation of the Pentland Hills Regional Park*

POSITIONS

Landowners and farmers – access interferes with land management
Ramblers – limitations on access are unjustified
Conservationists – species and habitats are seriously threatened
National park authority – planning can balance needs

FEARS

Landowners and farmers – disturbance from increased use is affecting livelihood; loss of autonomy
Ramblers – quality of experience hampered by 'inappropriate' activities', e.g., mountain bikes
Conservationists – disturbance from increased use affecting breeding success of ground nesting birds and trampling of vegetation
National park authority – lack of resources and failure to meet aims

INTERESTS

Landowners and farmers – minimal interruption to farming and sporting activities
Ramblers – safeguards for and improvements to existing access, e.g., routes along desire lines
Conservationists – protection of specific areas, e.g., breeding sites and wet areas in moorland
National park authority – cooperation of interests in management of moorlands to ensure natural qualities predominate

VALUES & BELIEFS

Landowners and farmers – sanctity of private property, autonomy of decision-making
Ramblers – right to roam at will
Conservationists – primacy of nature
National park authority – obligation to meet national park aims
All groups support park aims and conservation of moorland

Note: Positions, fears and beliefs were publicly expressed, while interests only became evident during Access Consultative Group negotiations (see Chapter 5)

Figure 3.3 *Assessment of Positions, Interests and Beliefs:
Moorland Access in the Peak District National Park 1990–1993*

However, at a local level, some members may be more willing to set principles aside to obtain tangible benefits from negotiation.

Attempts to Classify Conflicts

Various writers have attempted to classify conflicts using the metaphor of clinical medicine, in which the identification of symptoms leads to a diagnosis of cause and thereby suggests a remedy. However, Deutsch (1973) commented that the substantive issue (or apparent cause) may or may not be the most important for the disputing individuals and organizations. Conflicts are only partly about the nature of the dispute, and are as much about the relationships between the disputing parties within the broader context in which they are situated. Thus his typology is multi-dimensional, listing: the characteristics of the parties; their prior relationships; the social environment; the interested audience; and the strategy and tactics followed by the parties, as well as the type of issue in dispute. Van Doorn (1966) had earlier considered some of the same elements by differentiating between conflicts of interest, based on economic concerns; ideology, based on principles; and the distribution of power within organizations. However, he did suggest that many conflicts present combinations of these situations. Variations on this classification are suggested by Amy (1987) and Druckman (1993), distinguishing between three models of conflicts: conflicts arising from misunderstandings between different parties, from their competing interests or from their opposing beliefs. The purpose of Amy's typology was to identify those conflicts in which mediation may be an appropriate form of conflict resolution. The classification suggested that mediation is feasible in the first two of his categories but not in the third, as fundamental beliefs are non-negotiable. However, he recognized that these three categories are not mutually exclusive, and elements of each can apply in combination within a single conflict, which can be confirmed by examining the case studies presented in this book. There are elements of conflicts of interest, beliefs and misunderstandings in each case study, along with the constraints or legal demands of the decision-making process, which suggest multiple rather than single causality. In other words, it is not possible to identify mutually exclusive categories of conflict, which might be used for identifying appropriate forms of conflict resolution.

Pross (1993), in describing the operation of pressure groups in Canada, noted that many scholars attempt to classify groups according to the causes they promote, usually those pursuing self-interest or more general public interests. However, he considered the classification 'messy', as too many groups work simultaneously for both selective benefits and the public interest. Groups are difficult to categorize, as there is often a fine line between self-interest and public interest. Moreover, the approach ignores the relationship with government. He suggested that most pressure groups are chameleons: that is,

> *those that take their lobbying role seriously adapt their internal organisations and structure to suit the policy system in which they happen to operate.* (Pross, 1993, 147)

Thus the institutional context can also have an important influence on the course of a conflict.

The multi-dimensional nature of conflict has been recognized by various writers who give differing emphasis to particular characteristics of conflicts. Although certain relatively consistent patterns have been identified, no typology of conflicts has been generally accepted. The purposes of these typologies have not always been made clear; they tend to be generalized across a very broad canvas and have weak empirical bases. None appear to cover the full range of factors, and no one typology appears therefore to offer any practical advantage over any other.

Dimensions of Conflict

Despite their weaknesses, the existing typologies contribute to the identification of a number of consistent elements or dimensions of conflict, covering:

- beliefs: differences over what is right or wrong or how the world should be;
- interests: competition for resources;
- data: concerning the level of understanding of the issue, notably the lack of, relevance of, interpretation or assessment of information;
- relationships: personal emotions or enmities, tactics and strategies, poor communication and misunderstandings between the parties; and
- procedures: types of decision-making and concerns about the fairness of their outcomes (based on Moore, 1986; Amy, 1987).

During a conflict, the parties are likely to behave in a way that will harm or thwart the interests of their opponents, often attempting to discredit the other side rather than looking constructively for an equitable solution. Often it is the previous relationships between parties that determine whether they are likely to resort to conflict rather than cooperation. The contrasting aspects of conflict and cooperation are set out in Figure 3.4, based on the author's previous case study research (Sidaway, 1996), and can be viewed as two sides of the same coin. This shows how competing interests or opposing beliefs may lie at the heart of a conflict, coupled with misunderstandings over the nature of the dispute between different individuals and organizations, and from the way they interact within the prevailing system of decision-making.

The Social Function of Conflict

Max Weber suggested that society varies between conditions of equilibrium and conflict. From this standpoint, conflict is endemic in social life but tends to operate in favour of the powerful: that is, those with a vested interest in the status quo (Scimecca, 1993). Scimecca assessed Weber's main contribution to conflict theory to be the explanation he provided of how power is legitimized and stabilized in society. The major components of Weber's conflict theory are concerned with: the role of power; the emphasis on organized systems; legitimacy; and the individual who acts in his or her self-interest and marshals resources to achieve his or her own ends. These can be summarized as follows:

- Conflicts are endemic in social life.
- Power is differentially distributed among groups and individuals in society.
- Social order is achieved in any society through rules and commands issued by more powerful persons to less powerful persons and enforced through sanctions.

- Coercion proves to be an ineffective basis for maintaining power as it is seen to be illegitimate and it is the legitimate use of power that holds societies together.
- Powerful elements in society (or indeed the government) continually seek to convince others (e.g., the electorate) that their use of power is legitimate even though the distribution of power (power structure) favours the interests of the powerful.
- The powerful generally support the status quo and oppose changes that would reduce their power.
- Order is maintained by co-opting political challengers into the power structure or suppressing underlying conflicts.
- However, changes in a society occur as a result of action by persons who stand to benefit from these changes and who accumulate power to bring them to pass.
- If the powerful see that they can benefit from a particular change (e.g., industrialization of a 'backward' society), they will usually not hesitate to foster change (Scimecca, 1993, 216; Duke, 1979, 69–70).

CONFLICT	COOPERATION VIA CONSENSUS
Differences in Belief	
• Issues are elevated to matters of principle on which there can be no negotiation	• Differences in beliefs are respected and principles are laid to one side
Competing Interests	
• Each side aims for 'winner takes all'	• Efforts are made to accommodate everyone's needs
Data and Understanding	
• There is uncertainty over a contentious issue which is not fully understood	• The issue is understood
• Information is withheld and used as power	• Information is freely shared
Relationships and Procedures	
• There is a lack of direct and regular communication	• There is frequent contact and networking between partners
• A confrontational approach is taken towards the other side within an adversarial system of decision-making	• A conciliatory approach is taken towards partners within a collaborative form of decision-making

Source: based on Sidaway, 1996.

Figure 3.4 *Contrasting Aspects of Conflict and Cooperation*

Coser's perspective of social conflict also follows the Weberian view in relating conflict to social change.[1] He saw conflict as a stabilizing process in social groups, as it can serve the functional purpose of allowing adjustments to be made in social norms or power. Thus what he called 'flexible' social structures tolerate conflict, and may even institutionalize it

LOOSE-KNIT GROUPS	CLOSE-KNIT GROUPS
'Broad churches', which have multiple small conflicts of low intensity and act as ways of relieving tension. Any dissent is contained.	'Sects', showing a high degree of interaction and involvement of members. They suppress dissent so that grievances build up until a very intense conflict occurs with traumatic results.
Conflicts are about goals and interests, which allow readjustment of norms and power relations to benefit the social structure and are FUNCTIONAL.	Conflicts are about basic values and the legitimacy of the social structure and are disruptive and DYSFUNCTIONAL.
FLEXIBLE SOCIAL STRUCTURES	RIGID SOCIAL STRUCTURES
Tolerate and institutionalize conflict by allowing multiple small conflicts so that the social structure adjusts to new claims without a major line of cleavage developing and the balance of power is adjusted.	As conflicts are suppressed and no adjustment is possible, there is a risk of catastrophe.
Associations and coalitions may form during the conflict, which shape the future power structure. *Metaphor: earth tremor*	Diversionary 'non-realistic' conflicts may be created in an attempt to maintain the structure. *Metaphor: earthquake*

Source: Coser, 1956, 151–157.

Figure 3.5 *The Function of Social Conflict*

so that it can be used to eliminate dissatisfaction. The problems occur in 'rigid' social structures, which lack tolerance or the institutional mechanisms for dealing with conflict, and in these circumstances hostilities can accumulate. Conflict then becomes 'dysfunctional' as it tears the system apart (Coser, 1956). Some ten years later, Coser continued to argue that social systems need flexibility to adjust – his 'safety valve' thesis – and therefore argued for gradual social change to relieve tensions in society (Coser, 1967). The essential elements of Coser's propositions are summarized in Figure 3.5.

Like Coser, Thurlings (1962) suggested that conflicts may form a constructive role in society, in that groups are motivated to 'institute a new order which embodies their aspirations'. Thurlings used the distinction (made by Parsons) between role and position. Cultural groups compete for rights to resources, and conflicts may be defined in terms of social structures and social position, both of which are conditioned by norms or cultural standards that form part of the existing or proposed new order. Thurlings identified the interests of a cultural group as its rights (i.e., its social position), but he made a further distinction between the ability of the group to use these rights as it so wishes (autonomy) and whether it also has authority, i.e., has some say in the process whereby rights are allocated by society. In summary: the interest or social position of a cultural group is a combination of rights to resources that go with its role, comprising autonomy (the ability to exercise rights as wished), and authority (a say in the process of allocating rights).

Thurlings argued that the outcome of a conflict will be durable where it is based on consensus, and transitory where it is based on the exercise of power. Even though A's power may greatly exceed B's and there may be no conflict in the short term, their interests are irreconcilable and conflict is inevitable. B may work to counterbalance A's power by establishing the legitimacy of its claim to resources and gaining support from other groups on the grounds of injustice. Any enlargement of the field of conflict draws in other groups and presents a potential risk to them. In these circumstances, he suggested that organizations or individuals may attempt to mediate these claims. Thurlings recognizes that conflicts may be about the procedures whereby a social system or community allocates scarce resources, as well as the issue of how those resources are distributed and who gains access to them.

Coser's important insight was that group or social structure determines whether groups or social systems can tolerate internal dissent or cope with external threats and can therefore adjust to change without major disruption. This capability to deal with change overcomes one of the limitations of typologies: that they are based on static categories which are not easily applied to dynamic situations. By concentrating on the processes of conflict and how disputes escalate, rather than searching for root causes, it is possible to consider the immediate events which trigger conflict, the processes of politicization, the distribution of power and the possible forms of outcome to an environmental dispute. To advance this aim, the next section considers the contribution of theories which address the dynamic aspects of conflict.

The Dynamics of Conflict

Many writers have recognized the dynamic nature of conflict and the limitations of a static analysis in explaining the interaction between the various dimensions. In its simplest form, events can be seen to spiral out of control. What starts as a relatively simple problem increases in complexity, and communication and relationships deteriorate – sometimes rapidly, sometimes over a long period. This can be seen both in disputes between neighbours 'over the garden fence' and in more complex public policy disputes (see Figure 3.6).

In his analysis of conflict in organizations, Pondy (1972) considered the processes of conflict and how they develop:

> *Conflict may be more readily understood if it is considered a dynamic process. A conflict relationship between two or more individuals in an organisation can be analysed as a sequence of conflict episodes... Each episode or encounter leaves an aftermath that affects the course of succeeding episodes.* (Pondy, 1972, 359)

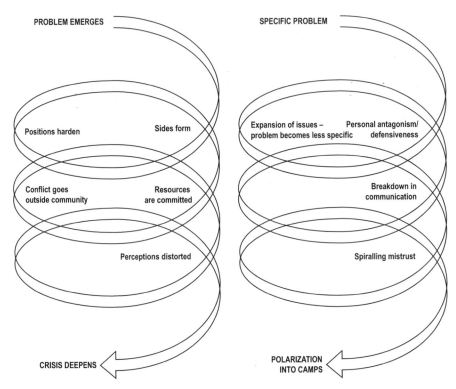

Source: based on Carpenter and Kennedy (1988); Mediation UK (1995).

Figure 3.6 *Conflicts Spiralling out of Control*

He used the labels 'aftermath', 'latent', 'felt' or 'perceived' and 'manifest' to describe the phases of a conflict episode. Other authors (e.g., Sandole, 1993; Fisher, 1990) agreed that a conflict passes through phases, tending to assume that it follows a linear path, which is not necessarily the case. In Thurling's description of conflicts between interest groups, his 'old' or 'existing' social order is equivalent to Pondy's 'aftermath' of the previous phase of conflict. During the struggle between established and new interest groups, their positions may converge to reach consensus and a durable outcome or diverge to perpetuate the conflict. Various logical outcomes are possible, including:

- existing groups being able to resist the claims of new groups and thereby maintaining the old order;
- existing groups making concessions to new groups, resulting in a transitory outcome;
- existing and new groups reaching consensus and a durable outcome; and
- the new order superseding the old.

Conflicts do not appear to arise spontaneously. The general proposition advanced by several authors (e.g., Deutsch, 1973; Mack and Snyder, 1957) was that whether a disagreement escalates into a conflict will depend on the standpoints of the interested parties and their relationships, which are in part conditioned by the aftermath of a previous conflict episode. However, none of them recognized that a particular tactical action taken by one of the parties, or some other external event, can escalate a dispute into a conflict. These constitute 'triggers of conflict'. A common feature of environmental conflicts is the disruption of an apparent state of equilibrium when a challenging interest group attempts to redefine (or gain some controlling authority over) the use of a resource. The challenge to the status quo might be a formal process whereby the primary land use is changed, ownership transferred or perhaps the area receives an enhanced conservation status from its designation by an official agency. Alternatively, change may occur less formally: the area could be 'invaded' by a new group of users or colonized by a bird new to that area, giving rise to demands for enhanced conservation status.

Established interest groups almost invariably react negatively to change. In each case there is an underlying formal decision – for example, about land use allocation – which concentrates attention on possible challenges to the status quo, i.e., the present distribution of interests in a natural resource. Uncertainty about the future and ambiguity of public aims are also contributory factors. Once primary land allocation decisions have been made, and particularly when the land is in public ownership and designated as a national park or wilderness area, its status is unambiguous as far as recreation interests are concerned. Hence the resistance to change based on fears that current activity will be curtailed (Sidaway, 1996).

The Pentland Hills and Peak District case studies illustrate such situations, but they are also exemplified in many archetypical situations in many countries where traditional community uses of forests are disrupted by the designation of national forest or park status by government agencies (see, for example, Doornbos et al, 2000).

Synthesis: A Dynamic Framework of Conflict

The key elements of these theories have been synthesized into a framework (Figure 3.7) which depicts the phases through which conflicts pass. The concepts on which this dynamic framework is based are:

- That each conflict consists of an episode which has an aftermath (Pondy). The aftermath conditions the following episode of conflict. This process of aftermath–episode–aftermath continues in a repeating pattern.
- That interest groups attempt to achieve *social position*, which consists of autonomy (the ability to exercise rights) and authority (being able to influence the process of allocation of rights). Together, these form the *social structure* (Thurlings).

Following this line of reasoning, conflicts concerning the access to resources are attempts to redistribute and/or ascribe a social position between interest groups.

- In essence, conflicts are resolved by the *exercise of power* or by *negotiation* (Coser, Pondy, Thurlings and others). Conflicts may or may not be resolved, in that the outcome of each episode may be either a durable or transitory one (Thurlings).
- To be effective, any decision-making process which attempts to resolve conflicts has to be perceived as *legitimate* by the recipients of that decision (Weber, Coser and Scimecca).
- The outcome of any conflict will be influenced (if not dictated) by the *balance of power* between the competing interest groups (Thurlings, Amy, Scimecca).
- The active phase of conflict is triggered by the arrival of a new interest group with a claim for social position (Thurlings).

The conditions in which such a dynamic framework might apply are likely to be as follows.

- Conflicts concerned with competition for access to resources, in which access is broadly defined as not only the ability to exercise socially defined rights in the use of those resources, but also as a controlling influence on how they are used by others.
- The interested parties are concerned to exercise those rights within a plural society, i.e., they are working within a broad structure of social institutions which are perceived as legitimate by all parties (in Coser's term, 'within the system').
- Although conflicts can occur at different levels, from the inter-personal to the international, the concern here is with an intermediate level of environmental conflict which may be local and/or site-based, and/or may have broader dimensions concerning a number of sites or larger areas. There may be some combination of local, regional and national issues contained within the dispute.
- Although some of the interested parties may be highly organized and bureaucratic agencies may be involved, the framework is unlikely to apply either to disputes within hierarchical organizations or to unstructured conflicts in which there is no representative framework within which organizations can operate.

The dynamic aspects of the framework are shown diagrammatically in Figure 3.7, where the possible outcomes of conflict (A) and a cooperative negotiation (B) are depicted. For simplicity of presentation, it is assumed that the outcome of power struggles within rigid social structures (as defined by Coser) can result in the maintenance or transfer of power or stalemate.

PROCESS OF CONFLICT	PROCESS OF COOPERATION
History of conflict Resistance to change Powerful defending status quo	*History of cooperation* Adaptation to change Power shared
Latent Phase Ideology maintains coherence of rival interest groups Weaker parties organize to gain influence Lack of information contributes to uncertainty Little direct communication between interest groups	Availability of information reduces uncertainty Regular communication between interest groups
Escalation Trigger - e.g., pre-emptive attempt to change legal status of resource	
Active Phase *Tactics of interest groups* Challengers formulate their case as an issue of principle, citing superior legislation to gain legitimacy Discourse confrontational via the media Coalition building to increase power	*Tactics of interest groups* Differences in beliefs respected Sensitivity shown to needs of others Discourse conciliatory using media to inform the wider public
Rigid decision-making Resistance to change Resulting balance of power favours victor	*Flexible decision-making* Accommodates change Power shared
Outcome transitory	*Outcome durable*

Figure 3.7 *Dynamic Analyses of Natural Resource Conflicts and Cooperation in Natural Resource Management*

Similarly, the only outcome of a power struggle within flexible social structures is a negotiation between parties in a situation of evenly balanced power. The figures attempt to portray the manoeuvring of interest groups as they seek power and legitimacy to maintain or gain social position. Each (coalition of) interest group(s) may be sufficiently powerful to dominate the other. Alternatively, they may reach a durable outcome via consensus, a transitory one by concession, or no outcome at all, i.e., a stalemate. The final section of this chapter illustrates the utility of the dynamic framework by further examining two of the earlier case studies.

A DYNAMIC ANALYSIS OF THE DESIGNATION OF THE PENTLAND HILLS REGIONAL PARK

Latent Phase

In this dispute, the ideologies of the conflicting interest groups did not appear as strong factors. The existing pattern of land use was defended by the landowners and farmers, while the conservation and recreation groups and local community associations also favoured the status quo. Although individual interests were affiliated with organizations, the pattern of political activity would be defined, in Coser's terms, as 'loose-knit'. While the landowners held considerable power, this was tempered by their being unable to control de facto open recreational access, and by the urban power base of the Lothian Regional Council (LRC). The LRC played a dual role, with one department (Leisure Services) acting as proponent of the regional park while another (Planning) acted as arbiter on development control decisions. Although a consultative committee with representatives from each interest had been formed, this proved to be an ineffective means of communication.

Escalation

The conflict was triggered by the publication of the Designation Order by the LRC. This was opposed in principle by the landowners, and they and the LRC proved to be the key players in the power struggle. The LRC's natural allies, the recreation and conservation interests, supported park designation in principle, but their support was so qualified that they were in effect opponents of the scheme. They were highly critical of the LRC for not setting out the implications of designation in the form of a master plan. This lack of information contributed to the uncertainty about the LRC's intentions. It failed to build a coalition with the recreation and conservation organizations, but it did gain legitimacy from the support of the national agency, the Countryside Commission for Scotland (CCS).

Active Phase

Many of the interests were formally represented at the subsequent public inquiry, but there was no formal coalition or umbrella group to lead the opposition, nor did an individual leader emerge. Each side took a confrontational stance and the local press was much used by the conservation interests, who challenged the legitimacy of designation by questioning the appropriateness of recreation development. Meanwhile, the LRC's authority and management aims were challenged by the landowners. This episode of the conflict was concluded by a public inquiry conducted in the traditional adversarial fashion. The Reporter adjudicated in favour of designation, and this was confirmed by the Secretary of State, but the confirmation of the designation was made conditional on the preparation of a management plan, when all interests would be consulted.

Aftermath of Episode

The preparation of the plan should have resolved the issue. Indeed, it was hailed by the planning profession as a model of its kind because of the detailed consultations that took place. This satisfied the recreation and conservation interests, yet by consulting but not fully involving the interest groups the LRC was unable to convince the landowners that their interests had been fully considered, and they continued their opposition. Successive attempts to reform the committee structure were seen to be tokenistic, as they failed to give the local interests, particularly the landowners, an effective say in the running of the park.

The decision-making structure had elements of rigidity and flexibility. Outwardly there were signs of flexibility in the appointment of advisory committees to aid communication, and in consultation procedures used during plan preparation. But it can be argued that the structure of decision-making contained considerable rigidity, as the LRC relinquished little real power. The conflict occured 'within the system', as the authority of the ultimate decision-maker, the Secretary of State, was unchallenged.

In one sense, designation can be interpreted as a concession by the established landowning groups. But as designation confers few executive powers on the LRC, the landowning lobby has continued to fight an effective rearguard action. As the LRC had failed to build an effective coalition and incorporate the recreation and conservation organizations into its power base, the situation is basically unstable. The changes in the advisory committee structure, most recently the establishment of a farmers' and landowners' panel, plus disagreements over development control decisions, suggest that the 'solutions' devised so far (i.e., designation, the preparation of a management plan, minor changes to committees) have produced no more than a transitory outcome. The situation was not helped by the abolition of the LRC in the 1996 local government reorganization, its functions being subsumed by three district councils. The outcome of this episode was continuing uncertainty in the relationships between the farming community and the local authorities. There is a sense of grievance among the farmers and landowners, and certainly no resolution. The dynamic analysis of the designation of the PHRP is summarized in Figure 3.8.

PROCESS OF CONFLICT

Aftermath of previous episode
Landowning, recreation and conservation groups seeking
to maintain their interests
Power dispersed favouring landowners
LRC does not depend on rural support

Latent Phase
No unifying leadership or political organization
No attempt to form coalitions
Lack of information on LRC's plans contributes to uncertainty
LRC develops Regional Park proposal, informs consultative committee
but fails to establish effective communication with wider community

Trigger
LRC seeking designation order for the park

Active Phase
LRC bases case on national legislation
Other interests oppose proposal on principle
Confrontational tactics using media to escalate conflict

Rigid decision-making
Consultation at late stage leads to formal objections
and public inquiry
Reporter (appointed by Secretary of State for Scotland)
acts as adjudicator finding that proposal meets designation criteria,
conditional on preparation of park plan. Decision supported
by recreation and conservation groups

Aftermath
Subsequent lack of public involvement in park management
leaves LRC with limited political support and vulnerable
to landowner pressures

Outcome unstable

Figure 3.8 *Dynamic Analysis of the Conflict over the Designation of the
Pentland Hills Regional Park, 1983–1985*

A DYNAMIC ANALYSIS OF MOORLAND ACCESS IN THE PEAK DISTRICT NATIONAL PARK

Latent Phase

The second example analysed in this way is that of moorland access in the Peak District National Park (see Figure 3.9). The present episode of the conflict has its antecedents in a long-running dispute between landowners, who were principally concerned about the disturbance of grouse shooting on their moorlands, and rambling organizations seeking open access to the moors. This conflict was detailed in Chapter 2. One of the first major successes of the ramblers' campaigns was the provision in the National Parks and Access to the Countryside Act 1949 to identify and to negotiate access agreements on privately owned open land. However, local implementation of this legislation depended on voluntary agreements between the landowners and the national park authority, in this case the Peak Park Joint Planning Board. Although open access to just over half of the moorlands in the Peak District was secured in this way, the Ramblers' Association (RA) continued to apply political pressure on the Board to enter into access agreements with the owners of the remaining moorland areas. Meanwhile, the RA also continued to press for national legislation for public access to 'open country', illustrating how an interest group may elevate its concerns into a matter of principle (a public interest) and seek broader support to legitimize its case. Those interests which are politically well organized are better able to advance their interests by securing legislation than those that are not.

In the 1990s, a third party to the dispute emerged: nature conservationists. They perceive open access as 'uncontrolled' and would prefer public access to be restricted to prevent disturbance to sparse populations of ground-nesting birds, such as golden plovers, which are not shot. Thus the landowning and nature conservation interests wanted to maintain (or ideally reduce) the present distribution of open access on the moors. Ultimately, the three interests were incompatible, particularly when expressed in terms of the ideological principles of 'freedom to roam' (ramblers), 'the precautionary principle' (nature conservation) and 'privacy and autonomy' (landowners) (see Figure 3.3). Thus, the competing interests of nature conservation and rambling had many of the characteristics of ideologically close-knit groups. Although the landowners might be said to form a loose coalition, they had a unifying ideology and held a considerable degree of power. Each surge of political activity attempted to redistribute power.

There had been little direct communication between the interests, and power was evenly balanced between them as each had strong political allies. But each had certain weaknesses in the eyes of the others: elitism on the part of landowners, the uncompromising aims of conservationists, and the

PHASE 1 CONFLICT 1980–1990

Aftermath of previous episode
Landowners resist RA attempts to extend open access areas

Latent Phase
Interest groups politically organized
Controversy about effects of access on grouse shooting
Little direct communication between groups
National park authority meets each party bilaterally

Escalation
RA exert pressure by staging mass trespass events on excluded areas

Active Phase
Both groups lobby effectively at national level and use
confrontational tactics to elevate issues to matters of principle
Media used to escalate conflict
Rigid decision-making dependent on legislative process

Aftermath
Power evenly balanced, stalemate

PHASE 2 COOPERATION 1992–1993

Latent Phase
Uncertainty about impact of access on ground-nesting birds

Potential escalation
Proposed conservation designation of moorland under European Directives

Change in institutional decision-making
Formation of representative Access Consultative Group provides
opportunity for mediated negotiation in which differences in interests
and beliefs are respected. Management aims clarified and accepted
Agreement on Access Management Planning Process

Aftermath
Power evenly balanced between interest groups,
each holding vetoing sanction
Agreement durable as long as momentum of negotiations maintained

Figure 3.9 *Dynamic Analysis of Moorland Access in the Peak District*

militancy of ramblers. Nevertheless, the claims of the three interests were legitimized within national park policy and the national park plan. The lack of information about the impacts of recreation on wildlife led to uncertainty, which all parties probably used to their advantage. In this situation the RA could afford to appear environmentally sensitive by accepting conservation policies in principle, while requiring proof that recreational disturbance was causing serious damage.

Escalation

Meanwhile, the preparation and revision at five-year intervals of a national park plan provided a method for responding to new claims on the moorland as the plan was reviewed. The most recent of these claims has been to give greater consideration to the nature conservation interests of the moors. The next episode of the dispute was triggered by two events:

1   the expiry of the existing access agreements and their renegotiation between the landowners' organization and the national park; and
2   the designation of the Dark Peak Moorlands as a Special Protection Area under European Union (EU) environmental directives.

Active Phase

Although each interest advanced its claims, each was also part of an established order resisting the changes demanded by the others. Certainly, these groups used the advancement of principles or arguments for appropriateness to advance their respective claims, used adversarial tactics and responded adversely to new claims. Although there were significant differences in the levels of organization between the three interest groups, each was highly organized with well established contacts at the national level. With the high degree of politicization of this issue, each party operated both tactically and strategically: the national situation influenced local action, while local action set a national precedent. The RA, in particular, acted in a confrontational way, following the 50th anniversary of the 1932 Kinder Scout mass trespass with a national Forbidden Britain campaign, with rallies in the Peak District in 1985 and 1991, attracting considerable media coverage (Holt, 1998). Conservation interests counter-attacked, proposing sanctuary areas to exclude 'inappropriate' use of breeding bird territories by walkers (although the principle of inappropriateness is probably used to greater effect by both parties to exclude active sports from the moorland areas).[2]

Each interest group attempted to influence the policies (management aims) of the Board. Although the national park plan was prepared using a consultative process and its main provisions were agreed, the Board's access strategy, which formed part of that plan, was challenged by conservation interests. This highlighted the need to get an agreement on both strategy and detailed management plans that would involve the interests directly rather than consult on firm proposals.

With power being evenly distributed between the parties and none being willing to make concessions to the other sides, the outcome appeared to be a stalemate. However, faced with uncompromising advice from English Nature (EN) on the threat to conservation, and the need to renegotiate existing access agreements with landowners, the board had to take an initiative. It proposed the establishment of the Peak District Access Consultative Group (PDACG) and engaged a consultant to devise arrangements acceptable to the interested parties (Sidaway, 1998a). As the workings of such a group could affect the social positions of all the parties, it was in their interests to be represented to ensure that they were party to the decision (authority) and could influence the outcome – the redistribution of access (autonomy) (Thurlings, 1962). Arguments of principle were submerged (at least temporarily) in the interests of direct negotiation, as each group wanted to seen to be reasonable to its national audience. The lack of communication evident hitherto was rectified by the establishment of the PDACG, and its workings increased the direct involvement of the interest groups in the preparation of local access management plans. The adversarial form of decision-making was changed to negotiation, and the PDACG provided a mechanism for brokering change. By accepting the PDACG's advice, the board could increase the legitimacy of its decisions. The process followed by the PDACG is considered in Chapter 5.

Aftermath of Episode

The phases of conflict over moorland access in the Peak District can be clearly recognized in the analysis set out in Figure 3.9. In effect, the conflict has run through several iterations in which the early episodes of trespass and campaigning for national parks can be said to follow the pattern of a power struggle. Legislation and the designation of the Peak District as a national park denoted a transfer of power to a new order from the established order of private landownership. Subsequently, the continual political pressure of the RA led to further concessions from private landowners in the form of access agreements. But as nature conservation built up a stronger power base, legitimized by European directives, a state of political stalemate was reached; no one lobby was able to amass superior power.

Central to this struggle was the board, which had some of the characteristics of a flexible social structure. It increased the degree of communication and public involvement in decision-making by establishing the PDACG. Ironically, this served both the local and national political aims of the RA, which benefits when local agreement is reached, while failure to reach agreement would further demonstrate the need for national legislation to override the local power of private landowners. Later developments in legislation and local negotiation over access to the countryside are described in Chapter 10.

CONCLUSIONS

Compared to the simple comparison of conflict and cooperation presented earlier in this chapter, the re-allocation of the influential factors into phases within a dynamic framework demonstrates the changing inter-relationships during a series of conflict episodes. A particular advantage of this analysis comes from the insights that it provides into the roles of ideology and arguments of principle in emphasizing group solidarity and tactics during the course of a dispute. For example, during the latent and subsequent phases, messages conveyed to the outside world may serve a more important function than the ostensible purpose of external communication by emphasizing the adherence of the group's representative to the ideology of the group. In this way, group solidarity is reinforced while basic beliefs remain intact and are not subject to negotiation.

Many conflicts are triggered by attempts to redistribute (access to) resources. The behaviour of the interest groups during the active phase of the conflict will be governed in part by their internal and external relationships and the ability of institutional decision-making to resolve conflict. The motivations and aspirations of the participating parties will influence how they act strategically and whether they seek to use existing methods of conflict resolution, either in a conciliatory way within the confines of this particular dispute or to meet wider political goals.

Tactics are chosen to improve legitimacy in the eyes of interested audiences. Thus, the elevation of interests to matters of principle enables competing parties to give legitimacy to their claims. Inappropriateness of the activities of others is advanced as a matter of principle which can be used to de-legitimize the claims of opposing parties. Thus arguments of principle can also be seen to be about social position. Interest groups advancing claims for enhanced social position will be proactive and agenda-setting, and will use the media for this purpose. These aggressive tactics will be matched by the defensive ploys of those with an established position. Either side may form coalitions to strengthen their power base. The distribution of power and how this changes during the course of the dispute is crucial in determining the outcome of a dispute and whether it will be resolved by the exercise or transfer of power, or by negotiation.

While this analysis gives some insights into decision-making structures, and their rigidity or flexibility in influencing the outcome of a dispute, these concepts are of limited application at the local scale of many disputes. This problem is examined in Chapter 4, which considers consensus building as a form of collaborative decision-making.

Part 2
Strategies for Cooperation

Chapter 4

Alternative Dispute Resolution – The Contribution of Negotiation and Consensus Building

Many of the decisions we face in the years ahead demand that we find ways to listen to opposing points of view, and find ways to accommodate deeply held and differing values. Conventional decision-making mechanisms tend to exclude rather than include diverse interests and do not cope well with the complexity that issues of sustainability present. (Canadian Round Tables, 1993)

SYNOPSIS

This chapter first describes the various ways in which societies attempt to resolve disputes, from avoiding the issues through to the use of force. Many of the 'novel' alternative methods of dispute resolution currently being advocated are not new, and have their antecedents in 'tribal' systems of decision-making. In essence, conventional systems of conflict resolution depend on claims being legitimated through the political process, often resulting in legislation. Such processes have strengths (that legal safeguards are provided to protect the rights of the powerless) and weaknesses (that the proceedings become adversarial).

The chapter then explores those alternatives which seek consensus rather than compromise, terms that are often confused. Consensus building processes are based on negotiations designed to remove misunderstanding, clarify interests and establish common ground between participants, which in turn leads to more relaxed, non-adversarial approaches. The process provides participants with the opportunity to treat others and to be treated with respect, and to gain control over the outcome. Consensus depends on trust gained through openness in sharing information, a balanced agenda and representation, early participation and having a genuine influence over decision-making. These principles are set out in an analytical framework depicting the conditions in which voluntary negotiation can lead to a 'principled outcome' to each party's advantage. This framework is used in subsequent chapters to assess the effectiveness of decision-making and the extent to which it leads to consensus.

WAYS OF RESOLVING DISPUTES

All societies have evolved methods of settling disputes that range from informal discussion to the use of force. The full range of techniques is often portrayed as a continuum that extends from letting the matter rest, through forms of negotiation and the legitimate use of power by the legal institutions of government, to violent exchanges such as industrial action or war. Slaikeu (1989) pointed out that the extremes of this continuum – avoiding the issue and unilateral use of power – represent the greatest losses of control and hence the greatest risks to the disputing parties. Who has responsibility for making the final decision in these matters is arguably one of the fundamental distinctions between the various methods. Figure 4.1 presents a simplified version of the continuum using this distinction and Ury's classification of the three basic approaches to dispute resolution:[1]

- those which determine who is right;
- those which determine who is more powerful; and
- those which reconcile the disputants' underlying interests (Ury et al, 1988).

Avoidance of the issue	Reconciliation of underlying interests	Determining who is right (forms of adjudication)	Determining who is more powerful
Decision left to chance: INACTION	Decision made by the disputing parties and unassisted by third party: NEGOTIATION Parties assisted by neutral third party: FACILITATION, MEDIATION and non-binding ARBITRATION	Decision made by higher authority: LITIGATION Decision made by third party: binding ARBITRATION	Decision made by the most powerful: COERCION

Source: based on Moore, 1986; Ury et al, 1988; Slaikeu, 1989.

Figure 4.1 *Ways of Dealing with Conflict*

If responsibility for determining the dispute is to move from the hands of the disputants to a superior adjudicator, the decision-making process must be perceived as legitimate and just by the disputing parties. The injustices and degree of coercion associated with the exercise of power led Thurlings (1962) to argue that the outcome of a conflict will be transitory where it is based on the exercise of power, and is more likely to be durable (resolved) where it is based on consensus. For the responsibility to determine who is right to be entrusted to a social institution, that institution has to be generally accepted by the community at large, usually because it is democratically accountable (albeit indirectly): for example, a court of law. This argument is supported by Creighton:

> *In every closely fought election, nearly half the voters 'lose' – their candidate isn't elected – yet the outcome of the election is accepted because there is a consensus that the decision-making process has been fair and legitimate. In effect, the decision-making procedure or process – the election – makes the outcome legitimate even if someone didn't like the outcome. One of the major functions of public involvement is to create sufficient visibility to the decision-making process so that decisions which result from it are perceived as fair and legitimate. While some of the people most directly impacted by a decision may not be impressed by the equity of the decision, their ability to undermine the credibility of the decision rests on their ability to convince the larger public that the decision was unfairly made.*
> (Creighton, 1978, quoted in Delli Priscoli, 1980, 9)

Legal processes may determine who is right, but they adjudicate in favour of one party at the expense of others without concern for future relationships, and can also be costly, time-consuming and present a degree of risk even to the stronger parties, as they cannot entirely control the eventual outcome. Most authors recognize that in principle the law should provide protection to the rights of the powerless, but they tend to emphasize the undoubted weaknesses of an adversarial approach (e.g., Acland, 1995). It is perhaps inevitable that the processes of arbitration, public hearing or inquiry have become institutionalized in the adversarial mould, as the disputants do their best to persuade the adjudicator of the merits of their case and the flaws of that presented by their opponents. This may also happen when the parties are represented by professional negotiators who play partisan roles, for example, in industrial disputes.

Not all conflicts lend themselves to legal remedies. It may be unclear who has jurisdiction. This means that aggrieved parties seek alternatives which do not demonstrate the perceived weaknesses of the legal system and offer a degree of autonomy and control over the outcome. Barach Bush suggests they try to avoid what they dislike (the unpleasant emotional exposure of legal proceedings with its delays, costs and risks of losing) and try to get what they prefer (the possibilities of treating and being treated with respect while ensuring their needs are met) (Barach Bush, 1995).

Arguably, the parties have the greatest degree of control when they are directly involved in decision-making, rather then handing responsibility wholly to an adjudicator – for example, a court or binding arbitration.

This is the case when they negotiate without assistance or are assisted by a neutral third party in the form of a facilitator, a mediator or an arbitrator (in non-binding arbitration). In each of these cases it is the disputing parties who make the final decision. The essential differences between these processes are as follows:

- facilitation – where the third party assists the disputing parties by suggesting the procedures to be followed in negotiation;
- mediation – where the third party takes a more active role in brokering the negotiations; and
- non-binding arbitration – where the third party suggests a solution for their consideration.

In practice, the differences between these roles are not always entirely clear, especially between facilitation and mediation. The terms may be used interchangeably and the third parties may follow individual preferences or styles.

> *A facilitator is always looking for consensus... But consensus should not be the goal of a facilitated process... The goal of facilitation is to improve communication and increase understanding, not to reach agreement.* (Moore, 1998)

In general, mediators do seek agreement and may be more interventionist as a result. Both mediators and facilitators seek to maintain neutrality, partly by not expressing opinions or recommending solutions. The issue of neutrality is explored in greater detail in Chapter 5.

Various forms of assistance using a neutral third party have been grouped under the term 'alternative dispute resolution' (ADR) to distinguish them from more traditional legal and administrative processes. Many of these alternatives are thought to be novel as they follow processes which are less familiar than legal ones and have come into greater prominence since the 1970s. But they are far from new and have their antecedents in 'tribal' systems of decision-making. For example, Scottish medieval law included arbitration and mediation (the latter termed an 'amicable compositor') as well as court procedures (Hunter, 1987).

Arguably then, only those procedures concerned with the reconciliation of interests, and that identify and recognize the needs of all the disputing parties have the potential to actually resolve conflicts. Ertel (1991) suggests the most effective approach to conflict resolution is to get agreement from the disputing parties on a desired model (or process) of decision-making before analysing their problems, thereby legitimizing its use (see Figure 4.2). The remainder of this chapter is concerned with analysing forms of decision-making which aim to reconcile interests and resolve conflict, namely consensus building.

- Clarifies the underlying interests of participants
- Builds a good working relationship
- Brings forward a range of options for consideration
- Is perceived as legitimate
- Recognizes the alternative procedures that are available to the parties
- Improves communication
- Leads to wise commitments

Source: Ertel, 1991.

Figure 4.2 *Attributes of an Effective Conflict Resolution Process*

CONSENSUS BUILDING

The term 'consensus' is often used loosely to cover general or widespread agreement, or as a synonym for compromise. Each word carries added shades of meaning: for example, 'compromise' can be seen to be honourable when concessions are made by both sides, although to some people any concession is a sign of weakness. Similarly, 'cooperate' and 'collaborate' can have positive and negative connotations. Focusing on the concept of obtaining general agreement, consensus building has been defined as 'a collaborative approach to making a decision in which the interested [or disputing] parties identify common ground and work voluntarily towards finding a mutually acceptable solution towards a contentious problem' (Environment Council, 1995). Throughout this book, 'consensus' and 'consensus building' will be used in this more exact sense.[2]

What is distinctive about decision-making by consensus is that:

- Decisions are reached collaboratively by all the parties. If they are to reach consensus, then minority views must have the right to block a decision (so-called veto power).
- The decision-making group is inclusive; all the interested parties are present and can take as active a role as they wish.
- Care has to be taken to ensure that the process is fully participatory, i.e., it will achieve and maintain consensus. This implies that the process is designed with this aim and is agreed by the participants.

The aim of reaching full consensus differs from that of informed consent, where interested parties may be aware of an impending decision and its consequences but feel sufficiently unaffected or indifferent to raise objections. Whether full consensus can be reached in all circumstances is debatable. There is a trade-off between reaching for the ideal and what is practical in a given situation. Many authorities accept the greater practicality of striving for informed consent (SPIDR, 1997; Canadian Round Tables, 1993) instead of full consensus. Both methods of reaching a decision have potential weaknesses: full consensus is open to weaker parties using veto power as a stranglehold, while the cut-off point for informed consent can be set so high by powerful agencies in control of a process that relevant interests are excluded.

Consensus building processes which aim to resolve conflict are based on negotiations geared to remove misunderstanding, clarify interests and establish common ground between participants, which in turn leads to a more relaxed non-adversarial approach. The process provides participants with the opportunity to treat others and be treated with respect, while retaining control over the outcome. As the process tends to be unfamiliar, a facilitator is often engaged to assist in designing the process and to ensure that the negotiations are conducted in a way that encourages the participation of all participants.

Important distinctions have been drawn between two types of negotiation, termed 'positional' (hard) and 'interest-based' (soft) by Ury et al (1998). In this context, 'positions' are defined as publicly stated demands or solutions, while 'interests' are underlying needs which are frequently not stated. Positional bargaining is adversarial in style (win/lose), each side being out to gain as much as possible and unwilling to make concessions. Offer is matched by counter-offer until an acceptable solution is found within the bargaining range. The outcome lies within a narrow range of compromise solutions. Interest-based negotiation (as advocated by Ury et al, 1998; Susskind et al, 2000) aims to meet the needs of the parties (win/win) on the assumptions that a cooperative relationship between them is important, and that there are probably several solutions to the same problem. Information is exchanged to establish each party's needs, and joint responsibility is accepted for solving a mutual problem by consensus.[3]

As implied by the word 'process', consensus building is usually undertaken in stages. In essence there are four steps, described by the Canadian Round Tables (1993) as:

1   assessment – talking about whether to talk;
2   getting started – talking about how to talk;
3   running the process – talking; and
4   implementing and monitoring the results – turning talk into action.

As with all other forms of decision-making, consensus building has its strengths and weaknesses. These are set out in Figure 4.3.

The main criticisms of consensus building, ADR and mediation focus on the disadvantages listed in Figure 4.3. For example, Palmer and Roberts (1998) suggest that disputes which cross lines of social stratification are those which involve gross imbalances of power and are seldom well resolved through negotiation. Which types of disputes are negotiable, how interests are represented and how imbalances of power are handled are discussed in greater detail in Chapter 5. It is also worth noting that the different forms of dispute resolution can (and arguably should) be used in combination. For example, industrial action can lead to negotiation, while the outcomes of an informal negotiation may be made binding by being expressed in a legally binding agreement.

Advantages	Limitations and constraints
• Increased understanding of issues and other viewpoints • Voluntary, less formal procedures allow the parties to meet face to face, to explore the problem and consider a range of possible solutions • Improved relationships engender trust • Control of process leads to commitment to outcome and its implementation • Savings in time and money, in the longer term	• Deeply held beliefs are non-negotiable • Informal processes can be manipulated by the powerful so that the less powerful need safeguards • Not all interests are easily represented in negotiations • Reaching consensus is time-consuming and may be difficult to sustain over time

Figure 4.3 *The Advantages and Disadvantages of Consensus Building*

ASSESSING PARTICIPATION IN DECISION-MAKING

The achievement of consensus depends on the development of trust between the negotiating parties, which is gained through a form of decision-making that is seen to be legitimate, fair, balanced and open. In essence, this hinges on:

- how the process is initiated;
- how inclusive it is;
- whether the relevant information is freely available to all parties; and
- whether the deliberations have genuine influence over the final decision.

These key points form the basis of the following framework (set out in Figure 4.4), in which the principles of consensus building have been re-formulated into a set of preconditions for collaboration in decision-making. This can be used to assess whether the process is likely to be seen as fair and legitimate in the eyes of all interested parties. The principles depict the conditions in which a voluntary negotiation can lead to a 'principled outcome' where no one party is disadvantaged, and can also be used to design a fair process. This framework is used in subsequent chapters to assess the effectiveness of decision-making in terms of the extent of participation in each of the case studies.

It must be emphasized that this type of assessment would form only one element of a full evaluation of the effectiveness of a participatory process. It covers inputs: the resources available to the exercise and the ways in which they are used. A fuller evaluation would also cover outputs and outcomes: specific products and longer-term effects of the exercise (see, for example, Barr, 2003).

INITIATION
Terms of reference and agenda
- Has the purpose and form of the exercise been agreed by all the parties?
- Is the agenda balanced to cover the full range of issues, or is it constrained by a pre-emptive policy or proposition made by powerful interests?

INCLUSIVENESS
Representation
- Is the representation of interests balanced at each level of decision-making?
Accountability
- How accountable are the representatives to their constituencies?
Openness of and involvement in decision-making
- Are all phases of the process open to all interest groups?
- What is their degree of involvement in each phase?

INFORMATION
- Is information freely available to all interests?
- How objective is the information, has it been gathered by independent sources?
- Is the information coverage of issues evenly balanced?

INFLUENCE
Delegation of authority in decision-making
- Who holds the power to determine and/or execute decisions, and do any imbalances of power between the parties hinder the process?
- To what extent has authority been delegated to the group and are the ultimate decision-makers committed to implement and resource the outcomes agreed in this process?

Source: Amy (1987); Canadian Round Tables (1993); Creighton (1978); Delli Priscoli (1980); Ertel (1991); Innes (1999); Lach and Hixson (1996); Madigan et al (1990); Murray (1989); Ozawa and Susskind (1985); Schwietzer et al (1999); Scimecca (1993); SPIDR (1997); Susskind (1981); Susskind and Cruikshank (1987); Ter Haar (1979).

Figure 4.4 *A Framework for Assessing Participation in Decision-making*

Initiation

The terms of reference, the purposes and content of decision-making processes can be drawn up to include or exclude the concerns of stakeholders, which raises the question of who controls the agenda and implies that all participants have a say in both the content of the agenda and way in which it is discussed. Being able to influence both the agenda and the process is one of many possible incentives to participate.

Inclusiveness

The underlying assumption is that representation should be inclusive, incorporating all relevant interests to achieve a satisfactory outcome. As far as possible, representation should be self-defining both in terms of which interest groups are present and which individuals are chosen to represent them. Effective processes also require consistency and continuity of representation, and the representative should have the authority, skills and resources to negotiate on behalf of the interests and the personal ability to enter into the give-and-take of a working relationship.

However, there is also the risk that the working relationship will take over, like the membership of an exclusive club, and it is vital that the representative maintains the trust of the constituency he or she represents and is accountable to it. This requires him or her to feed information back to members of the constituency and negotiate a new mandate with them, especially during the course of lengthy discussions.

The aim is that all interests can participate effectively at all stages of the process, with the caveat that participation is voluntary and that some may decide for themselves that their interests are more relevant at certain stages than others. In general terms, participants should expect consistency of treatment, and to be treated with dignity and respect. According to the situation, detailed procedures will be devised, and these details are considered for different processes in later chapters.

Information

Withholding information cannot be used as a source of power. There must be equal access to information, which must not be partial in its coverage nor in the way that it is gathered, analysed, interpreted and presented. This latter point is particularly crucial for lay audiences confronted with complex data of a scientific nature.

Influence

Where a process is being initiated by a powerful agency or organization, there must be a clear commitment to entering into a collaborative process at the highest level if negotiations are not to be abortive. This implies that the policy-makers are committed to accepting, or at least being strongly influenced by, the outcome of the negotiation; that the necessary resources are allocated to conduct the process; and that full consideration is given to how an agreement will be implemented and its effectiveness monitored.

CONCLUSIONS

The argument developed throughout this book is that consensus building, as defined in this chapter, is a generic process that can be used in a variety of ways to prevent or resolve conflict, as long as its application is tailored to the specific situation. Each application follows a conscious thought process – subsequently referred to as 'process design' – in which the key principles set out in Figure 4.4 are applied. Subsequent chapters examine the extent to which different consensus building processes and the accompanying case studies conform to these principles.

Chapter 5

Mediation and its Contribution to Resolving Environmental Disputes

You don't have to be a rocket scientist to be a mediator; you do have to be able to ask a lot of logical questions. (Lesnick, 1992)

SYNOPSIS

Mediation as a form of crisis management works on the principles of consensus building, tailored to the local situation. The neutral third party plays a crucial role in assessing whether negotiation is feasible and devising a negotiation strategy which gets the parties to the table. Participation is voluntary and depends on the mediator building conditions of trust, in which the interests of all parties are respected, their legal rights are not prejudiced and confidentiality is maintained. In part, the case for mediation rests on these principles being respected, but also on advancing the values of self-determination, compassion and concern for others.

This chapter examines the critiques of mediation and how mediators attempt to address them in designing negotiations. Many of these criticisms concerning access to justice and the use of power could equally be applied to other processes. During a preparation stage, mediators may spend considerable time making a preliminary assessment of whether direct negotiation is feasible or whether it would founder on a fundamental clash of beliefs or imbalances of power. Differences in beliefs and power may be set aside where there is external pressure to settle, the working relationship is important or stalemate has been reached. This chapter assesses how mediation can meet the consensus building criteria set out in the previous chapter, and presents pointers for good practice.

Two examples of environmental mediation are presented in this book. Later in this chapter, one episode of the conflict over moorland access is described, during which the deliberations of the Peak District Access Consultative Group (PDACG) in the Peak District National Park in Northern England were facilitated by the author. This account includes participants' retrospective views on the process. Chapter 6 is devoted to a second case study, mediation by the North Oxford County Coalition

(NOCC) of a conflict over the apparently high incidence of cancer in mill workers and their families in Rumford, Maine, USA.

THE PROCESS OF MEDIATION

Mediation is a voluntary process during which the parties to a dispute meet separately and together in confidence with an independent third party, who designs and conducts a process which enables them to explore and decide how the conflict between them is to be resolved. (Acland, 1995, 32)

Mediation was introduced in Chapter 4 as a form of collaborative interest-based negotiation which enables the parties to explore and understand each other's underlying interests, not just their bargaining positions. Assistance is provided by the mediator who, unlike a binding arbitrator, has no authoritative decision-making power and is concerned solely with managing the process and not the outcome. The other key element of mediation is the control it potentially offers to the parties. Because the disputing parties decide the terms of the agreement for themselves, they gain a sense of ownership by being party to a collective decision. But before negotiations can start, the need for assistance from a mediator has to be recognized.

Who Takes the Initiative in Starting Negotiations?

Depending on the nature and history of the conflict, which might have soured personal relationships, it can be difficult for the disputing parties to instigate direct negotiations. Conflict resolution is not just a question of expertise; there is also the question of neutrality, particularly the inability of an interested party in the conflict to initiate a negotiation or to mediate. At this stage, the crucial questions are as follows.

Which parties have a stake in the dispute and its outcome?
Who can act as an honest broker?
Those playing an active role in the dispute should rule themselves out as honest brokers as they have a conflict of interest. However, they might decide that negotiation offers a possible solution and want to make an overture to the other side. Alternatively, one or more of the interested parties may be sufficiently detached from the dispute to act as a go-between and make informal soundings on the desirability of negotiations.

Is there a need for an independent view?
A dispassionate view might be provided by someone not directly involved, but it is important to be certain that they really are seen to be neutral and impartial by all sides. In addition to neutrality, the crucial requirements are the ability and experience to make a careful and dispassionate assessment of

the situation, and the ability to conduct the negotiations. This combination of skills and experience is rarely found within organizations, hence the definite advantages of engaging an external, neutral third party with experience of handling other disputes.

Choosing a Mediator

The final choice of a mediator is dependent on their perceived impartiality and neutrality. They can be vetoed by any party, arguably at any time. Strict neutrality may be hard to achieve: everyone has values and opinions. Being perceived as impartial, fair, trustworthy and consistent is vital. The choice will also depend on what assistance is required to develop appropriate procedures, and whether technical knowledge of the issues or experience of similar previous negotiations is considered essential.[1] The mediator's acceptability will also depend on whether that individual or team can build a rapport with all the parties involved and can maintain their trust. A potential mediator can have no substantive interest in the controversy. Their interest is purely procedural – to see that the process is fair (Moore, 1996).

The role of the mediator is to help to design an acceptable negotiating process, and then convene and manage the discussions. The required skills include the abilities to listen and empathize, and to be sensitive and responsive while managing the process (Acland, 1995). As well as providing procedural assistance, mediators can help to improve communication between the parties, so that they develop a constructive relationship. This is done by facilitating contact, improving mutual respect, encouraging openness, working to help the parties gain equal status in the discussion, and getting them to work towards common goals (Fisher et al, 1997). Mediators adopt different strategies during the course of a negotiation, and may sense the need to question and be 'equally pushy' whilst maintaining an 'active impartiality' (Palmer and Roberts, 1998). The mediator's interventions need to be modulated by intervening to get agreement but keeping quiet when agreement is close (Pruitt, 1995). The mediator has the ability to alter the power and social dynamics of the negotiation, but there is a delicate balance between gaining the respect of the parties whilst not seeking to influence the outcome.

Complex environmental disputes require a major commitment of time and expertise on the part of a mediator, and it is unlikely that this will be done on a voluntary basis, as happens in many inter-personal disputes. Ideally, the cost of the exercise is borne by all the parties, or perhaps by an independent source, to emphasize the mediator's neutrality. Organizations without the resources to contribute in this way may well agree that others bear these costs, but they should still be satisfied that the mediator is and remains impartial. Where the government is the client, mediators have to consciously demonstrate their impartiality to counter any perception that they are influenced by the source of payment.

Deciding on a Mediation Process

Any initial discussions have to cover the form the negotiations will take and who should be involved. The most effective approach is to get agreement from the disputing parties on the structure and timing of the negotiations well before the substantive discussions begin. Typically, the process of environmental mediation is consistent with the phased process of consensus building described in Chapter 4. Usually, mediation of an environmental dispute takes place in three stages, set out in Figure 5.1:

1   a preparatory pre-negotiation stage, to establish the form negotiations should take;
2   the actual negotiations to obtain agreement; and
3   post-negotiation, to implement the agreement and review progress.

PRE-NEGOTIATION

1   Initiative to identify an acceptable neutral mediator.
2   Mediator meets the parties individually and makes an *initial assessment* of whether there is a basis for negotiation.
3   Mediator prepares a consultative document with proposals for a *forum and mediation process*. This outlines the purpose of negotiations, their scope, the size and composition of a negotiating group and the conventions and procedures to be used.

Agreement to negotiate – Yes/No

NEGOTIATION

4   If negotiation is agreed, an inaugural meeting of the negotiating group considers whether it is necessary to vary or agree the recommendations on procedures.
5   The mediator conducts collaborative negotiations in which the parties explore and understand each other's underlying interests, and develop and prioritize alternative solutions.
6   The parties work towards the form and content of a voluntary agreement, while also considering how it will be implemented and the criteria that will be used to evaluate its success.

Draft agreement

POST-NEGOTIATION

7   Agreement is ratified, implementation is monitored and reviewed.

Evaluation

Source: based on Madigan et al (1990).

Figure 5.1 *The Essential Stages Involved in Reaching Consensus in a Mediated Negotiation*

PRE-NEGOTIATION DISCUSSIONS – THE IMPORTANCE OF THOROUGH PREPARATION

This stage of negotiating about negotiating is often called 'talks about talks', or 'getting to the table'. A potential mediator may be assigned the role of making initial soundings and preparing proposals on the structure of negotiations, whilst at the same time remaining sceptical and questioning the likelihood of an eventual agreement. Indeed, the most crucial task at this stage is to assess whether negotiations are feasible and the likelihood of success. Only if negotiations are likely to be successful should a negotiating process be suggested. The ethics of mediation dictate that an honest judgement be made at this stage, and that the temptation to initiate discussions that are likely to be abortive is resisted.

The mediator's proposals should cover the scope of the discussions, how they are to be structured, a provisional timetable and who is to be represented. Thus the issues of recognizing and representing interests, the distribution of power between them and ground rules for negotiation, including equal access to information, are considered at the outset and form part of the recommendations from this initial assessment. The mediator ensures that each party is aware of any alternative procedures to negotiation, which they could use as fall-back positions.

The mediator's judgement will be partially dependent on the relationships and power balances between the interested parties, whilst ensuring that no powerful interests or stakeholders are isolated and ignored. This exercise is variously described as 'stakeholder analysis' or 'conflict assessment', and is principally concerned with the suitability of the dispute for negotiation and the ability to deliver justice in the face of the inevitable power differentials between disputing parties.

Who Should be Involved in Negotiations?

Susskind and Cruikshank (1987) suggest that four kinds of stakeholder are likely to be identified in conflict assessment: those with claims to legal protection, those with political clout, those with the power to block negotiated agreements, and those with moral claims to public sympathy. Various definitions of 'stakeholder' have been suggested which emphasize the interest or concern that people or organizations may have with the outcome of a decision (see, for example, Wilcox's definition in Chapter 3, p38). The criteria used to identify stakeholders are necessarily qualitative, suggesting that the interested parties should be directly involved in deciding who qualifies as a stakeholder in a given situation. This analysis is potentially contentious, as the decision about who should be represented is closely related to the way in which the problem is framed. By implication, whoever makes that decision – a convening organization, the disputing parties or a neutral third party – is in a position of power. The decision-maker can include or exclude contending parties, and give the impression of procedural justice or injustice, legitimacy or illegitimacy:

> *Where power is concentrated in the hands of an elite, the process of stakeholder identification, and boundary and problem definition will be distorted and manipulative.*
> (Ramirez, 1999, 107)

Thus there is a healthy debate in mediation circles about who should conduct the conflict assessment, with a range of options being suggested depending on the stance of the mediator. International negotiators tend to see their role as interventionist, going so far as to outline potential outcomes in their conflict assessment (Raiffa, 2002). Some mediators advocate total neutrality, preferring that the assessment be conducted by the stakeholders (Tonkin, 2002), whilst others suggest that the mediator's role should be flexible, working alone or with the convening agency during the assessment (Sobel, 2002).

The size of a negotiating group is another crucial consideration. There is a tendency for the major players to press for a small group of 'key stakeholders' on the grounds that this eases negotiation. Whilst consensus building is undoubtedly easier to develop in small groups, there is always the danger that someone – an individual or organization – who is excluded from the negotiations might exercise veto power at a later stage, such as initiating legal proceedings to overturn an agreement. Where there are large numbers of stakeholders, it might be better to consider one of the following options:

- establishing a large inclusive forum which agrees that separate aspects of the dispute or its solution are negotiated by sub-groups and referred back to the forum for ratification; or
- establishing a small task force to conduct the negotiations, ensuring that the representatives of each sector refer back to umbrella groups during the negotiations according to previously agreed procedures.

Confirming the Basis for Negotiation

The mediator's findings are presented in a consultative document and, if negotiations are recommended, the parties are asked to confirm their agreement on the establishment of a negotiating group. There is no point entering negotiations if one or more parties are set on another course of action. It is important at this stage to confirm that the responsible authorities are committed to a process controlled by the participants, and to be sure how this is to link into existing responsibilities for decision-making (influence) – one of the vital criteria of consensus building identified in Chapter 4 (see p71). For example, the failure to implement the agreement reached by the PDACG, described later in this chapter, emphasizes just how crucial this commitment is.

THE NEGOTIATION AND POST-NEGOTIATION STAGES

The inaugural meeting of the negotiatiors considers whether it is necessary to vary the mediator's recommendations before they are finally agreed. Attention then turns to exchanging information, understanding each other's interests, building trust and agreeing a common goal. It is vital that the negotiating group agrees or redefines the nature of the underlying problem before attempting to develop a range of alternative solutions. The two case studies partly describe how this was done, whilst the details are covered in many standard texts and manuals (Acland, 1995; Carpenter and Kennedy, 1988; Moore, 1996; Susskind et al, 2000; Mediation UK, 1995).

If the negotiations are to reach consensus, it is vital that everyone is treated equally and respects the interests of others throughout. Thus the issues of recognizing and representing interests and the ground rules for negotiation, including equal access to information, have to be considered at the outset. Examples of issues that may be covered in the ground rules are given in Figure 5.2, while the ground rules used by the NOCC are set out in Chapter 6.

- *Terms of reference*: particularly the precise role of an independent mediator or facilitator
- *Decision-making*: the use of consensus rather than voting
- Mutual *recognition of the legitimacy* of each party's concerns
- The *role of representatives* of interested organizations, particularly with regard to consulting their organizations during negotiations and reporting back to the forum (according to any agreed ground rule on confidentiality)
- *Confidentiality* of any discussions during the negotiations, including deciding who has responsibility for issuing prepared public statements and informing the media
- The availability of *information*, providing equal access to all parties
- The responsibility for *organization and recording* of meetings
- The time to be given for *consideration* of any recommendations from the discussions

Source: Sidaway, 1998b.

Figure 5.2 *Issues to be Considered in the Ground Rules for Mediated Negotiations*

During the course of the negotiations the group has to agree the type and form its recommendations should take, and how they are to be implemented. When the agreement has been ratified by all the parties and possibly put in a legally binding form, there must be a system of monitoring to keep the agreement under review. This helps to maintain trust between the parties.

Criteria	Pre-negotiation stage	Negotiation stage	Post-negotiation stage
INITIATION			
Terms of reference and agenda	Determine the purpose of negotiations	Establishment of common ground Coverage of agenda Search for mutually acceptable agreement	
INCLUSIVENESS			
Communities and representation Accountability Openness of and involvement in decision-making	Identification of stakeholders and who is to be in negotiating group Relationship of negotiations to other groups and wider constituencies (suggested ground rule)	Two-way feedback to constituencies (dependent on ground rules agreed by negotiating group) Provision of information to the media (ground rule)	All parties concerned in monitoring and evaluation Time allowed for ratification (ground rule)
INFORMATION			
	Guarantee of equal access (ground rule)	New information sought from neutral sources Equal access to information	
INFLUENCE			
Delegation of authority in decision-making	Purpose of negotiations and commitment to implementing outcome Potential role of mediator	Confirmation of role of mediator (ground rule) Consideration of draft agreement and how it will be implemented Decision-making by consensus (ground rule)	Commitment to monitoring and evaluation of agreement

Source: based on Sidaway, 1998b.

Figure 5.3 *How Mediated Negotiations Fulfil the Criteria for Participation in Decision-making*

Mediation as a Form of Consensus Building

By using a conscious process of design during the pre-negotiation conflict assessment, mediators conform to the criteria of consensus building set out in Chapter 4. Figure 5.3 summarizes how, in each stage of the mediation process, the criteria are met.

The assessment should ensure that all the issues of major concern to the stakeholders are included in the terms of reference (*initiation*); that all stakeholders are represented and that they understand their responsibilities towards those they represent within any agreed ground rule on confidentiality (*inclusiveness*); that the limitations of existing *information* should be revealed and accepted, and joint responsibility taken to fill essential gaps; and that the negotiation will have genuine *influence* on the final decision.

CRITIQUES OF MEDIATION

A detailed critique of environmental mediation has been provided by social scientists, notably Amy (1987) and Scimecca (1993), although many of their criticisms apply to other forms of participatory decision-making based on negotiation. Their basic arguments are that negotiation is an inappropriate form of dispute resolution when non-negotiable principles are at stake and power is unequally distributed, putting the weak at a fundamental disadvantage.

Amy (1987) suggests that mediators recognize two types of dispute (those concerning misunderstandings and conflicting interests) and tend to ignore a third (disputes over basic principles, which feature in most environmental conflicts). He considers environmental mediation to be an inappropriate method of settling such disputes:

> *It can be argued that issues involving principles are best dealt with in more traditional political institutions like the courts, administrative agencies, and legislatures. After all, it is the purpose of these political institutions to establish and enforce certain societal norms and principles. But by obscuring the principled nature of environmental disputes, environmental mediation may divert participants from these institutions that may be more suited to their political struggle.* (Amy, 1987, 185)

Misunderstandings might arise because of the stereotypical perceptions that disputing parties have of their rivals' positions, or because of disagreements over the scientific and technical aspects of the dispute. The value of direct contact and negotiation between the disputing parties is that it can remove these misconceptions and clarify the technical issues.

By working on conflicts of interest, he suggests that mediators follow the assumptions of Fisher et al (1997) that the parties' bargaining positions are negotiable, and that their underlying interests can be served by revealing a hitherto unconsidered option or by a straightforward compromise between the respective positions. In Amy's view, this type of negotiation cannot and should not compromise non-negotiable principles which are based on deeply held values or beliefs concerning the way society should function. In his view, environmental values are a case in point:

> *In any case, there is a real difference between seeing environmental disputes as conflicts of interest or as conflicts of principle ... more activist organisations, such as Greenpeace, Earth First! and Friends of the Earth ... tend to see themselves not so much as another interest group, but as part of a movement which is dedicated to creating an environmentally sane society ... more like a campaign or crusade to get basic ethical and ecological principles embodied in law.* (Amy, 1987, 175–176)

Amy concedes that many environmental mediators recognize that they cannot mediate conflicts of principle. He also points out that 'environmental disputes are often multi-faceted, involving a mixture of issues, some negotiable, some not' (Amy, 1987, 190).

Before deciding whether or not to negotiate, the parties will make their own assessment of the risks involved, the likely outcome, whether a solution will be imposed by politicians or the courts, and what the effects of such a decision might be on their interests. Fisher et al (1997) argue that the only reason for negotiating is to obtain better results than can be obtained by other means, and that both parties will and should assess the likely outcome of the negotiations against their 'best alternative to a negotiated agreement' (BATNA). Furthermore, they argue, 'the relative negotiating power of two parties depends primarily upon how attractive to each is the option of not reaching agreement' (Fisher et al, 1997, 106). They argue that the power of the weaker party increases when it has other options to pursue and that, once it realizes this, its negotiating position is strengthened.

From a sociological perspective, this approach to rectifying imbalances of power would seem a somewhat simplistic view of a fundamental problem concerning the distribution of power within society. Scimecca (1993, pp216–218) identifies certain limitations of alternative dispute resolution (ADR), including:

- ADR is based on the concept of individual responsibility and assumes that rational individuals should be able to resolve their conflicts. It further assumes that improving processes of communication and increasing understanding between disputants will lead to resolution. Yet many environmental disputes reflect sharply contrasting views about fundamental values and the parties may understand their opponents 'only too well'.

- The atheoretical approach of ADR ignores a main source of conflict – the unequal distribution of power – which is legitimated in established social institutions, such as the planning and legal systems. Thus by backing the status quo, ADR becomes a tool of social control. Scimecca considers it significant that ADR in the main concentrates on inter-personal, organizational and industrial disputes. Environmental disputes are in a separate category as they challenge the political order.
- The neutrality of the third party is likely to favour compromise, existing predominant values and the status quo. Mediators are unable to change the distribution of power or justice, which is more properly the role of the political process.

Furthermore, it would seem unlikely that those who have gained power through political struggle will voluntarily relinquish it during a negotiation.

Amy (1987) also argues that mediation will be used by powerful business interests or the government to co-opt environmental groups who lack the resources or the organization to use the political process. In these circumstances, the powerful might restrict the political agenda and manage conflicts to their advantage. This point is examined in greater detail in Chapter 10.

Amy further suggested that the informality of mediation (when compared to litigation) may present inherent difficulties for weaker parties if the safeguards of more formal procedures are lacking. However cumbersome, legal procedures are often designed to protect individual rights. In addition to being seduced by the cordial atmosphere, the weaker parties' inexperience of negotiation may leave them vulnerable. He also suggests that informal procedures place heavy responsibilities on mediators, who might set the agenda and reframe issues in possibly manipulative ways that could mislead innocent parties. The impracticalities of negotiation within very large groups may favour reducing the size of the group, with the effect that only the most powerful are included whilst the weak and unorganized are ignored. He concedes that the accountability of the representative to the constituent group is a partial safeguard (Amy, 1987).

In summary, Amy sees a very limited role for environmental mediation, arguing that it assumes a pluralistic view of politics in which power is evenly distributed between the interested parties, or that some at least of the many sources of power are available to the weaker parties. Citing some mediators, again he postulates that mediation is only a viable option when power is evenly distributed, and when the parties have reached a political stalemate and a state of mutual frustration. 'Only when the politics of power have been exhausted can the politics of co-operation become a viable possibility' (Amy, 1987, 92).

THE MEDIATORS' RESPONSE – CONFLICT ASSESSMENT AND PROCESS DESIGN

Most mediators are sensitive to these arguments, although their reservations are expressed in slightly different terms. For example, Barach Bush (1995) discusses the risk of justice being privatized if mediation attempts to bypass the protective legal framework of rights, or justice being denied if the less powerful are excluded. On a practical level, most mediators attempt to address these pitfalls in their initial conflict assessment and subsequent process design. Indeed, the first of Amy's criticisms is tacitly acknowledged by the emphasis that mediators place on their initial preparatory assessment of the likelihood of mediation being effective. Factors that are typically taken into account are summarized in Figure 5.4.

When mediation is likely to be effective	*When mediation is less likely to be effective*
• There is a history of cooperation or willingness to act in good faith • There are limited numbers of parties and issues and little anger • The working relationship is important • The parties will accept help from a neutral third party • There is external pressure to settle • Impasse has been reached by other means • Each party has some influence or leverage on the other parties and agreement is within the parties' power • The representatives are trusted and have some flexibility • The relevant information is available	• The fundamental interests of the disputing parties are mutually exclusive • There are many disputants and key stakeholders are not identifiable • A larger policy is at stake, e.g., local resolution could have wider implications in a national ideological debate • Clearly identified representatives with the ability to negotiate are lacking • The long-term consequences are unpredictable so that there is no commitment to the resolution of the dispute

Source: based on Talbot, 1983.

Figure 5.4 *The Feasibility of Mediated Negotiations*

Contrary to Amy's view, it is at this point that mediators consider whether fundamental differences in values can be negotiated. For example, Acland (1995) rates the degree of complexity mediators may face, culminating in differences in beliefs and values which relate to personal identity and deeper meaning, which he considers to be non-negotiable. Burton goes further and draws a distinction between 'disputes', which are negotiable, and 'conflicts', which stem from deeper needs, in which case the basic causes have to be addressed if the conflict is to be resolved. Talbot (1983), in examining a series of environmental disputes, links the presence of mutually exclusive fundamental interests with wider implications that local resolution might have in setting a precedent when larger policy issues are at stake. He concludes that mediation is likely to be feasible when the following conditions pertain: the conflict matures to the point where the issues are clearly defined; the various sides perceive the existence of a balance of power; and the perceived objectives cannot be achieved without negotiation. These conditions equate with Amy's. This often comes down to a question of timing (many mediators talk of assessing the ripeness of a dispute). Taylor wryly observes that in one of the cases he studied negotiations were possible after eight months, while in another case it took 17 years to reach a similar point.

The mediation literature is much concerned with how to deal with disparities of power and, as was noted earlier, it is generally recognized that gross imbalances of power may present an insurmountable barrier to negotiation (Palmer and Roberts, 1998; Leibmann, 2000). Where the situation is less clear, there are those who argue for intervention and those who argue that the mediator's most effective contribution is to maintain strict neutrality.

The interventionists seek to deliver justice, seeing it as their duty to ensure that any agreement does not favour the stronger party (e.g., Forester, 1989; Susskind, 1981, in Moore, 1986). Remaining neutral in such circumstances is to preserve the existing order, rather than attempting to change it. This is, in part, an argument for empowering the weak. For example, Ramirez (1999) sees the need to give a voice to weaker parties by transforming them from stakeholders to social actors. The former are at risk of being marginalized by the more powerful, while the latter are those with the 'capacity to make decisions and act on them'. Moore (1996, 69) suggests that there are circumstances when the stronger parties may welcome power-balancing to assist negotiation, although he recognizes that such interventions by mediators could put their neutrality at risk as they come close to advocacy on the weaker party's behalf. Moore also draws the distinction between 'recognising, organising and marshalling the existing power of the disputant' and 'assisting in generating new power and influence' [i.e., being partial]. He admits that there is no easy answer to the dilemma.

The tools that a mediator can use to balance power are limited to securing equal access to information and/or insisting that research is undertaken where information is lacking; providing training in negotiation skills; and ensuring that weaker parties are aware of such powers that they have, notably veto power, and are accorded equal opportunities and respect during the course of the negotiations, by reference to agreed ground rules. Moore (1986) suggests that it is helpful if the parties conduct their own power assessment, listing their sources of power and assessing those of other parties, and vice versa, and then exchange the information. The opposing school of thought considers that such interventions put the neutrality of the mediator at risk, and that such tasks are more properly those of the political organizer (Bellman, 1992).

Chornenki (1997) counters these views by arguing that by entering into a collaborative process, the parties exchange any power they have over others for sharing power collectively with them – the power of the team. More exactly, in interest-based negotiation the collective power of the team is focused on common, problem solving goals. Meanwhile, Carpenter and Kennedy take a pragmatic view:

> *The familiar theoretical argument that a 'balance of power' must be achieved before meaningful negotiations can begin seems irrelevant… The issue is not one of 'balance' but whether or not one party can influence the behaviour of another.* (Carpenter and Kennedy, 1988, 218)

However, the related issues of power and justice present an unresolved dilemma. This concerns whether the parties should retain control of the process and negotiate an agreement that they consider acceptable, with the risk that the powerful will manipulate the process to gain an advantageous outcome. Alternatively, control of the process can be handed over to a third party to secure justice and a fair outcome. In this case, the more the third party intervenes to redress an imbalance of power, the less likely it is that they will be seen to be neutral. Marks el al (1984) argued that the decision should rest with the stakeholders:

> *Whether inside or outside the courts, the goal of consensual dispute resolution is agreement between the parties on terms all find acceptable, not what the law or a third party 'justice seeker' determines is fair.* (Marks et al, 1984, 53)

The same authors also comment on the susceptibility of seemingly impartial processes to the blandishments of the powerful.

> *Courts and other adjudicative forums theoretically correct for power disparities by deciding cases on the basis of neutral principles applied equally to rich and poor alike. In practice, of course, such disparities are not overcome because parties with less means cannot afford equally competent representation. But mediation and such approaches may reinforce rather than correct existing imbalances.* (Marks et al, 1984, 53)

Summarizing the arguments about the potential denial of justice because of power differentials, Barach Bush (1995) agrees that ADR and mediation pose possibly greater risks than the legal system, but that these risks, especially the denial of justice, exist within the legal system too.

Whilst debate about the role of the mediator in respect of power is in part about perceived neutrality, successful mediators undoubtedly gain respect and authority as the negotiations progress. They are able to influence the course of events by controlling the structure of the process, by meeting stakeholders individually in caucus, and by controlling the flow of information from such meetings (especially when dealing with inter-personal disputes). Kolb and Babbitt (1995), in reviewing research on mediator behaviour, suggest that mediators may only communicate 'reasonable and fair' offers and direct parties towards settlements, in other words control the process of mediation more than they admit. The role is potentially a powerful one. These observations should not be used to negate the good that mediators do, but rather to promote acceptance of the idea that mediators are biased towards obtaining agreement (note the distinction between mediation and facilitation in Chapter 4). Tactics designed to obtain agreement are acceptable when all the disputing parties have agreed in advance that the mediator may need to use them. However, if the mediator transgresses the agreed norm, his/her contract should be terminated.

APPLICATIONS OF ENVIRONMENTAL MEDIATION

The use of ADR techniques to resolve public policy disputes in the USA is based on growing frustration over the delays and costs of administrative and legal processes of decision-making, coupled with the complexity of environmental problems in which large numbers of interests are involved. Mediation can also be seen as an attractive alternative to confrontational politics, satisfying a yearning in Western societies for peace, cooperation and reconciliation (Amy, 1987). These techniques have been applied to different levels of decision-making in the USA: for example, in the formation of public policy, such as getting agreement on the content of federal legislation or the detailed regulations which implement legislation (negotiated rule-making). Many site-based disputes about contentious developments, such as the disposal of hazardous waste, major water schemes, highway construction and airport expansion, have been settled in this way, together with disputes over wildlife and fisheries management and habitat conservation (Moore, 1996). A wide range of USA case studies are described in Talbot (1983), Susskind and Cruikshank (1987) and Susskind et al (1999), with international examples in Buckles (1999). However, even in the USA, the vast majority of environmental disputes are resolved by administrative or legal procedures.[2] Amy (1987) quoted a civil litigation research project in Wisconsin which found that only 10 per cent of disputing parties went to a lawyer. Of these, half filed a suit and 92 per cent settled out of court. Bellman also pointed out that most settlements are reached without mediation, and estimated that only 10 per cent of environmental disputes can be mediated (cited in Talbot, 1983, 93).[3]

Liebmann (2000) provided an overview of mediation in the UK, and traces its development over a very similar path as in the USA. Apart from historical precedents, the earliest initiatives were in industrial relations and employment disputes, and legislation heralded the establishment of the Arbitration and Conciliation Advisory Service (ACAS) in 1974. Family mediation started at about this time, whilst peer group mediation in schools, victim–offender mediation (latterly termed 'restorative justice'), and the mediation of neighbourhood disputes and commercial cases all represent different strands of mediation, which originated in the UK in the 1980s. The 1990s saw mediation applied to medical disputes within the National Health Service, as well as disputes concerning services for elderly people, organizations and the workplace, and applications within the civil justice system. Liebmann's edited volume contains a review of each of these topics. The most striking growth has been in community mediation services dealing with neighbourhood disputes. Two services had been established in 1984, rising to 124 by 1999; their caseloads rose from 7890 in 1998 to 11,504 in 1999 (Liebmann, 2000). Whilst there is some interest in mediation in the environmental field in Britain, hitherto there has been little activity, but this situation is likely to change with government interest in reducing costs and delays within the planning system (see Chapter 11).

CULTURAL VARIATIONS

Different forms of mediation are to be found in various cultures and there are historical precedents within most Western societies, indicating that the current interest signifies a rediscovery rather than an invention of a form of dispute resolution. For example, in colonial North America, following Puritan and Quaker traditions, conflict and legal disputation were viewed as disruptive to the fragile foundations of unity, harmony and group solidarity. Recourse to the official courts was rejected in favour of dispute resolution within local religious and ethnic communities on more consensual grounds (Auerbach, 1983). Moore (1986) also highlights the role of the clergy and rabbis in mediating family disputes within their respective faiths, the role of mediation in Islamic and Hindu cultures, and its practice in Japan, 'where religion and philosophy place a strong emphasis on social consensus, moral persuasion and striking a balance or harmony in human relations' (p20). A fuller account of mediation or quasi-mediation in different cultures would cover African moot courts, settlement by consensus in Melanesian, Latin American and Hispanic cultures, and the revival of mediation in a decentralized, professional form in the Republic of China (Palmer and Roberts, 1998). Kolb and Babbitt (1995) contrast the emphasis in Western cultures on the neutral outsider as mediator with the role performed in many non-industrial societies of the elder, who is well known to the disputing parties – indeed, may even be related to one or other of them – but is not directly involved in the dispute, and advocates a settlement in accordance with agreed cultural norms and values. These distinctions are highlighted in Figure 5.5, based on Augsburger (1992).

The salient point to recognize is that environmental mediation based on a Western model assumes common values which may not be shared by other cultures, and care should be exercised before assuming that these are universal

Western	'Traditional'
Process	*Process*
• structured, task oriented and directed towards agreement which satisfies disputing parties	• dynamic directed to resolving tension in community; emphasis on responsibilities of disputing parties and reconciliation
Mediator	*Mediator*
• technical specialist on contract, whose relationship to clients is professional and impersonal	• agreements may be suggested by others
Communication	*Communication*
• direct, with mediator controlling a formal process via ground rules. Such formality provides security and stability when discussing volatile issues	• recognized leader or go-between, known to disputing parties • indirect using go-between to save face, reduce threat, balance power and equalize verbal skills
Time	*Time*
• linear, one thing at a time within defined schedule of discreet sessions	• issues and relationships are interwoven • tasks and schedules are secondary to relationships and social rituals

Source: Augsburger, 1992.

Figure 5.5 *Western and 'Traditional' Models of Mediation*

and appropriate to all cultures (Chevalier and Buckles, 1999). While there are similarities in approach, environmental mediators need to respect and work with local cultures, rather than advocate a preference or false claim to universality of a dominant (Western) cultural system over others.

> *Ethical concerns are being raised as commentators have become concerned about imposing dominant cultural standards on minority groups or in the case of international work, neo-colonialism in the form of exportation of dispute resolution processes based on Western values.* (Palmer and Roberts, 1998, 159)

Cultural differences can be compounded by power differentials, and the communication problems of translation and interpretation are likely to be exacerbated when third party intervention comes from a mediator of a different culture to the disputants (Avruch and Black, 1993). The same authors envisage a risk that:

> *profitable jobs go to a new breed of hired 'have process, will travel' mediators, missionaries of United States democracy offering a menu of McMediation techniques designed to cool things down across the world.* (Avruch and Black, 1996, 52–53, quoted in Chevalier and Buckles, 1999, 18)

Case Study: Access Management by Local Consensus – Mediated Negotiations in the Peak District

The Establishment of the Peak District Access Consultative Group

The long history of the struggle to establish rights of public access on privately owned, uncultivated land in Britain has been described in Chapter 2. The analysis of moorland access in the Peak District National Park in Chapter 3 culminated with the controversy over the perceived risk to wildlife in the moors, and noted the change in decision-making following the formation of the PDACG. This case study reviews the process of mediated negotiations conducted within the PDACG.[4]

Specific provisions in the National Parks and Access to the Countryside Act of 1949 enable local authorities to enter into access agreements with landowners. The Peak District was the first English national park to be designated in 1951, and the park authority (the Peak Park Joint Planning Board) has been most assiduous in negotiating access agreements. By 1970, the Board had negotiated 19 access agreements covering 76 square miles of the park, about 60 per cent of all agreements made in England and Wales (Peak Park Joint Planning Board, 1992). Under the terms of an agreement, landowners and their tenants receive compensatory payments, and they are able to close their moors to the public for up to 14 days a year when grouse-shooting is taking place. By-laws regulating public access are enforced by the park's ranger service. The 1978 national park plan took account of the possible effect of wander-at-will access to open country on the breeding populations of upland waders by proposing limited access to areas of the highest wildlife importance. A subsequent review of the plan promoted the concept of limiting public access to 'corridors', and advocated research into the effects of access on wildlife (Peak Park Joint Planning Board, 1992). However, whether the effects of recreational disturbance were seriously damaging has been the subject of some controversy, with the scientific basis of work undertaken on behalf of the Board (Anderson, 1990) being contested on behalf of the Ramblers' Association (RA) (Watson, 1991). The RA continued to apply political pressure on the Board to enter into access agreements with the owners of the remaining moorland areas, whilst conservation interests advocated a stricter application of the precautionary principle and restrictions on access. Their arguments were supported by the designation of the South Pennine Moorlands as a Special Protection Area under the EU Conservation of Wild Birds Directive (79/409). By this time, many of the existing access agreements were due to expire and needed renegotiation, which increased the pressure on the Board to resolve these issues.

In 1992, the Board consulted approximately 50 organizations about a draft access strategy, which drew on principles of good conservation practice and a description of the limits of acceptable change (LAC) which had been set out in national guidance (Sidaway, 1991a). The strategy proposed the establishment of the PDACG, upon which the principle interests would be represented. It was envisaged that the PDACG would examine whether the LAC approach could be applied in the Peak District to deal with the controversy over recreational disturbance to ground-nesting birds. The strategy envisaged that access plans might be prepared as part of renegotiated access agreements, and that approaches would be made to all landowners in the national park to gauge their interest in any new arrangements (Peak Park Joint Planning Board, 1992).

Initiation – Pre-negotiation Stage

The feasibility of establishing the PDACG was investigated by the author in a series of pre-negotiation meetings with the individual stakeholders. These meetings considered what work the PDACG might undertake, its size and composition, and the procedures under which it might operate. This phase of work concluded that there was support for establishing the PDACG and that its remit should include preparing advice to the Board on the procedures which might lead to the production of agreed access management plans. The preference was for the establishment of a small task force of nine members, evenly balanced so that three representatives were drawn from each of the landowning, access and conservation interests. There was resistance to the group being chaired by a member or officer of the Board, as the Board was not perceived to be neutral. However, it was agreed that the Board would provide logistical support and that officers would attend PDACG meetings. The group would be led by a neutral facilitator, and hold monthly meetings over a period of six months under a set of agreed procedures.

These findings were set out in a report which was circulated first to the key interests for comment, and then more widely by the Board. The report explained why particular organizations would be represented on the PDACG, with the assumption that the representatives of these organizations would relate to a wider network within their sector of interest. For example, a particular onus was placed on the Sports Council to liaise with a wider community of active recreation interests. This pre-negotiation investigation lasted from February to June 1993.

Negotiation Stage

Following an exploratory meeting in June 1993, the PDACG met on six occasions between September 1993 and June 1994. During the initial meetings, members made presentations on their organization's interests in access to the moorlands and the qualities that they were concerned to maintain or enhance. Although their objectives differed, they were able to identify a mutual interest in conserving and managing the moorlands within the national park. Each member then made a list of considerations which their organization would like to be covered in local access management plans, and the group applied these in a pilot planning exercise for Crowden Moor.

The later meetings of the PDACG were concerned with preparing a report that could be agreed and submitted to the Board. The report emphasized the quality of moorlands in the national park, their value to landowners, farmers, conservationists, climbers and walkers, and set out the case for access management planning. For planning to be worthwhile, it had to offer potential benefits to each party and to recognize that each has a legitimate interest in the moors. A plan could offer reassurance that the important qualities of the moorlands would be safeguarded, as each interest had been directly involved in its preparation.

The report suggested that the Board should adopt the following management strategy:

• a commitment to the preparation of local access management plans using a voluntary and collaborative approach;
• the adoption of a management strategy based on a moorland code of behaviour, management by the Board's ranger service and the development of its interpretive strategy, and the establishment of a viable network of wildlife sanctuary areas for certain species and conservation management measures for others;
• the agreement of a programme for the preparation of access management plans linked to the renegotiation of access agreements and the search for voluntary agreements on new areas; and
• a commitment to undertake a programme of monitoring which would be subject to annual review (Peak District Access Consultative Group, 1994).

The report was completed in July 1994, having been circulated for detailed comment and endorsed by the member organizations. The main findings were reported to the Board in November 1994.

Assessment

The work in the pre-negotiation stage was funded by the Board. The negotiation stage was funded by the Countryside Commission and English Nature (EN), and this required the facilitator to assess the exercise. The assessment was prepared following a series of telephone interviews with members of the PDACG. At that point (November 1994), the mood was understandably cautious, welcoming the report but realistic in recognizing that there was still much to be done. Most members of the group felt that they now had a better understanding of others' points of view, and that a workable document had been prepared which provided a basic framework for further work. Even a small measure of agreement was seen to be encouraging, given the very low expectations that members had had at the outset because of the previous conflict. There were some reservations about whether the basic conflicts had been addressed; whether trust had been established; and whether the management approach was sufficiently detailed.

Most members thought that the initial approach of identifying common ground between interests was worthwhile, rather than dwelling on conflicts with which they were only too familiar. The strengths of the mediation and its attempt at consensus building were its inclusiveness, that it had been fair, and that it had enabled personal relationships to develop. The main weakness was the apparently long timescale. As one member of the PDACG commented: 'It was long-winded, but that is inevitable in democracy. We made heavy weather as everyone had their say, but they would have been frustrated if they had been cut short. Given the outcome, it has been worthwhile.'

Many procedural details were important. The size of the group was considered to be about right, but probably at the upper end of what is practical when implementing this kind of procedure. The composition of the group was seen to be fair, but there needed to be clearer arrangements about how other interested organizations could become involved. The PDACG had opted for evening meetings, but these frequently overran. With hindsight, most members considered that full-day or weekend meetings, each with a clear goal, would have been more productive. The employment of an independent facilitator was seen to have been necessary at this stage, and most members doubted that any other arrangement would have worked. While some members thought it would have been disastrous if the mediator had strayed from a neutral role, others felt he could have been more directive and possibly provided a greater technical input, although it would be difficult to combine both the technical role (a consultant making recommendations) and the conciliatory role (the neutral facilitator).

The PDACG had agreed a series of ground rules at the outset, which specified that decisions would be taken by consensus, that others' views would be respected, and that representatives had a responsibility for reporting back to their organizations but that confidentiality should be maintained. Information would be treated as a common resource, and only agreed statements would be issued to the media. With hindsight, reporting back to member organizations was seen to be a crucial issue, particularly when the PDACG's work extended over such a lengthy period. At times this conflicted with the confidentiality rule, which some thought hindered discussion, making representatives cautious about their contributions and stopping them from sounding out their colleagues. The difficulty stems from the different ways in which organizations work. Professionals working for organizations frequently have considerable autonomy, and are used to taking responsibility when negotiating and reporting back later. Voluntary officers representing democratic organizations may have difficulty exploring other group members' positions without the risk of premature disclosure, which could upset the organizations they represent.

The open-ended approach to discussions proved difficult when the PDACG tried to apply the LAC principles. It led to an abstract debate which sidetracked the PDACG, although several elements of LAC were adopted in the proposed planning method, such as the collaborative approach, the monitoring of potential impacts and the agreement of consequent management action. It was the Crowden pilot planning exercise that grounded and focused an otherwise abstract discussion, and gave some confidence that a collaborative approach (using mediation) which takes all interests into account can probably resolve most practical problems. One unresolved problem concerns how this approach would be developed for individual access agreements. Initial soundings suggested that individual landowners might be willing to cooperate, but it would be necessary to bring in people with local knowledge who had not previously been involved in consensus building. The park-wide PDACG would lack that local knowledge, and its members envisaged it would meet only occasionally in future as a review body.

Consensus building with an independent mediator appears to have succeeded where conventional committee working might not have done. The PDACG produced a planning approach which reflected the range of interests around the table but was not imposed upon them. Although the process was undoubtedly time-consuming, it is worth remembering that this was the first occasion in which representatives of all three interests had met and worked on matters of common concern. The PDACG largely achieved the task that had been defined in the access strategy two years earlier. If the timescale taken to achieve that task appears extended, it should be seen in the context of a long-running conflict, elements of which extend back some 70 years. Final agreement was contingent on further work being done to resolve outstanding technical issues, such as the scale of wildlife sanctuary areas, and on resources being obtained to monitor and evaluate a wide range of factors. Success at each stage was likely to reinforce confidence in collaborative management planning as a way of resolving new problems.

However, the Board did not act on the recommendations of the PDACG, and with hindsight the failure to obtain a firm commitment to do so in advance was a fundamental weakness of the exercise. Various reasons were given for inaction, which certainly contributed to scepticism on the part of the Ramblers, at least, about the value of voluntary negotiations (Holt, 1998). This was an echo of the reservations the Ramblers had held in earlier episodes of the conflict over rights of access (see Chapter 2). The extent to which these mediated negotiations met the principles of consensus building is set out in Figure 5.6.

INITIATION
Terms of reference: the agenda covered the interests of the principal stakeholders
identified in preparatory stage and the discussions focused on finding common ground.

INCLUSIVNESS
Representation was deliberately balanced between the major interests but limited to
ease decision-making. It was intended that representatives should report back to
provide *accountability* to their organizations.

Openness: the meetings of the group were confidential and this inhibited full discussion
of progress within member organizations.

INFORMATION
During the negotiations information was made freely available to members of the group,
although conclusive evidence on the effects of disturbance on bird populations was not
available.

INFLUENCE
Agreement was reached on the process of access management planning but the lack of
commitment to accepting the group's findings meant that their recommendations were
not implemented.

Figure 5.6 *Peak District Access Consultative Group – Assessment of
Participation in Decision-making*

Postscript – The Stanage Forum

However, the Board subsequently decided to prepare a management plan
using consensus building for the 542-ha North Lees estate, which it owns
and is situated about 10km from the centre of Sheffield. The estate includes
Stanage Edge, an important site for rock climbing, as well as farmland and
moorland of high recreational value. The Stanage Forum was established in
2000 with open membership, and nominated an 18-member steering group
whose meetings were independently facilitated. The group met 22 times,
reporting back to the Forum at significant stages in the plan's preparation.
The plan was publicly launched at the Forum's fourth meeting in September
2002. Active participation was and is being sought throughout this
continuing process, both at the Forum meetings and via the website
(www.peakdistrict.org/stanage).

CONCLUSIONS

This chapter has described the process of mediation and examined how
mediators attempt to design a fair and equitable process of negotiation. It
also shows that they are aware of many of the criticisms they face,
particularly that informal, non-legal processes are less likely to deliver justice
in the face of unequally distributed power. The initial conflict assessment or

stakeholder analysis is pivotal in meeting these criticisms. An example was provided in the working of the PDACG, which agreed a collaborative process to be used in preparing access management plans within the national park. The plans aimed to reduce the potentially harmful effects of unregulated access on protected species of ground-nesting birds. Although the PDACG contained representatives of the three main interests and followed most of the principles of participatory decision-making, it was lacking in one vital respect: the failure to obtain a firm commitment that the Board would act on its recommendations. Thus the PDACG lacked influence, reinforcing the scepticism of the RA about participating in voluntary negotiations. Chapter 6 gives a fuller account of a mediated negotiation: the NOCC in Maine, USA.

Chapter 6

'Clearing the Air' – The North Oxford County Coalition

I'm sure there'll be another issue that comes up sometime and now they've learned – this community's gone through a process and they've learned how to deal with conflict in a constructive way. I think that's invaluable for the community to know that. (Health professional)[1]

SYNOPSIS

This chapter presents a detailed case study of the North Oxford County Coalition (NOCC) in Maine, USA, which was formed to bring together members of the local community, government regulators, representatives of local industry and others to consider the potential health effects of emissions from a pulp mill in the town of Rumford. The conflict was precipitated by sensational TV coverage of the apparently high incidence of cancer in mill-workers and their families, which deeply divided the community. During the course of three years of negotiation, most of the initial fears were allayed following an assessment of the medical and scientific evidence by independent experts, and the main outcome of the group's deliberations was a health education initiative: the River Valleys Healthy Communities Coalition (RVHCC). The process was facilitated by the Consensus Building Institute (CBI), Cambridge, Massachusetts, and has been investigated by the author. This chapter covers the process followed by the mediation team, charts the turning points in the discussions, considers how the process was seen in retrospect by participants and shows how the NOCC process met the preconditions for consensus.

CONTEXT

The small town of Rumford lies in the wooded valley of the Androscoggin River in Western Maine, close to New Hampshire border. Although its pulp mill is a dominating feature, outwardly Rumford seems an unlikely setting for a bitter conflict over the health risks from environmental pollution. In many ways, this town, along with its immediate neighbours (Mexico, Peru and Dixfield), is very similar to many others in New England, in that it is largely dependent on a single employer – in this case the pulp mill. The mill was originally opened in 1899 by the Oxford Paper Company, later owned by Boise Cascade and now by the Mead Paper Corporation. Like other mill towns, this economic dependence meant there was a reluctance to voice concerns about the local incidence of cancer, matched perhaps by a reluctant acceptance that health risks were a necessary price to pay for steady employment and a better chance for one's children.

But what really makes this community different is the way in which that conflict was resolved, how it has moved on to tackle a wider range of health problems and how the town can now live with itself. This chapter concentrates on the process which helped to resolve the conflict and does not dwell on the conflict itself. What is worth noting, however, is how in the earlier stages, before that healing process began, this conflict followed a familiar pattern of escalation (described in Chapter 3), threatening to spiral out of control from relatively small beginnings (see Figure 6.1).

The beginnings of the conflict lay in an increasingly commonly held view in the community that the incidence of cancer in mill-workers and their families was unusually high, and the suspicion that this was due to emissions from the mill. These allegations were denied by the then mill managers, only to be 'confirmed' by a tragic case: the death from cancer of a teenage girl. The publicity that this case attracted was highlighted in a television programme which labelled the community as 'Cancer Valley', and this had far-reaching implications, typified by the outsiders' response of 'Boy, I'm glad I don't live there'. The reactions of the mill managers were defensive, as they saw themselves complying with the federal and state regulations. This response was matched by the scepticism of many health professionals, as the study on which the programme was based has never been traced and subjected to professional scrutiny. But in such an emotive situation, many people were prepared to make up their minds without recourse to hard data, although preliminary monitoring by the Maine Department of Environmental Protection (DEP) did suggest that there were increased levels of certain air toxins that might be of concern, and the discharge data from the Maine Bureau of Health suggested increased incidents of respiratory illness in the valley (Roscoe and Weiss, 1999).

In many cases, judgement was clouded by resentment towards the mill so that the community became increasingly polarized. Such suspicions added salt to the wound from a 1986 labour dispute, and the only opportunity for resolution proved to be more of an adversarial event – a public hearing in 1992 for a licence application by the then owners Boise Cascade to install new boilers and change the manufacturing process to burn sludge. At this hearing, community concerns about dioxin emissions were not alleviated and local people were angry that the State Air Bureau did not appear to be protecting the community. This led to further mistrust, in this case between

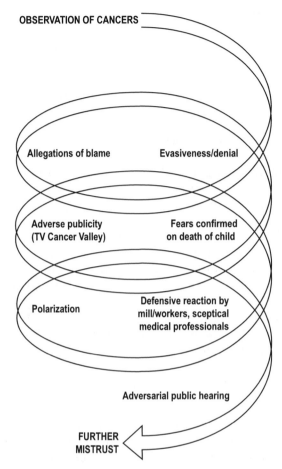

OBSERVATION OF CANCERS

Allegations of blame   Evasiveness/denial

Adverse publicity   Fears confirmed
(TV Cancer Valley)   on death of child

Polarization   Defensive reaction by
mill/workers, sceptical
medical professionals

Adversarial public hearing

**FURTHER
MISTRUST**

Figure 6.1 *Rumford, Maine: Perceived Cancer Risk from Pulp Mill
Emissions – Spiral of Conflict*

the community and public officials. As far as local people were concerned,
the state environmental and health agencies were part of the problem.

INITIATION

The public pressure on the state agencies, particularly the DEP, resulted in a
personal initiative by the DEP's director to engage consultants to conduct a
dialogue between labour and mill representatives, health care providers,
local government, and state and federal agencies. Ad hoc meetings in 1993
led to the first formal meeting of the NOCC in June 1994. While the task
was reasonably clear – to investigate concerns about cancer rates, levels of
river and air pollution, and whether these were linked – the process was

novel and also more problematic. Part of the task was to assess what was technically feasible within available resources, and which problems could be investigated with a reasonable hope of success and might therefore lead to a practical outcome. Mediation was required to help a local group with very differing interests address these issues in an un-emotive way.

However, the initial attempt at mediation made little progress; several facilitators and consultants failed to build a good working relationship with the group, and the process faltered. It was at this point that personal contacts between the Environment Protection Agency (EPA) in Boston and the CBI initiated a fresh start. The lack of funds was limiting the exercise, as much of the initial funding from the EPA had been spent in the early stages. However, the CBI had access to independent funding from the Hewlett Foundation, which enabled it to work initially on a pro bono basis. Thereafter, the EPA was able to draw on a new initiative, community-based environmental protection projects, to cover the cost of research investigations and subsequent CBI fees.

Even more critical was the lack of data on which to base justifiable judgements on the incidence of cancer in the valley. Although the complexity of the issues and the limitations of epidemiological studies would not become evident until later, it was vital to move from a debate based on emotion to one grounded by facts from studies that might provide some reassurance to the community.

PRE-NEGOTIATION STAGE

Once appointed, the two CBI mediators went back to square one.[2] They conducted interviews with potential stakeholders with the aim of identifying and including all relevant interests in the subsequent discussions, irrespective of the wide differences of opinion. The written report of this stakeholder analysis, equivalent to the first stage of a negotiation strategy as described in Chapter 5, was presented to the coalition at the first meeting facilitated by the CBI in June 1995, and debated at the subsequent one-day retreat. The contacts made during this exercise began to establish the credibility of the mediators within a community weary of the conflict. The mediators found a reluctance to participate in the NOCC discussions, and much scepticism that consensus could be built: '[I thought] is this another of those dry runs which go down the drain?' (former selectman, i.e., a member of the town board).

NEGOTIATION STAGE

The CBI's approach was to be as open and inclusive as possible, which meant deliberately seeking representation from all shades of opinion, including the mill's most outspoken critics as well as its representatives and

---

Box 6.1 CBI's Approach to Stakeholder Analysis

The purposes of the stakeholder analysis were to summarize community concerns, to ensure all stakeholders were represented and to devise a work plan.

The CBI interviewed 48 respondents, starting with people who were already involved with the coalition and going on to interview others with a direct interest in the subject. 35 interviews were conducted face-to-face and 13 by phone. The CBI discovered a wide range of differing views on air quality, public health, economics, plant–community relations and concerns about the NOCC discussions to date. Three main areas of agreement were identified:

- the need to gather detailed factual information on air quality and public health;
- the need to inform the public about air quality and public health issues; and
- the need for the group to work in a more structured way, with a work plan to provide direction over a defined time period, using sub-committees to draw on the expertise within the group to develop specific tasks.

The CBI suggested that the membership of the coalition should be extended to include an additional representative from each of the following interests: state and federal agencies, business, organized labour, environmental advocates, and state-wide health non-governmental organizations (NGOs). Four more representatives should be drawn from health care providers, and seven more should be ordinary citizens. The coalition would then increase from 19 to 36 members.

---

those occupying the middle ground. This led to the early meetings of the NOCC being variously recalled as 'wild', 'hot and heavy', 'accusatory and ghastly' and 'very, very long'. At this stage the representatives of industry and the DEP were equally mistrusted and encountered the hostility of the environmental activists and elected representatives: 'As we say in Maine, we were loaded for bear' (retired teacher).

These feelings took time to subside as participants adjusted to a novel process. To some of the initial participants, the process appeared to be going nowhere. They grew frustrated and left. Even those who stayed had their doubts, although they see in retrospect the value of letting people talk things out.

> *Well, I guess, facilitators are necessary in this kind of situation just because you have a group of people with different backgrounds, who are ... coming to talk about a particular subject and because of their differences ... you need to be able to ... focus – what are the issues that are important to us? What are the issues that we can deal with? ... Because so many problems were identified and I don't care what community you're in, you can find lots of different things that you feel should be better – but what you then need to do is say – what can we actually do? ... Once we decided that we broke into the groups to tackle these issues and come back with some kind of*

meaningful format in which to report it and, as often as possible, some kind of action plan. (Medical practitioner)

Thus, the mediators provided a structure for the discussions and kept them focused, yet they kept their fingers on the pulse of the group, learnt to understand the stakeholders and let them have their say.

> *I have to give enormous credit to Pat and Sarah, because they put up with so much, both taking the brunt of what were basically local arguments, and they learned very quickly not to use any of the classic – you know those cute little ice-breakers that people do at the beginning?... I had been part of a lot of different kinds of problem solving basically in the school and that's so scary. A lot of people are sitting in a trench with something over their heads saying 'This day will pass'. You really have to be awfully sensitive to what the group will bear.* (Retired teacher)

The patience of the mediators paid off. They worked with the community's agenda of concerns, which included sorting out the priorities for investigation, building trust between warring parties, and carefully documenting each stage. They provided direction by setting out a road map and targets for the group, which could be altered by mutual agreement.

In part, this planning came from the group going into 'retreat' at its second meeting – a day-long workshop which included negotiation training. Views varied on the success of this retreat when the group was not yet ready to act collectively, but it provided a framework which was re-visited and developed as discussion proceeded. The more usual pattern of three-hour

---

Box 6.2 NOCC Ground Rules (Revision of June 1996)

1 Listen when someone else is speaking in order to encourage respect among all members.
2 Give others a chance to express their views.
3 Describe your own views rather then the views of others.
4 Encourage discussion not speeches.
5 Speak to the point not the person.
6 Stay on track with the agenda.
7 Members should signal a 'time out' if they think other members are not following the ground rules. When a time out is signalled, the facilitators will ask the group if the ground rules have or have not been followed.
8 When necessary, the facilitators will use an egg timer to limit individual comments to a reasonable time period.
9 Facilitators will play an active role in enforcing the ground rules.
10 There will be a 'disagreement list' to post outstanding issues and disagreements.

meetings, held in the evening at approximately monthly intervals, limited the amount that could be done at any one session, but it was the group's choice and fitted into their daytime schedules (see Chapter 5 regarding meetings of the Peak District Access Consultative Group – PDACG).

Part of the strategy that emerged was the establishment of sub-groups which investigated particular aspects of the controversy in greater depth, and which were able to call on appropriate outside expertise. Three groups were formed: a technical sub-group, which considered sources of independent advice to the NOCC and investigated cancer rates in the valley; a public health sub-group, which considered community health issues; and, later, an air quality sub-group, which considered air pollution. The air quality sub-group was supported by the air toxics section of the DEP, and instigated an extensive programme of air quality and fog monitoring undertaken by the DEP. The technical sub-group was supported by the Maine Board of Health, and also studied the incidence of asthma. However, its principal task was an epidemiological investigation led by Dr Wartenberg from Rutgers University in New Jersey. The choice of advisor was influenced by two factors: neutrality (one of the experts nominated earlier was found to have worked with the unions and was rejected by the mill) and cost (CBI contacts identified an expert who was willing to work on a pro bono basis).

> Well ... when we got what seemed to be valid information, for instance, [about] the cancer rates or the air quality sampling rates, of course we needed somebody to explain that to us ... and ... like any scientific literature, people debated the validity of it and so we spent a lot of time bringing in experts ... explaining ... what's statistically significant because most of the people just took, for instance, the cancer rate at face value. (Health care provider)

Not all the animosity was directed at the mill and its representatives. Initially, there were other lesser tensions within the group, between the community health care workers and the hospital and between group members and the research scientists brought in to conduct the epidemiological studies. In the latter case, hostility was provoked by a careless turn of phrase:

> We would study something, and the epidemiologist would say, 'Well, you don't have enough people to be statistically relevant'. I did say to them at one point, 'If my mother had died of cancer, I wouldn't have found that a very appropriate thing to say to me, thank you.' (Retired teacher)

Sensitivity to how a turn of phrase can be interpreted by others is only one element of respecting their views. Other more basic civilities tend to be neglected in adversarial debate, so that agreeing and enforcing ground rules for discussion is one of the mediator's first tasks. Although the CBI got the group to set out ground rules at the first meeting, it took a while for the disciplines of listening and not interrupting to take hold. Indeed, some participants felt the rules should have been applied more rigorously in the early meetings, as the critics tended to dominate the discussion. Later, as the group realized the value of rules of engagement, they re-visited, re-wrote and took ownership of the ground rules.

> *Ground rules were something that were always being reviewed. I guess they were necessary, certainly at the outset with some of the more vocal people that had axes to grind. They could monopolize a meeting in a way that was not respected, so I can understand why those rules were used. I think it's important that people can be civil and accord each other respect and the opportunity to voice an opinion and to listen. But I guess you've got to have rules to make sure that the process doesn't get out of hand somewhat.* (Selectman)

The CBI's practice of inclusiveness extended to ensuring that NOCC meetings were open to the press, a policy not invariably followed by mediation professionals. This paid off handsomely, for unlike television – which has a short attention span and looks for sound bites that can distort a situation – the local press showed a sincere interest and commitment to the community and its wellbeing. The local press maintained its interest throughout the lengthy NOCC process, and its coverage was considered by NOCC members to be fair, responsible and constructive. Certainly, in this case, the major benefit of this procedure was that the local community was kept informed of the discussions, and there were no grounds for being suspicious of what was happening behind closed doors, as the doors were already open.

The health sub-group's findings that cancer rates in the valley were a matter for concern but were not of epidemic proportions proved to be very contentious within the NOCC. It was an important statement to be making to the community, coming at the end of three years of research and hard discussion. The NOCC deliberated for a long time over the wording of its report. It had decided that even if it could not be totally unanimous, then everyone had to be able to live with the document and that there were to be no minority reports.

STRENGTHS AND WEAKNESSES OF THE NOCC PROCESS

The determination to reach consensus over the report was perceived to be one of the strengths of the coalition. It presented a united view to the community and the perception of a positive change. This view had been reinforced all along by the policy of open access and responsible reporting in the local press. To reach consensus required a major commitment of time

Perceived strengths	Perceived weaknesses
MEDIATION CBI mediation: experience, commitment and attitudes of mediators, that gained the trust of the group and kept discussions focused. CBI kept the same team throughout	LENGTHY PROCESS 'False start' with change of mediators; lengthy discussions Ground rules might have been more strictly enforced at start. CBI should have redressed balance of power Lack of preparation for press launch
OUTSIDE RESOURCES AND EXPERTISE Federal and state agencies: the commitment of EPA and DEP, in terms of expertise and resources Access to outside technical expertise, coupled with expertise within the community Support and data from mill	Need for outside intervention questioned and whether such commitment could be repeated elsewhere
STAKEHOLDER COLLABORATION Commitment and time dedicated by stakeholders Getting stakeholders together, wide range of opinions represented, opportunity to discuss issues and ask questions and to network Collaboration provided ownership of NOCC process, which has carried over into RVHCC	REPRESENTATION Lopsidedness of representation (few town leaders) Delays due to changing representation
CONSENSUS OVER REPORT Epidemiological findings Insistence of consensus on report Perception of positive changes Press presence, openness with community during course of negotiations	UNRESOLVED ISSUES (minority views) Air pollution issues unresolved Air quality monitoring Clarification of health issues – for many attitudes to mill unchanged Limited resources for data collection

Figure 6.2 *Retrospective Views of Stakeholders on the NOCC Negotiations*

by the members of the NOCC. They had to learn how to collaborate, to raise their concerns and to discuss them productively. This sense of ownership, developed so strongly in the NOCC, has persisted into the RVHCC. NOCC members were asked in this study what they saw as the strengths and weaknesses of the mediated process, and their responses are summarized in Figure 6.2.

Although one NOCC member questioned whether it should have been necessary to bring in facilitators 'from away' (from outside Maine), the majority thought it was the mixture of neutral mediation and technical expertise from outside, coupled with expertise within the community, which helped to gain the support of the mill and developed the process of collaboration. The experience, commitment and welcoming attitudes of mediators were seen to be major strengths of the process of building trust, and their facilitation kept discussions focused and moved things on.

The perceived weaknesses tended to be the downsides of many of the strengths, and were generally minority views. A corollary of attempting to reach consensus was long drawn-out discussion, which tempted some members to drop out, coupled with the delays incurred by changing representation, which required old ground to be re-visited. It was suggested that representation was 'lopsided', i.e., few town leaders attended meetings, and that neutral mediation tended to be 'more than fair' to the mill. Although some members were impressed by the commitment of federal staff and the resources they provided for research, to others resources for data collection were too limited, so that many of the air pollution issues were thought to remain unresolved. One unforeseen eventuality was the extent of media interest the day before the release of the final report, when some members were caught unprepared.

TURNING POINTS IN THE DEBATE

Three main factors were highlighted by NOCC members as turning points during the discussions: changes in group dynamics, the production of scientific evidence in the epidemiological study, and changes in mill processing.

The changes in the group dynamics resulted from several causes. The attempt at team building during the retreat had some influence, along with the gradual building of trust both within the group and between the group and the mediators. More significantly, as adherence to ground rules became stronger, so the group became more impatient with the adversarial stance of the mill's critics:

> *The turning point that I remember was after a lot of people in the group sort of got tired of hearing the very vocal critics regarding, you know, 'Maybe the mill is a high contributor to the air quality problem and we need to do something about that,' and the group kind of thought, 'Well, wait, maybe what we need to do is focus on what's good in this for the valley. Let's get away from what's bad here [and focus on] what is really good here and try to promote what's really good.'* (Health care provider)

Coupled with this was a positive change in the attitudes and approach of the mill's representatives when the ownership changed hands from Boise Cascade to the Mead Paper Corporation in 1995, followed by a major reduction in chloroform emissions from the mill, triggered (at least in part) by impending environmental regulations.

Box 6.3 Key Questions in Process Design Illustrated by the NOCC

Who takes the initiative in starting negotiations?

The DEP initiated mediated negotiations, although it was a stakeholder in the dispute. The commitment to mediation shows the value of having an internal advocate for consensus building at a senior level in the DEP. The NOCC was crucial in the early stages.

How to choose a mediator

Having facilitators from out of state proved crucial to ensuring that they were perceived to be neutral. When the initial choice proved unsatisfactory, others were tried until a successful partnership was achieved. The initial rapport established by the CBI during the preliminary conflict assessment enabled it to gain the trust of stakeholders.

Who pays the mediator?

The main funding was provided by the EPA. The CBI had access to independent funding from the Hewlett Foundation, so that it could initially work on a pro bono basis.

Who are the stakeholders, and who should be involved in negotiations?

The CBI conducted a stakeholder analysis to identify the interested parties and their concerns, and this led to an expanded representation in the negotiations (see Box 6.1).

The need for clear ground rules decided in advance

The CBI insisted on ground rules at the initial meetings, and these were regularly re-visited and revised (see Box 6.2).

Does the preliminary assessment confirm that there is a basis for negotiation?

The CBI presented its findings in written form, proposing both the composition of the negotiating group and a structured framework for discussion. These findings were accepted by the NOCC.

For the health professionals, the changes in dynamics were also linked to a growing emphasis on research, which could provide a factual rather than an emotional basis for discussions. Later, as the results of the epidemiological study became available, the group came to appreciate both the limitations of that study and the complexities of trying to unravel the local causes of cancer. Realizing the effort it had taken to get that far and the costs of attempting further work, the NOCC decided to devote its energies and resources to more feasible investigations, like a radon study, and to health education.

> *I think people came out with a better understanding of the complexity of this health problem; that you can't just point a finger at one thing and say, 'Stop doing that and you're going to cure cancer'. That this is a very, very, very complicated problem with many causes, and this community has a poor lifestyle – unhealthy lifestyle, not poor lifestyle, an unhealthy lifestyle. (Interviewer: 'Such as?') I think overweight, underexercised, smoking and drinking. Maine has, and I'm sure this community has, one of the highest smoking rates in the nation.* (Health professional)

ACHIEVEMENTS AND OUTCOMES OF THE NOCC

According to the members of the NOCC, the coalition's achievements fell into four main categories:

1 the investigation of health issues;
2 the formation of a new coalition to promote the health of the community;
3 growing cooperation between the neighbouring towns on other issues; and
4 improvements in the relationship between the town and the mill, typified by greater openness about its operations on the part of the mill.

From the work of its sub-groups, the NOCC gained a better understanding of the local incidence of cancer and, just as significantly, a better understanding of the multi-causality of cancers and the difficulties and costs of clarifying cancer risks. However, there remain differences in emphasis, if not opinion, based perhaps on different expectations about what could be achieved. The professionals emphasize the value of focusing on aspects of the problem which can lead to a practical outcome, while a small minority of lay sceptics see the task as incomplete, so that some uncertainty remains.

The decision not to make further investigations into cancer rates was not reached without some soul-searching. It was partly a pragmatic decision made when the resource implications became clear, in terms of both the volunteer inputs from the NOCC and the financial costs. But it was also a conscious decision that more positive things could be done with the remaining funds, which would contribute to health in the community. Indeed, several NOCC studies, such as the dioxin workshop and the radon survey, made a practical contribution to community wellbeing. At the same time, due to EPA and state regulations, the mill went from using chlorine for bleaching to chlorine dioxide, which produces much less dioxin.

BOX 6.4 REFLECTIONS ON THE OUTCOME

I think from [the agency's] perspective, we achieved … all our goals – that we provided assistance to the community to answer some of the questions about the pollutants that they had. And I think that we raised a lot of awareness about cancer rates through the multiple factors that go into cancer, that it's an environment problem as well, but there are also a lot of other components. We did the air monitoring as best we could. It was very difficult with all the problems, but we gave it an incredible effort to do the best we can … the technology just wasn't quite there … and now they're working on issues that are important to them. (Agency representative)

I think there are a lot of people in the town who had the same kind of knee-jerk reaction to the issues they had 12, 20, 30 years ago – that the mill was responsible for a lot of the bad things that happened to people; and I think it is going to be hard, it may take generations, to eradicate that position. (Selectman)

It was fully completed. What it did was sort of hypothesis-generating. It was just looking at incidence rates, and what it showed was there were certain types of cancer that had elevated levels, and some of those could have an environmental component to it… Could it have been taken to a lot more levels?… I really think with the population size, it would be almost impossible to [do] – you know, they're talking about a million-dollar type study to do that. (Agency representative)

One issue was radon in that community… They have treatment control so they don't have radon in their drinking water supplies, but it's just a naturally-occurring area of very high levels of radon, and [in] that part of Maine … the granite has quite a bit of radon. So the EPA said that [it] would provide assistance by providing 500 radon sensors to the community and … a lot of people had tests for free – they could test their homes for radon… That was very successful, because it would involve a lot of the community. We had the Boy Scouts help put together the canisters, and then we had the fire department provide a place for them to be picked up, and I think we had like over 400 homes tested. (Agency representative)

An accurate summary of the NOCC's research findings was given by a coalition member, who also highlighted the importance of focusing on other health factors in the community:

Rumford does have a slightly elevated cancer rate, but it isn't a hot spot … and the more they worked at it, the more it appeared that while the mill certainly was a polluting factor, the geography of the valley traps [pollutants], and then you get a lot of traffic through here. So it's [also] cars and auto-body shops and cleaning establishments. There's a lot of junk getting into the air that isn't just the mill, which some people didn't want to hear. (Retired teacher)

The decision to move the agenda on by forming the RVHCC was, for most NOCC members, the most tangible legacy of their deliberations:

I think the real success of the NOCC is that we came out of it, and we were able to develop the Healthy Communities Coalition. I really think that that's a major thing for this community, and I hope that people realise it, that that is important. (Medical practitioner)

Some NOCC members also feel that the NOCC certainly contributed to, even if it did not initiate, a growing realization in the valley that there should be greater cooperation between towns:

It was a situation where everybody was running in different directions. Rumford hated Mexico, and Mexico didn't like Rumford, and they were excluding all the little towns; and over the last seven or eight years we've done a lot to bring [them] together. We've formed committees of different town officials so we sit down and say, 'Hey, what can we do to better our communities?' We can buy stuff together ... to save money. And ... I think that really, from my point of view, it happened when that group started to form, because that group was so deep-rooted in this whole area, [it] went way out to Oxford, Mexico, Peru and Dixfield. (Former selectman)

Certainly, one of the lessons the community appears to have learnt is the value of talking things through and getting things done, and this restored its faith in the system. At the same time as community confidence has been restored, the image of the community to the outside world has improved dramatically:

And another outcome is that the so-called 'cancer valley' talk has died down a great deal, the negative public relations [for] the community has decreased. It was very strong at that time. The community had a very poor reputation... When I first lived here, people would say 'Why did you move there? We don't understand why you'd want to live there.' I found it extraordinarily difficult to recruit physicians into the community at that time, and if I did, I lost them after a year or two, and that's not true anymore. (Health professional)

I think that the town feels a lot better about itself, and I say that as a subjective statement, but I think there's less worry about things and the hot items have changed. (Business representative)

The other aspect of improved community relations is the way in which the mill now understands the community's concerns and communicates with it, for example by establishing a Community Advisory Panel, which meets regularly, and by holding public meetings, which contribute to a sense of openness. This is largely attributed to the NOCC.

> *The mill, for the first time since I've arrived in town, actually had public meetings every six months letting you know, and they still do that. There are three or four different things that they have done over the past three years... The environmental engineer would sit down with anyone who showed up and tell us what they had planned, how much money they were going to spend and answer questions. That's never happened in this town until then.* (Retired teacher)

Whilst there may be greater understanding of the mill and the importance of its survival for the economic benefit of the towns, there is still healthy scepticism about what its spokespersons choose to say:

> *I thoroughly believe in [environmental regulations], not least the fact that industry fights them all the time. But this is an industrial town... You know, people come here and they want to change it, but without the mill they wouldn't have the quality of life. So if you choose to live in an industrial town, I think it's more responsible to try to make them be compliant and maybe even forward-looking in terms of environmental stuff, but don't wish them away. That's really cutting off your nose to spite your face. I think you can work together, but it takes some more trust and some more honesty on both sides.* (Retired teacher)

> *It has become more open ... but the PR department lets out what they want. You don't get a specific answer to a specific question. But it is easier to talk to someone from the mill now.* (Journalist)

THE VALUE OF OUTSIDE INTERVENTION

Given what the NOCC finally achieved, the thought has crossed several minds that the community might have reached similar conclusions on its own. Certainly, the view was expressed that things were moving that way and that a community-led initiative was a possibility. However, most NOCC members confirmed the view that the towns could not have afforded either the much-needed technical expertise to ask the appropriate questions, or the research provided by federal and state resources, which was backed by the regulatory powers of these agencies.[3] Indeed, a mill representative felt it was imperative to have the regulatory agencies represented within the coalition, as they provided independent verification of the improvements in plant processing.

> *This would have never gotten done. The group might have talked itself out, but there certainly wouldn't have been any research done.* (Health professional)

> (Interviewer) *Do you think this would have happened without the involvement of the EPA?*

> (Health care provider) *Absolutely not.*

> (Interviewer) *Would it have been just a local initiative?*

> (Health care provider) *Absolutely not. The group probably would have met twice and disbanded. Absolutely not.*

CONCLUSIONS

The events that led to the formation of the NOCC illustrated only too vividly the spiral of conflict described in Chapter 3. Nevertheless, this desperate situation was transformed from a community in conflict to one at ease with itself and engaged in improving community health. Both external and internal factors were crucial to the success of this mediated process. External support from the environmental regulatory agencies came in the form of internal advocacy for mediation, persisting when the initial attempts failed. External resources were also vital to obtain an objective interpretation of the risks of cancer in the community. The strength of the mediated process depended on designing an inclusive and open process, which allowed critical activists to air their views and ensured that meetings were open to the press and public. The mediation team showed great patience and commitment in gaining the trust of the negotiating group, and kept the discussions focused. But it was the inner strength of the group which showed through in its growing determination to reach consensus over the final report. The extent to which the mediated negotiations conformed to the criteria for participatory decision-making set out in Chapter 4 is summarized in Figure 6.3.

Criteria	Pre-negotiation stage	Negotiation stage	Post-negotiation stage
INITIATION			
Terms of reference and agenda	CBI conflict assessment identified stakeholder concerns and the purpose of negotiations	Facilitators established the common ground between participants in clarifying cancer risks	Community health agenda developed by new coalition and frequently reviewed
INCLUSIVENESS			
Communities and representation	CBI identified enlarged negotiating group to cover community interests	No explicit ground rules to cover consultation and feedback to/from wider constituencies (but open process)	Open membership
Accountability			Meetings open to the public with media present
Openness of and involvement in decision-making	Some participants represented agencies (EPA, DEP), towns (selectmen), mill and trade unions, health organizations	Meetings open to the public with media present	
	Inclusive process designed by CBI		
INFORMATION			
	Investigation of environmental and public health issues part of terms of reference	New information obtained and analysed for the group by neutral assessor	
INFLUENCE			
Delegation of authority in decision-making	Negotiations initiated by regulatory agencies with implicit commitment to outcome Role of mediators agreed	Final report agreed by consensus	Monitoring and evaluation of agreement conducted by regulatory agencies reporting back to the community

Figure 6.3 *The NOCC and the RVHCC – Assessment of Participation in Decision-making*

Learning Resources
Centre

Box 6.5 Epilogue – the River Valleys Healthy Communities Coalition

Mission statement

Measurable improvement in the quality of life in the river towns of North County through co-ordinated, ongoing community health promotion, including physical, mental and spiritual health, economic and recreational opportunities, and a clean environment.

How RVHCC is organized and funded

The board has representatives from a wide range of local organizations, nine of the towns in the river valley and over 50 local organizations involved in its activities. This broad base of community support means that the coalition reflects the needs of the community, and is not dominated by any one agency. Initial core funding came from the EPA, the Bingham Foundation and the Mead Paper Corporation; the latter still provides substantial funding. More recently, funding from the State of Maine's allocation of settlement funds from tobacco companies has allowed a second full-time member of staff to be employed.

How the RVHCC works

The RVHCC started with a community forum (which has been repeated annually), where local people were asked what was good about the area and what needed improvement. The coalition has subsequently reviewed its priorities via a monthly open planning meeting and an annual retreat for board members, which prepares an action plan for the year. The open meetings provide an opportunity for local organizations to exchange information on their activities, so that rather than attempting to do everything, the RVHCC often facilitates the co-ordination of projects between local organizations to avoid duplication of effort. By following the philosophy of letting people choose for themselves, the RVHCC has focused on lifestyle issues relating to health which are of direct concern to most people. For example, there is more concern about teenage pregnancy rather than the environmental risks of cancer, which concerned the NOCC. Much of the RVHCC's work is undertaken in schools, trying, amongst other things, to counter advertising targeted at young people.

RVHCC projects

In addition to its educational work, producing a newsletter and promoting regular health columns in the local press, the RVHCC has tobacco use-prevention and cessation programmes, and addresses the issues of 'passive' smoking. It has task forces on the prevention of lead poisoning from old paint and on lung health, working with the American Lung Association. In 2000, it co-ordinated work camps that brought over 400 volunteers from throughout the USA to refurbish the homes of needy families in the river valley towns using materials donated by local businesses.

Chapter 7

Public Participation in Decision-making and Partnerships

You cannot achieve sustainable economic development without participation by people. You cannot achieve genuine participation without profound commitment and a change of heart. Even with such commitment the costs are high.
(Lineberry, 1989, xi)

SYNOPSIS

Chapter 4 emphasized the role that negotiation and/or the development of consensus can play in the resolution of conflict and in reaching more stable outcomes to episodes of conflict. This chapter is in two parts. The first reviews methods of decision-making and the arguments for increasing public participation to resolve conflicts by reaching consensus among stakeholders. These arguments pivot around two main concepts: firstly, the democratic ideal that people ought to be involved in decisions that affect their lives; and secondly, that decision-makers can work more effectively when they have active public engagement and support for their proposals. Both arguments run counter to the 'decide, announce and defend' school of public consultation, an approach that still appears to be endemic despite its failures. It is based on the principle that experts plan for people, rather than with them.

The second part of this chapter sets out the principles of 'process design'. Typically, the consultation element of a planning exercise is improvised, with no clear objectives; techniques are used because they are in vogue; and it is unclear how the results will be related to decision-making. If public involvement in planning is to prevent conflict, a participation strategy is required which is designed to overcome these failings and is deliberately constructed on consensus building principles. It should consider the purposes that participation can achieve and the role of the initiator. A strategy needs clear aims; it needs to assess how and when different stakeholders are involved and the techniques to be used to engage them. The suitability of different participation techniques to encourage different levels of involvement is assessed, as well as their strengths and weaknesses. The chapter concludes by setting out principles of participation on the grounds that clarity of purpose, integrity and commitment to listening to the public on the part of decision-makers are more important than choosing the most appropriate technique.

PARTICIPATION – OPPORTUNITY OR PROBLEM?

Somewhat similar issues to those relating to consensus building (discussed in Chapter 4) and mediation (Chapter 5) are raised about participation. In the case of participation, these are based on the idealistic advocacy of public involvement, criticisms of previous (government) practice or a combination of both factors.[1] The idealistic arguments revolve around the exercise of rights in a democratic society, often coupled with the need to redistribute resources to the less favoured sections of the community via their empowerment.

> *Many people would answer the question 'Why involve the community?' with the answer 'The community has a right to be involved.' This reflects the view that citizens have the right to be involved in decisions that affect them in a much more direct way than merely through their right to vote in periodic elections.* (Department of Environment, Transport and the Regions, 1997, 13)

This concept of participation is enshrined in the ethos of sustainable development and has been actively debated in environmental planning, social welfare and international development from the 1950s onwards.

Critics of government question the motives of agencies, and their criticisms stem from public dissatisfaction with the effects of decisions allegedly taken in the public interest, and the suspicion that public participation has not been fully accepted in principle by the bureaucracy. The problem is not new, and certainly continues to extend across many areas of public policy; indeed, Barry and Sidaway (1999) have highlighted the parallels between environmental planning and social work practice in this respect.

In 1977, Sewell and Coppock wrote of the challenge of accommodating mounting political pressure for greater degrees of public participation. This critique still holds good, and for that reason is considered in some detail below. In their view, the then current dissatisfaction with decision-makers arose from a failure to establish effective channels of communication to disseminate information and to get feedback from the public. This brings the effectiveness of the planning system into question, when the public mood can swing so easily from support to opposition if it loses confidence in the system. This happens when decision-makers fail to identify public preferences correctly or to deal with the problems of minorities and the environment, when there are few incentives to participate, and few direct benefits from public involvement (Sewell and Coppock, 1977). Confronted by officials who are resistant to change, interest groups move from lobbying to protest and demonstration. Examples of such controversies in the UK in the 1970s were to be found in urban redevelopment (with the relocation of communities and the construction of high-rise dwellings), highway construction and reservoir construction for water supply.

The situation is much the same today, and while some of these issues remain as contentious as ever (e.g., major road building schemes), others have emerged, such as waste disposal, genetically modified foods, the environmental impact of fish farming and energy generation. The failure to get effective public participation over all these years is not simply a matter of professional incompetence, but depends more fundamentally on the power relationships between decision-makers and communities of interest.

THE CASE FOR PARTICIPATION

The full range of arguments for public participation centres on two main aspects: ideological and pragmatic. These are depicted schematically in Figure 7.1.

Agency perspectives tend to emphasize effectiveness, pragmatism and legitimacy, whilst interest groups focus more on ideals, democracy and having more functional relationships with agencies.

Thompson (1977) identifies some of the pragmatic needs for participation as follows:

- when action in the public interest may have a severe adverse effect on a minority, as in the case of a major road scheme;
- when the democratic process fails, because those in authority are not in touch or in sympathy with the majority of people affected by their decisions; and
- when local government officials are incompetent, and their plans are approved by councils or committees which have neither the time nor the qualifications to examine them properly.

McCool (1986) notes that public consensus in favour of US Forest Service planning is critical to the agency obtaining financial support for and successful implementation of its policies. He further argues that decision-making should be an open process with each stage easily traced, and that an informed public can assist the service in reaching high quality decisions. But participation goes beyond incorporating representatives of interest groups on management boards or commissions, to a commitment in principle to open and collaborative decision-making.

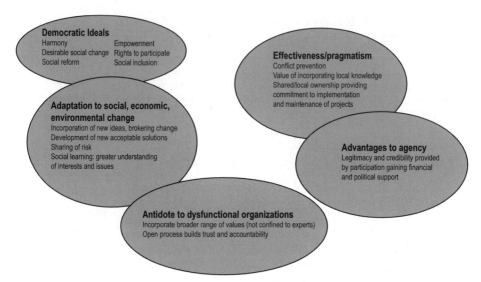

Figure 7.1 *Arguments for Public Participation*

Direct representation and openness of decision-making are crucial to ensuring that public policy decisions are accepted as legitimate. This argument is supported by Creighton:

> *In effect, the decision-making procedure ... makes the outcome legitimate even if someone didn't like the outcome. One of the major functions of public involvement is to create sufficient visibility to the decision-making process so that decisions which result from it are perceived as fair and legitimate. While some of the people most directly impacted by a decision may not be impressed by the equity of the decision, their ability to undermine the credibility of the decision rests on their ability to convince the larger public that the decision was unfairly made.*
> (Creighton, 1978, quoted in Delli Priscoli, 1980, 9)

At a more practical level, it is argued that environmental regulation, for example in the form of a nature conservation designation, requires a high degree of public acceptance if it is to be successfully implemented (Sidaway and van der Voet, 1993). The rationale is that policies will only be fully accepted and implemented when interest groups understand and are involved in determining the solution to mutually recognized problems. If regulation is imposed on people, there may be a broad level of compliance in the short term, but it may not be generally accepted and this could have serious long-term consequences. In other words, the effectiveness of regulations depends upon the strength of political support, and if this is lacking the regulations may be unenforceable. Delli Priscoli (1980) argues that a further advantage of public involvement is that it can affect the way an agency carries out its mission and adapts to changing social values by redefining problems and considering a broader range of alternatives.

DEFINITIONS OF PARTICIPATION AND THE VALUES THEY EXPOSE

Definitions of participation range from the radical, seeking social change, to the more managerial. For example:

> *the redistribution of power that enables have-not citizens, presently excluded from the political and economic processes, to be deliberately included in future ... In short, it is the means by which they can induce significant social reform which enables them to share in the benefits of the affluent society.* (Arnstein, 1969, 71–72)

> *A process through which stakeholders influence and share control over development initiatives, and the decisions and resources which affect them.* (World Bank, 1996, xi)

> *The process by which public concerns, needs and values are incorporated into government decision-making.* (Creighton, 1992, 10)

What the definitions have in common is the commitment to people having a say in decisions that affect their lives. This is explicit in the core values of participation adopted by the North American-based International Association for Public Participation (IAP2), which sees the purpose of participation as being 'to make better decisions that reflect the interests and concerns of potentially affected people and groups'(IAP2, 2003). IAP2 also requires members to adhere to a second core value: that 'Public participation includes the promise that the public's contribution will influence the decision'. In IAP2's view, the public participation process should:

- communicate the interests and meet the process needs of participants;
- actively seek out and facilitate the involvement of those potentially affected;
- involve participants in defining how they participate;
- provide participants with the information they need to participate in a meaningful way; and
- communicate to participants how their input affected the decision. (IAP2, 2003)

Thus there is a responsibility for both the practitioner and the client agency to ensure that involvement serves the needs of both agency and public. Yet, as has already been suggested, it is the ambivalence of decision-makers about public involvement in decision-making that gives rise to so many problems.

TOKENISM AND THE EXERCISE OF POWER

Sewell and Coppock's review pointed out that there had been successes and failures in public participation, and that the failures came from too high public expectations, when the process 'did not immediately deliver the Promised Land', or did not deliver the political change that some of the participants wished to accomplish. Indeed, many exercises failed because they merely furnished a means of endorsing what the planners or the politicians had already decided, and were therefore perceived to be tokenistic by a sceptical public (Sewell and Coppock, 1977).

Two examples from different continents and different eras demonstrate the risks of public participation apparently being used to endorse what planners and politicians had already decided. The first concerns the construction of a new runway at Edinburgh Airport, affecting the neighbouring community of Cramond. Although the public inquiry held in 1972 to consider objectors' concerns ruled in favour of them, the decision was taken at a political level to proceed with the plan. This provoked the following comment from an aggrieved Cramond resident:

> *This case showed the serious inadequacy of the planning system, in that, quite deliberately, the planners could keep their scheme secret from the community until there was no flexibility in it and until it was too difficult for society to fling it out and tell the civil servants to try again. The real tragedy was the demonstration of absolutism among professional planners and administrators who closed ranks whenever an effective objection was raised; it made a mockery of public participation in environmental planning.* (Mutch, 1977, 58)

More recently, Walker and Daniels (1996) described the ill-feeling that results when a purported participation exercise proves to be a sham. They analysed in some detail the attempt by the Clinton administration to resolve a conflict of ten years' standing (or more) over timber harvesting in the Pacific North-west of the USA. In 1993, the President and Vice-President co-chaired a one-day conference in Portland, Oregon. This was greeted with much enthusiasm, as both politicians invited participation and it appeared to offer a long overdue opportunity to stimulate communication between the forest industry, the lumber workers and the environmental groups. With hindsight, the researchers concluded that the proceedings closely resembled an arbitration hearing, as the Clinton team controlled who was able to make presentations, and took evidence rather than provided real opportunities for a genuine exchange of views. The conference was followed by the establishment of a scientific team, which worked intensively to a tight deadline to produce a technical solution to the problem. The solution was rejected by all sides, and was subjected to a legal challenge because the scientific group had met privately, contrary to legislation which requires federal committees to operate in public. In effect, the initiative reverted to a tokenistic consultation exercise and the loss of good will is judged to have set back the establishment of a well-supported long-term solution by 20 years.

A recent extensive review of UK government practice from 1979 to 2002 concluded that:

> *Conservative and New Labour governments have taken public participation to mean participation in dialogue with government. This form of participation allows local people to have a greater say in decisions only to the extent that decision-makers act in accordance with their views. Both governments have encouraged but have not forced local agencies to act in accordance with the views of the participating public.* (Williams, 2003, 7)

THE DISTINCTION BETWEEN CONSULTATION AND PUBLIC INVOLVEMENT

The key elements of participatory decision-making are concerned with ensuring that there is a balanced, open process, which is seen to be legitimate in the eyes of each of the parties. In a closed, non-participatory process there is neither public consultation nor involvement. In a semi-participatory process, policy is developed within an organization without reference to the public, and it is only when a number of options have been eliminated and a preferred proposal agreed that this is subject to consultation. In a fully open participatory process, interest groups or a wider public are involved at each successive stage of planning. Thus a key characteristic of public involvement is collective decision-making, whilst consultation may be no more than the dissemination of information, or public relations, which aims at placating the public. Public participation gains its legitimacy by involving the parties throughout the process, starting in the initial stages of problem definition and analysis, and including the setting of objectives and the consideration of alternative strategies. These options are set out in Figure 7.2.

But the main distinctions that are being made between consultation and involvement revolve around:

- the role that the public plays in decision-making, for example whether members of the public are equal parties in the planning exercise;
- the timing of such involvement, i.e., whether the public is being consulted on a draft plan or whether it has been involved from the outset in the definition of problems and the formulation of options; and
- the initiators' motives in seeking involvement and how they perceive its risks.

These issues are discussed in greater detail in the following sections.

Stages of decision-making	Non-participatory Planning of people	Consultation Experts planning for people	Participation Experts planning with people
Identification of issues	Neither consulted nor involved	Identification of issues	*Involvement throughout all stages*
Generation of options		Generation of options	Identification of issues
Selection of proposals		*Consulted once a proposal has been selected*	Generation of options
Policy decision			
Evaluation		Policy decision	Selection of proposals
		Evaluation	Policy decision
			Evaluation
When are people involved?	Excluded	Late in the process	Early in the process
What are they asked to do?	Acquiesce	Agree to proposal put forward by decision-maker	Identify the problem, provide information and develop and assess alternatives
Advantage to the agency	Control	Saving time? Efficiency in the short term	Public acceptance Effectiveness over the longer term
Risk to the agency	Public resentment and opposition	Public rejection and delay through prolonged conflict	Delay, loss of control

Source: based on Burton, 1976; Creighton, 1978; Delli Priscoli, 1980; Ter Haar, 1979.

Figure 7.2 *Participation in Alternative Planning Models*

The Public's Role in Decision-making

During the 1960s and 1970s, considerable attention was paid to increasing public participation in planning. Burton (1976) recognized the following planning philosophies:

- planning of people, based on strong ideological principles, legitimating the justification for certain measures;
- planning for people, based on the rational planning model and the contribution of scientific research; and
- planning with people, i.e., participatory planning, recognizing the normative base of decision-making, the uncertainty principle in future development and the limitations of scientific knowledge.

The first philosophy is concerned with the interests of the powerful, the second emphasizes technical expertise and places power in the hands of professionals, whilst the third aims to empower the relatively powerless and at least enable them to influence decision-making. Similar arguments are advanced by Creighton (1978), who suggests that public involvement ranges from knowing about, to having an influence on or being party to a decision.

The Timing of Involvement

Ter Haar (1979) pinpointed the dangers of formal consultation procedures which tend to polarize the participants. Often, the only possibility available to aggrieved members of the public is to form action or protest groups to appeal against administrative decisions and delay the process. This contrasts with more democratic systems of planning, in which the preliminary phase is open to the public. Ter Haar argued that limiting participation to a late stage of the planning process so that there can be very little real discussion is likely to lead to conflict. He distinguished between the preliminary, discussion and decision phases of planning, and advocated public involvement in the preliminary phase, when problems are identified and analysed and goals and objectives are defined. He accepted that politicians will set the financial constraints of a plan and will attempt to balance the representation of interests. However, he considered that the public should be involved in the consideration of alternative strategies in the discussion phase of a draft plan.

This highlights one of the most important distinctions between public consultation and public involvement: the point at which discussions begin with interest groups and the public generally (see Figure 7.2). Whilst it may be quite legitimate for private organizations to operate a closed system of decision-making, as has already been mentioned, the common practice of government agencies is to operate a semi-participatory process of consultation. In this case, decision-making is far advanced before the public is invited to participate, with discussion being invited on a draft plan based largely on technical assessment and in which the future options might be limited to one preferred solution.

The time-consuming nature of a fully participatory process is one of the principal objections of agency decision-makers. They see it as unnecessary delay which reduces the efficiency of decision-making. This ignores two factors: the time taken to formulate proposals within the organization before other views are sought; and the potential effectiveness of public involvement in avoiding conflict over the longer term.

Delli Priscoli (1980) compares the timescale of administrative decisions and alternative dispute resolution. He points out that criticism of public involvement may not be valid if the time taken to implement a decision is taken into account. Without public involvement, the initial decision may be taken more rapidly, but if the outcome is unacceptable there may be a prolonged period in which the decision is contested and implementation is delayed. Public involvement may delay the initial decision, but if that decision is acceptable to the interest groups, implementation should be assured and the total process will be shorter than under the original, non-participatory procedure. Nevertheless, there is little doubt that public involvement is a time-consuming process. These distinctions between consultative and participatory planning are highlighted in Figure 7.2.

Ter Haar (1979) notes that the extent of the area and the complexity of the projects are important factors in obtaining participation. Small-scale, low profile projects are more likely to encourage participation, while the influence of professionals is extended in large-scale, more complex projects.

Agency Purpose and Preoccupation with Risk

Sidaway (1992) has pointed out that the purpose of most government agencies is to execute one or more aspects of public policy, and that as a result few are politically neutral or exist to mediate change. Constitutionally they are accountable to their political masters for executing a limited set of activities; to operate outside this remit would be *ultra vires*, and this provides a very real constraint on their decision-making, which is not always accepted by interest groups.

> *Agency missions embody values – packages of views on how the world ought to be [which service] some segment of society's values.* (Delli Priscoli, 1980, 12)

Yet, too often, agency motives for public participation appear to be mixed and uncertain, stemming from a combination of factors as identified by a number of authors. For example, Schatzow (1977) presents the following perspective on federal environmental decision-making in Canada:

1   *A belief that government through the political process represents the public and that more public participation is a challenge to that political process;*

2 *A belief that politicians know what the public want and do not require input on each decision;*

3 *A belief that public participation is cumbersome and time consuming;*

4 *A desire not to expose the decision-making process to public scrutiny;*

5 *A belief that much of government decision-making requires merely technical advice and that the public is not qualified to provide such advice;*

6 *A fear the forums for public participation will become platforms for radical 'unrepresentative' groups to spout their concerns, and will lead to conflict and noise.* (Schatzow, 1977, 151)

Hesitancy and reluctance, if not outright refusal, to engage with the public stems from what Delli Priscoli calls the 'enduring myths of public involvement', namely:

• Public involvement leads to paralysis and inaction. This is only true when sufficient time and resources are not made available. This approach is likely to result in frustrated opponents in the community exercising veto power.
• Public involvement is misused by single issue groups.
• Vocal minorities are unrepresentative and public officials represent the silent majority. This criticism assumes officials invariably know what the majority want and majority voting is the appropriate way to reach decisions, as opposed to ensuring that the full range of values are represented within a consensus process.
• Arguments put forward by the public are irrational and emotional, are invalid and are not based on facts. The alternative view is that science is not objective, that feelings are valid expressions of social values and that decision-makers should devise a process to synthesize values.
• Public involvement is subversive, a point with which Delli Priscoli agrees, as 'subversion' promotes change. He considers this to be an argument put forward by bureaucrats resisting change and unwilling to share power (Delli Priscoli, 1983).

The latter point is echoed by Sewell and Coppock:

Perhaps there is also an underlying concern that increased public participation will result in a reduction of power and prestige for the planner, administrator or the politician. (Sewell and Coppock, 1977, 6)

Too often, then, it seems that agency responses tend to be cautious and minimalist, based on fears of increased time and costs. They also have to be seen in the context of a general decline in trust in government; increased competition between the agencies of government for scarce resources; and a government agenda for the public sector which has more recently stressed service delivery over policy-making (Lowe, 1994).

Those organizations that are not well versed in public participation may well be constrained by internal problems, ranging from tensions between technical and political interests to the lack of experienced and skilled staff. In such situations, organizations are vulnerable to plausible consultants, whose experience may be limited to a narrow range of techniques. Often, the purpose of the exercise may not be clear and techniques may be used almost at random. As well as sorting out such internal differences and acquiring skills through training programmes, it is vital for organizations to relate public involvement to their internal decision-making, particularly by ensuring that sufficient time is allowed to develop consensus and build trust with the public. Internal problems may be compounded by a lack of agency co-ordination (possibly competing public involvement programmes), rival agencies seeking centralized control, or public involvement procedures written by government being too prescriptive (Delli Priscoli, 1983).

Ragan, writing about US Corps of Engineers' district planning, noted that effective public participation requires:

- *Well developed objectives and policies*

- *Committed district personnel*

- *Facilitative organisation*

- *Clear assignment of responsibilities*

- *Adequate resources*

- *Well developed public plan for each study*

- *Regular and systematic program review and monitoring.*
  (Ragan, 1983, 167)

Fifteen years later, Warburton (1998) arrived at a similar assessment, arguing that if sustainable development initiatives are to be successful, new relationships between institutions and the public are required. To achieve this, institutions must give staff with experience in participation greater influence, enter into a long-term commitment to participation, and assess how successful their participatory programmes have been.

COMMUNITIES AND PARTNERSHIPS

Warburton's critique has two implications for the relationships of agencies: for working with communities and for working with other organizations, i.e., in partnership. All too often, agencies portray the communities with whom they are supposed to be working as problematic. The key question to ask the agencies is: 'Are the problems with us or are the problems with them?' The standard reply is 'them', revealing that the problems are really internal to the agency or their organizational partners. Mackie sums up the common problems:

> *At the same time as improving the liaison between and within agencies and communities we should be examining the processes of delivery. They are opposite sides of the same coin. More work needs to be done on the processes, structures and vehicles of partnership working. Too often a partnership is just a bunch of people from different organisations who just happen to be present in the same room, giving the impression of dancing together while actually standing still.* (Mackie, 2004)

Working with Communities

Participatory approaches to development in developing countries have attracted considerable interest, not least from funding organizations such as the World Bank; so much so that they have been labelled the 'new orthodoxy'. The guru of the allied methods of participatory rural appraisal and rapid rural appraisal (subsequently termed participatory appraisal (PA)), Robert Chambers, is quoted as claiming that participation constitutes a new paradigm for development (Cleaver, 2001). This comment appears in probably the most pointed critique of participation in recent years: *Participation: The New Tyranny?* (Cooke and Kothari, 2001). The use of the term 'tyranny' in the title of this edited volume is quite deliberate. In their introduction, the editors define 'tyranny' as the illegitimate or unjust use of power, and various contributors attempt to show that while participatory development aims to empower local communities as an alternative to top–down, outsider-led projects, it has failed to demonstrate significant results.

> *Despite such significant claims, there is little evidence of the long-term effectiveness of participation in materially improving the conditions of the most vulnerable people or as a strategy of social change. While the evidence for efficiency receives some support on a small scale, the evidence regarding empowerment and sustainability is more partial, tenuous and reliant on assertions of the rightness of the approach and process than convincing evidence of outcomes.* (Cleaver, 2001, 36)

Henkel and Stirrat identify the common themes of participatory development:

- A stress on bottom–up rather than top–down approaches – *bottom–up approaches deliver and they are morally superior – its beneficiaries are morally bound to participate*

- A stress on empowerment – *it is unclear what empowerment involves and it becomes an end rather than a means*

- A stress on the marginal – *the excluded, as defined in formal power relations*

- A distrust of the state – *NGOs are seen as virtuous*

- A celebration of local or indigenous knowledge – *scientific or external technical knowledge is depreciated.* (Henkel and Stirrat, 2001, 170–171)

Given that many of the prime arguments for participation are ideological (see Figure 7.2), passionate beliefs on the value of this approach are hardly surprising. But, in the case of PA, many practitioners appear to adopt an almost religious fervour in advocating participatory development (Henkel and Stirrat, 2001). More significantly, the successful conversion of the development agencies to the participatory approach has led to its widespread application in a very routine way. Chambers himself has expressed concerns about the proliferation of bad PA practice (Hailey, 2001). In a scathing criticism of the way in which the World Bank has used PA, Francis quotes its own reports to the effect that the Bank now classifies many information-sharing and consultation exercises as fully participatory (Francis, 2001). While individuals in the Bank may be sympathetic to participatory approaches, the organizational framework within which they work is not. Support for participatory development in the higher echelons of the Bank is derived from perceived savings in transaction costs (Hildyard et al, 2001).

The dependency of the agencies of delivery (non-governmental organizations – NGOs) on sponsors (like the World Bank), and NGO naivety about local communities and their internal power relationships, have also caused problems. The NGOs are under many pressures, including pressure from their sponsors to meet targets, and are reliant on their contacts with local communities, who are only too well aware of the NGOs' bureaucratic needs. Participation is tailored accordingly, with the implication that such collusion suits the powerful in the community while the excluded remain powerless (Mosse, 2001). What passes for participation frequently serves to sustain and reinforce inequitable economic, political and social structures, to the detriment of marginalized groups. Hildyard et al (2001) take this argument further in asserting that NGOs need to take a more politically committed approach to the problems of inequality, and seek to change the structural dominance of the more powerful groups. Identifying stakeholders, getting around the table and hoping to reach a consensus is not enough. They also argue that the NGOs should begin by putting their own houses in order.

> *Indeed, perhaps the first step that the agencies that are serious about participation and pluralism might take is not to reach for the latest handbook on participatory techniques, but to put their own house in order: to consider how their own internal hierarchies, training techniques and office cultures discourage the receptivity, flexibility, patience, open-mindedness, non-defensiveness, humour, curiosity and respect for the opinions of others that active solidarity demands.* (Hildyard et al, 2001, 70)

Hailey also questions how NGOs interact with local communities, and whether participatory techniques are culturally appropriate. He observes that 'some successful NGOs appear not to rely on formulaic participative technologies, but place greater reliance on personal contact and a process of personal engagement' (Hailey, 2001, 100), implying that effective participation does not rely on techniques alone, a theme that is further developed later in this chapter.

Other themes emerge from this brief review of working with communities. Some are familiar from earlier chapters, such as the questioning of neutrality in the face of imbalances in power and whether to assume the role of the political activist, which confronts mediators (Chapter 5, p85). The analysis that participation tends towards tokenism and ignores the realities of power is not confined to development projects, as will be seen later in this book (Chapter 9), but has parallels with labour–management relations and largely unsuccessful attempts to get employee participation (Taylor, 2001). The analysis of the relation between consensus building and political processes is considered in depth in Chapter 10. What starts as an ideological belief in the value of participation per se (or a particular approach such as PA) may then become self-justifying. This needs to be tempered by a cooler look at both the appropriateness of the process and its outcome. This is recognized by Cleaver, and emphasizes the need for rigorous assessment, however intrinsically difficult it may be.

> *I am not a complete pessimist about such approaches [community-based development] rather I see them as promising but inevitably messy and difficult, approximate and unpredictable in outcome. Subjecting them to rigorous critical analysis is as important as constantly asserting their benefits.* (Cleaver, 2001, 37)

Agencies Working in Partnership

The benefits of engaging in partnerships are widely acknowledged and span the more efficient use of resources, the reduction of duplication and the delivery of comprehensive services. For example, Slee and Snowdon (1997) identify such benefits as:

- a shared vision: scope for creating agreements with a broad base of support;
- strategic thinking: agreement on long-term goals, priorities and the targeting of resources;
- stimulus: co-ordinated action attracts funding;
- skill development: sharing of skills leads to greater efficiency and cost saving; and
- synergy: better links between sectors and the local community, and the opportunity to tackle all aspects of the problem.

But if the benefits attributed to inter-agency working in, say, the rural development and social work sectors are very similar, so too are the difficulties encountered in changing the delivery system (Barry and Sidaway, 1999). Collaboration may be hampered by internal agency reorganization and the changed responsibilities of successive policy initiatives from government, giving little time to assimilate the first before yet another new initiative descends from on high. All too often, the problems lie in the terms of reference: 'a common recipe for failure was to burden a team with vague purpose, squishy deadlines, fuzzy success criteria and then instruct the team to "work out the specifics"' (Bolman and Deal, 1992, 36). There is a tendency for organizations to drift into partnership and fail to consider in a structural way the extent of their planned cooperation. Liddle and Gelsthorpe (1994) describe five possible models ranging from the least communicative to the most communicative, as follows:

1   The communication model – *where agencies recognise that they have a role to play in relation to each other, but do not go beyond communication with each other. The communication may be one-way or two-way, and may involve full or partial disclosure of information.*

2   The co-operation model – *where agencies maintain separate boundaries and identities, but agree to work on a mutually defined problem. This may involve joint action, or it may involve one agency (or more) consenting to another taking the initiative to act.*

3   The co-ordination model – *where agencies work together in a systematic way; there are defined agency boundaries but agencies may pool resources to tackle mutually agreed problems.*

4 The federation model – *where agencies retain their organisational distinctiveness but also share some central focus. The agencies operate integrated services.*

5 The merger model – *where the agencies become indistinguishable from one another in working on a mutually defined problem and they form a collective resource pool.* (Ibid, 2)

Agency preferences are often for an unthreatening world of co-existence at the level of communication rather than exploring the unfamiliar territory of fuller forms of cooperation. It is as though the slippery slope of cooperation will inevitably lead them to merger and loss of identity.

Part of the problem may be internal, relating to the different cultures within an organization, whereby professions have limited contact or communication with each other. They have different values and conditions of working and respect inter-disciplinary boundaries (Newberger, 1975; Handy, 1985). These occupational or organizational cultures share assumptions and models of reality that define 'insiders' and 'outsiders'. Such are the worlds of professional status between, for example, consultants, doctors, nurses, social workers and administrators. Most marked are the cohesive tribes with private language, heroes and rituals: for example, the police (canteen) culture with its overwhelmingly masculine overtones of 'fighting crime' (Young, 1991).

In other words, to be effective, partnerships have to move away from the familiar culture of committees to collaborative decision-making based on the principles established in earlier chapters. The archetypal committee relies on the authoritative chairman, who is ruthlessly pursuing his own goals, aided and abetted by a secretary who controls the agenda and re-writes history (in the form of the minutes) when necessary. Members are selected to rule out divergent views, as there is no agreed method of handling disagreement: indeed, there is little advance discussion of procedure and process. Propositions are concealed in papers produced at short notice by officers so that they are rarely read, and participation is reduced to rubber-stamping their recommendations. Whilst it would be grossly unfair to represent all committees in this light, the elements are sufficiently familiar to draw our attention to the attractions of the more democratic processes of consensus building (Sidaway, 2002). The contrast is highlighted in Figure 7.3.

The problems of agency partnership are well illustrated by the failure to find solutions to the multiple problems of rural land management in upland parts of the UK. There have been successive calls for the integration of policy-making and concerted government action (Burt et al, 2002). Previous attempts at integration have been based on the assumption that the problems (or ways of dealing with uncertainty) are technical ones, to be solved by acquiring information and specialized technical expertise. Such a

Criteria	Committee culture	Consensus building
INITIATION		
Terms of reference and agenda	Selective and limited to soft options	Mutually agreed
INCLUSIVENESS		
Representation	Exclusive and inconsistent	Inclusive and consistent
Accountability	Left to individual discretion	Responsible to
Openness and involvement in decision-making	Late with 'consultation' on firm proposals	constituents
		Early involvement in formative stages
INFORMATION	Selectively gathered and presented	Impartially gathered with open access
INFLUENCE		
Delegation of authority in decision-making	Discretionary with scope for unilateral action	Clearly defined delegation or sphere of influence
	Power differentials maintained	Equal respect for all stakeholders

Source: Sidaway, 2002.

Figure 7.3 *The Contrasting Worlds of Committee Culture and Consensus Building*

diagnosis inevitably leads to pleas for more scientific research. Yet it has been suggested that addressing the problems of partnership would be just as fruitful as the further technical specification of either problems or solutions (Sidaway, 2002). What has been lacking is an understanding of the sectoral nature of government, in which departments and agencies are engaged in a struggle for survival. This struggle to maintain autonomy and to compete for resources is typified by demarcation disputes, the failure to delegate power, unrelated initiatives and unconnected levels of decision-making. Underpinning this is a system of accountability which rewards performance based on narrowly focused, short-term criteria, such as readily quantifiable 'products', rather than longer-term processes of development, which are intrinsically difficult to assess. In writing prescriptions for further action, changes to these reward systems are needed which benefit cooperation, if joined-up government is to become more than fashionable rhetoric. If this cannot be achieved, then it would be as well to jettison the rhetoric of integration and to concentrate on clarifying objectives and setting realistic limits to intended cooperation (Sidaway, 2002).

The realities of attempting to adopt alternative approaches to decision-making are spelt out by Slee and Snowdon (1997) as a series of changes in working practice that have to be adopted if rural partnerships are to be effective. Namely:

- participating organizations may have to delegate some authority to the partnership;
- compromise may be required concerning attitudes and issues on which partners are used to being partisan;
- sharing power may be both uncomfortable and time-consuming for partners;
- the aims of a partnership may not fit the more limited remits of some member agencies; and
- partners need to be open about their objectives and indicate aims that are non-negotiable and potential areas of disagreement.

PROCESS DESIGN

A more systematic approach to public involvement is enshrined in the concept of deliberately designing the participation process and devising effective participation strategies (Creighton, 1992). In essence this requires agreeing on *procedures* in advance, i.e., designing the process, having clear *aims* at each stage, getting the desired *level of involvement* from *interested parties* at the right time, and using the most effective *techniques* to secure their involvement. Thus the designer and/or the initiator (who may not be one and the same) set the agenda and can steer, if not control, the process.

Clarifying the Aims of Participation

Wilcox's *Guide to Effective Participation* (1994) poses a crucial series of initial questions for the designer of the process (set out in Figure 7.4). These entail the partners being clear about their intentions, and the purposes of participation, from their point of view. Bearing in mind one of the criteria for consensus building identified in Chapter 4 – namely *authority and power of decision-making* – it needs to be clearly established whether the partners intend their authority to take the final decision to be retained, influenced by or delegated during participation. There may be no opportunity for an agency with statutory responsibilities to delegate its powers, in which case the other parties need to understand why the agency is seeking participation. Whilst its remit may not be negotiable, the way it exercises its responsibilities can be. What is important is for all partners, and others invited to participate, to know where the agency stands. One way of addressing the problem of conflicting agendas is to adopt a twin-track approach, in which the agency declares its agenda and asks existing groups in the community to compare this with their aims. Meanwhile, the agency works with the groups to develop an issue-based agenda drawn from the locality and the groups' own experiences (Fagan, 1997).

Who are you?
Someone in a position of power controlling funds or other resources
Someone with influence because you are planning or managing a participation process
Someone with professional expertise or knowledge

What do you want to achieve?
To try and develop plans that meet people's expectations
To give people a say in the plans
To give people control over the solutions

Whose needs will be considered?
The community as a whole
Disadvantaged sectors of the community
Managerial needs of an organization

Who has the final say?
Yourself
A management team
Everyone who gets involved
A political institution or other body

How ready are people and organizations to work in a participatory way?
Do they have the desire?
Do they have the skills?
Do they have the authority?

Source: Wilcox, 1994.

Figure 7.4 *Aims and Intentions – Setting the Agenda*

Assessing Who Should be Involved

This entails considering both who should be involved and their desired level of involvement. The first of these considerations requires a stakeholder analysis to be undertaken, as described in Chapter 5 (p77). The emphasis on stakeholders, rather than communities, stems from the complexities of defining 'communities' when it soon becomes evident that the networks of different 'communities of interest' extend way beyond local geography. Creighton (1992) lists some of the alternative communities which can be considered (see Box 7.1), but as Wilcox (1994) suggests, whilst identifying stakeholders helps to understand participation, trying to analyse communities in detail can be a hindrance.

Creighton (1992) points out that different interests emerge at different stages with differing levels of involvement, and that the number of interests tends to increase with controversy and closer to decision time (the threat of imminent change providing an incentive to participate). It can be revealing to map these relationships according to the different issues that the development strategy will cover, the most powerful occupying the central area of the map (see Figure 7.5). Indeed, in a fully participatory exercise,

BOX 7.1 COMMUNITIES OF INTEREST

- Proximity: people who live in the affected area.
- Economics: people who will gain or lose.
- Use: existing and potential users.
- Rights: of minorities, equal access.
- Environment: impacts on environmental quality.
- Responsibility: to take technical or policy decisions.

Source: Creighton, 1992.

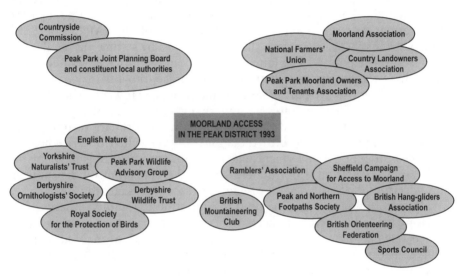

Figure 7.5 *An Example of a Stakeholder Map*

this mapping exercise forms part of the appraisal undertaken by members of the community, probably during a series of workshops. In that way a consensus can emerge on who are the key stakeholders.

Identifying the Desired Level and Timing of Involvement

The other assessment that can clarify both the desired level and timing of involvement is to position the stakeholders on a 'ladder of participation'. The ladder is based on Sherry Arnstein's (1969) seminal paper on US urban planning, which advocated the empowerment of urban communities and demonstrated their exclusion by manipulative decision-makers (see her definition of participation on p119). Positioning stakeholders on the ladder assumes that people have differing degrees of interest or concern in an issue, and that some may be content to be informed about what is happening whilst others wish to become more fully involved. They may want to contribute to a greater degree at specific stages but not at others, according to the nature of the exercise. That should be their decision. Others may wish to play a more central role throughout.

Although it was probably not intended to be used in this way, numerous versions of the ladder have been produced which elaborate on or, in some cases, omit certain stages. Figure 7.6 sets out three versions of the ladder: Arnstein's original and two simplifications designed to make the ladder into a more operational tool (Wilcox, 1994; IAP2, 2003; Burton's (1976) planning philosophies have been added). Perhaps the most important distinctions are those made by Arnstein between the levels where citizens have autonomy (planning by people), influence (planning with or for people) or are excluded (planning of people). Certainly, her stance in advocating empowerment is somewhat different from that of the IAP2. The IAP2 clarifies the distinctions between the various levels by setting out 'goals' and 'promises to the public'. The latter clarify (along with the associated set of values that practitioners/members should embrace) the integrity of purpose and commitment to lay participants in the process. However, the wording of these promises demonstrates an underlying assumption of a partnership between the practitioner and the sponsor, with the ultimate responsibility for decision-making lying with the sponsor. Even when one reaches the uppermost rung of empowerment when the ultimate decision is made by the public, implementation is not undertaken by the public but by the sponsor. This is certainly not the degree of empowerment envisaged by Arnstein or even Wilcox, who envisages the need to support autonomous initiatives.

Using the ladder certainly helps to clarify who may want to be involved at each stage of the participation strategy and the basis of their subsequent involvement, notably their role in decision-making. It also helps the initiating agency to clarify its own aims when seeking participation. The crucial decisions concern who decides which stakeholders are to be included, at what level of involvement and the techniques that will be used to engage them.

Certainly there is a trade-off between efficiency and effectiveness in using methods which seek broad participation on ideological grounds, or limit participation for more practical reasons. In large group processes, often it is not practical to reach consensus; instead one should settle for establishing priorities by voting or reaching tacit agreement by informed consent (see p67).

> *Consensus is a noble ideal, but it can give every participant a veto. Seek consensus, but be prepared to settle for informed, visible, majority public acceptance and support.* (Connor, 1997, 24)

The alternative may be to devise and gain acceptance for a representative structure, perhaps by convening a conference which agrees on issues and the process of decision-making. One outcome may be the establishment of

Ladder of participation (Arnstein, 1969) (Planning philosophies based on Burton, 1976)		*Levels of participation in planning (based on Wilcox, 1994)*	*Goals of IAP2's Public Participation Spectrum (2003)*
	*(Planning **by** people)*		
Citizen control		**Supporting independent community initiatives:** in doing what they want	**Empower:** to place final decision-making in the hands of the public
Delegated power	Degree of citizen power	**Acting together:** deciding on and forming partnerships to carry out strategies	
Partnerships	*(Planning **with** people)*	**Deciding together:** providing ideas before a joint decision	**Collaborate:** to partner with the public in each aspect of the decision including the development of alternatives and identification of the preferred solution
Placation/ involvement			**Involve:** to work directly with the public throughout process to ensure public issues and concerns are consistently understood and considered
Consultation	Degree of tokenism *(Planning **for** people)*	**Consultation:** offering options for feedback	**Consult:** to obtain public feedback on analysis, alternatives and/or decisions
Informing		**Information gathering:** obtaining important factual information which will improve the quality of the decision	
		Information giving: telling the community what is planned	**Inform:** to provide the public with balanced and objective information to assist them in understanding of problems, alternatives and/or solutions
Therapy/education	Non-participation *(Planning **of** people)*		
Manipulation			
		Exclusion: the community is unaware of decisions that are being made	

Figure 7.6 *Levels of Participation*

working groups which address issues and report back to a second conference. This may result in a widely circulated consultation paper so that comments will be considered by a third decision-making conference. The strengths and weaknesses of these alternatives are set out below.

Selecting the Most Appropriate Techniques to Secure Effective Involvement

Once the appropriate level of involvement has been identified for the various stakeholders, careful consideration should be given to the selection of appropriate techniques to obtain their involvement. A wide range of techniques is available to inform, obtain the views of, consult with and involve interested parties in decision-making. An indication of the techniques that may be considered for different purposes is set out in Figure 7.7. Generally speaking, techniques that encourage direct contact are more effective at higher levels of participation. This is shown by the way techniques in the third column of the figure are ranked alongside the levels of participation in the second column. However, several techniques can be used for more than one purpose and, resources permitting, a combination of techniques is more likely to encourage participation by different types of stakeholder and to ensure that particular groups are not excluded from the process. The first column of Figure 7.7 sets out three different scales of operation, from local to national, and who is likely to be involved in decision-making at each scale. Comparing entries in the first and third columns gives a further indication of the situations in which various techniques can be applied.

A number of special considerations could affect the choice of techniques:

- *The duration of decision-making*: during long periods when technical studies are being considered, brief progress reports or other feedback can sustain an agency's credibility.
- *Specialist expertise*: it may be necessary to employ specialist skills to ensure certain techniques are used effectively. These might include facilitation or mediation by a neutral third party; or writers and graphics specialists to present technical information in language the general public can understand.
- *Issues of particular public importance*: where large numbers of people or interest groups are involved, cost may become a major consideration in the choice of technique.

The Strengths and Weaknesses of Various Techniques

Informal techniques which encourage face-to-face discussion, such as workshops, staffed exhibitions and PA, can be more effective than formal public meetings, which tend to polarize views. For example, the purpose of any meeting or workshop should be clearly explained to the participants in

Scale of exercise (level of decision-making)	Purpose of involvement (level of participation)	Techniques to consider
Local planning/community engagement (decisions made by community or jointly)	**Supporting independent community initiatives:** in doing what they want	Grants, advice, visioning workshops: Planning for Real, participatory appraisal, site visits, development trusts
	Acting together: deciding on and forming partnerships to carry out strategies	Joint working groups, advisory groups, team building, facilitated (visioning) workshops
Regional planning/project development (decisions made jointly by stakeholders)	**Deciding together:** providing ideas before a joint decision is made	Facilitated workshops: brainstorming consensus building and action planning, face-to-face meetings, interviews
	Consultation: offering options and requesting feedback	Meetings and interviews, staffed exhibits, reports, social surveys, consultative committees, forums and panels
Project development/policy initiatives (decisions made by politicians)	**Information gathering:** obtaining important factual information which will improve the quality of the decision	Social surveys, telephone hotlines, participatory appraisal
	Information providing: telling the community what is planned	Press releases and briefings, reports, factsheets and brochures, exhibits, presentations at public meetings, advertising, websites

Figure 7.7 *The Range of Participatory Techniques*

advance. Large meetings may need to be divided into plenary and small group sessions. Workshops are effective at involving small groups to achieve more precise aims, such as developing, evaluating and prioritizing alternatives, and it may be necessary to use facilitators who can concentrate on conducting the meeting rather than debating the issue. When a clear outcome or agreement on a contentious topic is required, a neutral person with consensus building or mediation skills is likely to be needed, particularly to make the necessary careful preparation for the event. A brief assessment of the strengths and weaknesses of each technique is given in Figure 7.8. More detailed assessments of participatory techniques are to be found in a number of handbooks, such as those by the Department of Environment, Transport and the Regions (1997), World Bank (1996) and IAP2 (2003).

PRINCIPLES OF PARTICIPATION

Various authors echo Barach Bush's (1995) comment that alternative dispute resolution[2] (ADR) is not an exact science, and recognize that participation is as much a philosophical approach as it is a panacea, and certainly not a set of techniques looking for a solution. Thus there is no single way to 'do' participation: some methods work in some situations but not in others. Furthermore, participation should be complementary to, not a substitute for, representative political democracy (Delli Priscoli, 1983). To that end, several authors identify general principles which contribute to a fair process aimed at gaining trust and credibility. Thus there is considerable emphasis (as in mediated processes) on careful preparation. An example of this principled approach can be paraphrased from the headings of Widditsch's article as:

> *Start early, plan carefully, know what you want, be flexible, know who is doing what, provide useful information, work for broader participation, make meetings convenient, get lots of publicity, be organised but informal, and report conclusions adequately.* (Widditsch, 1983)

It is suggested that the process should comprise four phases: initiation, preparation, participation and continuation, and that the second of these phases should take 80 per cent of the time. In reality, it frequently happens that agencies fail to give careful consideration to phase one, skimp on phase two, do not think ahead to phase four and wonder why phase three fails to work.

Phrases that constantly re-appear in this advice are the need for clarity of purpose, role and stance; flexibility to alter processes as one learns from experience; allowing adequate time and resources; honesty; relevance; accessibility; and commitment. Not surprisingly, given the earlier criticisms

Techniques	Strengths	Weaknesses
Collaborative techniques		
Conferences (e.g., 'Future search', consensus conferences)	Combination of plenary sessions and workshops useful in presenting information, developing ideas and getting feedback from wide range of participants. Value of opportunities for networking	People may be reluctant to speak in open forum. Costly and long lead time for planning. Audience may be self-selecting
Participatory appraisal (e.g., PA, Planning for Real)	Use of visual techniques particularly effective at encouraging participation by all sections of the community. PA uses a variety of techniques and provides triangulation. Able to move from values to action plans relatively quickly	As in other techniques, careful consideration needs to be given to the influence community appraisals have on subsequent decision-making to ensure that expectations are not raised falsely
Forums and panels (e.g., citizens juries/panels)	Allows lay representative to interrogate experts and organizations and provide dispassionate assessment	May not reach consensus. Difficulty of obtaining representative or randomly selected group. Cost of providing facilitation, expertise, briefing and steering committee
Joint working groups, advisory groups, task forces	Valuable ways of tapping expertise, undertaking detailed analyses and gaining credibility. Can operate on continuing basis	Terms of reference have to be clear and achievable. Composition has to be representative. Administration can be costly
Facilitated workshops	Effective way of exchanging information, developing and evaluating alternative proposals	Need to be carefully designed and facilitated by experienced specialists. Costly if they have to be replicated to cover a wide range of opinion
Consultative techniques		
Websites	Comparatively fast to set up. Can provide links to wide range of information	Not accessible to large sections of community. Concerns about confidentiality and security
Site visits	Increases awareness and understanding in selected interest groups	Time commitment to preparation and staffing. Likely to reach limited audience
Staffed exhibitions/ open houses	Attractive way to present information. May reach beyond interest groups. Staff can obtain feedback and build rapport in informal discussions	Requires specialist display skills. Staffing exhibit is time-consuming and costly

Figure 7.8 Strengths and Weaknesses of Participatory Techniques

Techniques	Strengths	Weaknesses
Public meetings	Attract general public interest	Agenda and procedures need careful consideration. Rarely represent the full range of public opinion. Tend to polarize views, be dominated by vocal minority and discourage general participation
Information gathering techniques		
Focus groups	Opportunity to test proposals and gain rapid response from selected target groups	Relatively expensive to get representative groups
Face-to-face meetings and interviews	Provide important information on issues and the extent to which interest groups wish to participate	Provide limited representation of public opinion. Labour intensive to administer and analyse
Telephone 'hotlines'	Convenient way to communicate with relatively large numbers of people. Easy to update	Impersonal. Staff must be briefed to deal effectively with critical public comment
Social surveys	Provide a cross-section of opinion to set against views of interest groups	Cost of obtaining a statistically reliable sample likely to be high
Information providing techniques		
Reports and brochures	Direct way of conveying a large amount of information economically	Presentational skills may have to be obtained from outside an organization. Direct mailing expensive and frequently disregarded
Press releases/media events	Reach a wide public and can encourage participation. Quickly organized	May be difficult to control unless regular contact maintained with media. Liable to reduce message to soundbites

Figure 7.8 *continued*

INITIATION
Terms of reference and agenda
- Clarity of purpose, mutual understanding of aims, process and expectations
- Honesty of intentions and mutual commitment to the purpose of gaining trust and public credibility
- Participants agree to the way the process is designed
- Careful preparation using existing networks and building on previous initiatives

INCLUSIVENESS
Representation and accountability
- Work for broader participation, identify and include all key parties
- Ensure participants are mandated to represent their organization or constituency

Openness of and involvement in decision-making
- Flexible process which is open to all interest groups, receptive to their ideas and geared to mutual respect, trust and transparency
- Meetings at times convenient to all participants

INFORMATION
- Commitment to shared knowledge with information freely available to all interests
- Common access to resources and expertise

INFLUENCE
Delegation of authority in decision-making
- Clarity on how final decision will be made and what influence participants will have
- Feedback to demonstrate participants' effort has been worthwhile
- Process relates to existing formal decision-making
- Clear responsibility allocated for monitoring
- Adequate time allowed with clarity about duration of process at the outset

Source: Canadian Correctional Service, 1997; Delli Priscoli, 1983; De Marchi and Ravetz, 2001; Warburton, 1997; Widditsch, 1983; Wilcox, 1994.

Figure 7.9 *Principles of Participation*

of tokenistic consultative processes, the key issues centre on sincerity and integrity of purpose, with a clear link being established to decision-making. In other words, 'Participation is useless unless there is a prior commitment to implementation' (Wilcox and Mackie, 2003).

These principles have been collated and summarized in Figure 7.9 under the headings used in the evaluative framework in Chapter 4 (see Figure 4.4), showing how they conform to the criteria for a legitimate, balanced and open process of decision-making. These criteria can also be used to assess whether the process designed for participation in the rural development strategy is likely to prevent conflict. Figure 7.10 sets out a checklist of considerations which helps to avoid the usual pitfalls of a improvised process (Sidaway, 1998b).

Criteria	Problems that can arise	Options to consider
INITIATION		
Terms of reference and agenda	Setting too narrow an agenda	Consider a twin-track approach
INCLUSIVENESS		
Communities and representation	Excluding vital interests who can influence or delay the final decision by other means	Conduct a thorough stakeholder analysis
Accountability	Representatives fail to feedback to their organizations	Ensure representatives understand their responsibilities. Establish a policy of open information to ensure information is conveyed to interest groups by other means
Openness of and involvement in decision-making	Devising a closed process of decision-making which excludes interests until the vital decisions have been made	Initiate participation at the earliest stages of strategy formulation and maintain it throughout to obtain shared ownership of decisions
INFORMATION	Information is withheld	Recognize that interests who contribute information expect feedback Share information with them
INFLUENCE		
Delegation of authority in decision-making	Misunderstandings about responsibilities and influence	Clarify the purposes of participation, the stance of each partner and the influence participation is intended to have on the final decision

Source: Sidaway, 1998b.

Figure 7.10 *Checklist for Troubleshooting in a Participatory Strategy*

Nevertheless, as Warburton, Wilcox and Mackie remind us:

> *Methods and techniques are only as good as the context and process in which they are employed. Planning the whole process is more important than choice of individual techniques. A major complaint from participants about participatory techniques is being left in the dark after the event, not about the effectiveness of technique.* (Warburton, 1998, 10)

> *Commitment is the other side of apathy: people are committed when they want to achieve something, apathetic when they don't... I think people care about what they are interested in, and become committed when they feel they can achieve something.* (Wilcox, 1994, 5)

Since the key issue for engagement and commitment is trust, the more lousy participation we do, the less trust people will have. (Wilcox and Mackie, 2003)

These perspectives should be set alongside the attitude of those agencies which limit public participation on the grounds of low response and apparent 'consultation fatigue', a factor (when it exists) which is just as likely to be the result of ineffective or uncoordinated work by the agencies.

CONCLUSIONS

Lack of trust on the part of both decision-making agencies and the communities they serve has been a continuing theme throughout this chapter. Initially it seemed that the problem could be solved by devising a participation strategy and selecting the most appropriate techniques at various stages of the process. Whilst this approach is intrinsically sound and much preferable to the alternative of muddling through, the problems of community disillusion with consultation (as defined earlier in this chapter) are not entirely technical. The problem of a lack of commitment on the part of decision-makers, which leads to community apathy and mistrust, is basically political and hinges on the distribution and use of power. These issues have been recurring themes over the years; witness the reviews edited by Sewell and Coppock (1977) and Creighton et al (1983) and, most recently, the comments of Warburton (1998) and Wilcox and Mackie (2003). Chapter 8 re-visits these issues in reporting on varying degrees of success in case studies of partnerships, whilst the final chapters dwell on the issues of power.

Chapter 8

Building Trust – Crucial Lessons in Participation and Partnership

Synopsis

The key principles of participation set out in the previous chapter emphasized the importance of building trusting relationships between decision-makers and stakeholders, rather than concentrating on particular techniques. The case studies in this chapter illustrate the often long and arduous task of building trust, which can be lost all too quickly and be hard to regain. The case studies cover two studies of participatory planning and two of the development of successful partnerships, as follows:

- An initiative to develop a collaborative vision for the future of the island of Texel on the north-eastern coast of the Netherlands met with some initial local opposition. The agenda of Texel 2030 was seen as having been set by outsiders, and it presented a challenge to the existing power structure. But five years later the debate about the future continues within a range of local forums, and several practical projects on sustainability are being developed. The lack of leadership from the local municipality, which was ambivalent about the original project, has resulted in mistrust between politicians and the community that they represent.
- The earlier history of Pentland Hills Regional Park (PHRP) (described in Chapter 2) provides the background to a recent attempt to develop an integrated management strategy for the regional park by engaging local communities in participatory workshops and surveys. Care was taken to trace how ideas from these workshops could be taken forward into the plan and related to the priorities and decision-making of the local authorities, which sponsor the regional park. However, since the strategy has been completed there has been limited feedback to the public and the local authority partnership has yet to realize its full potential.
- The Morecambe Bay Partnership in north-west England was established following a national campaign by conservation organizations promoting the concept of integrated coastal zone management. The long-term commitment by the Partnership to community involvement over a ten-

year period has enabled national agencies and local government to develop a programme of coastal zone management projects with broad community support.

- Plans to introduce traffic management in Glen Muick on Upper Deeside in Scotland met with a critical response from mountain users and the community of Ballater, who feared restriction and charging for access, and the loss of its tourism income, respectively. However, the establishment of a partnership trust and the appointment of a project team led to practical improvements in recreational access to the benefit of visitors. The Upper Deeside Access Trust (UDAT) has gained further credibility from its open style of governance and willingness to explain its proposals to the public. This has enabled the Trust to reach consensus on proposals that probably would have provoked conflict a few years earlier.

The case study analysis follows the evaluative framework from Chapter 4, covering:

- *initiation*: the institutional context and the terms of reference of the exercise;
- *inclusiveness*: in terms of the representativeness, accountability and openness of the process, when participants became involved and what attempts have been made to secure their continuing involvement;
- *information*: its availability to participants and the methods used to assist their understanding of complex issues; and
- *influence*: the effects of their inputs on major decisions.

Needless to say, relatively few cases can be assessed thoroughly on all of these criteria as they have not been recorded with this task in mind, and little systematic evaluation occurs in this field .

CASE STUDY 1: Planning for the Future of Texel

Context

Communities have intrinsic difficulties with discussing the future, partly because it may affect their interests in unpredictable ways, and partly because many people are uneasy with or feel threatened by change and associate it with impending conflict. The technocratic approach is to attempt to predict the future. But whatever technical model is used, such forecasts are only as valid or reliable as the quality of the data inputs and the assumptions that are made about future behavioural patterns. Hence the interest in devising collaborative approaches framed in terms of desirable rather than inevitable futures.

This case study examines an initiative to develop a collaborative vision for the future of the island of Texel on the north-eastern coast of the

Netherlands. The planning exercise, conducted in 1999 and 2000, was called Texel 2030, and this account is based on a variety of sources, notably literature reviews, interviews and surveys conducted by social researchers from Wageningen University. In addition to the quoted sources, much of the initial analysis was undertaken by Jan Philipsen, who also participated as a facilitator during the project. The material has been updated during study tours made in 2000 and 2004 with students from the university. The most recent visit allowed me to reflect on the legacy of Texel 2030 and the continuing process of change that has occurred since that exercise was undertaken.

The merit of examining small island communities is that whilst they are in many senses unique, they also provide a microcosm of change and reaction to change in wider society. In an island setting issues are somewhat starker, boundaries are clearer and relationships are thrown into sharper relief. Historically, living with the sea has enabled island communities to develop ways of dealing with adversity and uncertainty and to devise collective solutions to common problems. The story of St Kilda is a classic case in point: the community as a whole bore the responsibility for survival in its lonely predicament in the Atlantic, way out beyond the Outer Hebrides. However, such communities can also be more vulnerable, in that case leading to the eventual evacuation of the island (Steel, 1965).

The Geography and Changing Economy of Texel

Texel is the westernmost of the Wadden islands, which lie between the Dutch mainland and the North Sea and extend eastwards to Germany and Denmark (see Figure 8.1). The association with the sea is a vital part of Texel's history. The island provided an important staging point for sailing vessels of the Dutch East Indies company that used the port of Amsterdam during the Golden Age of the 17th century. Fishing was formerly an important industry, and Texel ownership of the ferry has been influential in stimulating economic growth (Duim and Lengkeek, 2004).

There is a marked contrast between the sand dunes of the western part of Texel and the open landscape of agricultural land in the rest of the island. The dunes occupy about one-quarter of the island and have been designated a national park in recognition of their high nature conservation value. Some farmland close to the dunes has been acquired by conservation organizations for conversion to reserves, making nature conservation a significant land use on the island. Biological research establishments within the dunes, such as Eco-mare, have become educational centres and important visitor attractions in their own right.

In contrast with many parts of the Netherlands, the traditional form of agriculture on the island has been a mixed pattern of dairy cows, sheep, bulb and arable farming. In line with the rest of the country, employment in this sector declined as the number of farms on Texel decreased from 160 in 1985 to 112 in 2000. Whilst the agricultural sector has economically,

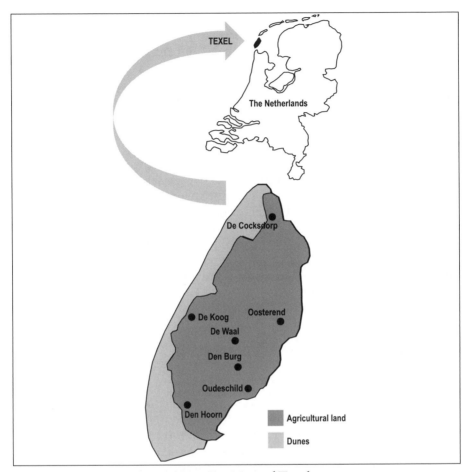

Figure 8.1 *Map of Texel*

culturally and politically dominated the island for centuries, over the last 50 years tourism has become the main source of income for the island. For example, approximately 25 per cent of the population are currently employed in tourism and about 75 per cent of the population are economically dependent on the industry. In terms of gross turnover, in 2001 tourism accounted for about 91 million euros, compared to 55 million for agriculture and 32 million for fisheries. There is a resident population of 13,450. The main village is Den Burg, with a population of approximately 7000, and the six other villages range in size from Oosterend (1400 inhabitants) to De Waal (400 inhabitants). Most tourist accommodation is concentrated in two centres: De Koog on the west coast, which attracts most of the tourists to the island, and De Cocksdorp in the north (Duim et al, 2001; Philipsen et al, 2003).

People from Texel are generally proud of their island, and this is expressed in a number of ways, most simply by displaying green and black flags and stickers on the backs of their cars. There is an active programme of marketing local produce as 'real Texel products'. There is a local party called 'the Interest of Texel' (Texels Belang) and an action group called 'Tien voor Texel' (literally, 'Ten (out of ten) for Texel'). The main aim of Tien voor Texel is to preserve the open landscape of the island by increasing sustainable tourism and developing a more extensive system of agriculture. All these things are expressions of the wish to preserve and strengthen local identity and distinguish Texel from the '*overkant*' ('the other side', referring to the mainland).

However, the local culture is far from homogeneous. Islanders make conscious distinctions not only between themselves and '*overkanters*' (mainlanders) but also between 'genuine' people of Texel, from a family with roots going back several generations, and people 'from away' who may have lived there for many years, or who have recently retired there to seek a more relaxed quality of life. These 'incomers' share the romantic feelings of living on an island, while at the same time introducing values, norms and lifestyles from elsewhere. The result is a degree of cultural fragmentation (Duim and Lengkeek, 2004).

Meanwhile, there is considerable uncertainty about the economic future of Texel, arising partly from changes in agriculture and tourism. These are compounded by external influences, such as climatic change and European Union (EU) policies, over which the islanders have little control. Moreover, it is unclear how decisions about the future will be made and by whom.

In the case of climatic change, the sea level is expected to rise between 25cm and 75cm in the next 30 years. This is likely to result in the salination of the most important polders of Texel and the compaction of their underlying clay layers, which would have important consequences for soil fertility and agricultural yields. In addition, agriculture is strongly affected by European policies and potential reductions in subsidies. The future of small-scale family businesses providing tourist accommodation is also under threat. Parallels are drawn with the retail sector and the global trends towards concentration of ownership. Between 1960 and 1990, small family retailers in the Netherlands lost about 75 per cent of their market share to a few large national supermarkets. The question is whether small-scale accommodation providers on Texel will be affected by the appearance of large hotel chains or the affiliation of existing small-scale businesses to larger franchises. A ceiling on the amount of tourist accommodation was set in 1972 at 47,000 beds. While this is widely accepted as a crude measure of capacity, the ceiling has not been reached and the total currently stands at 43,000. This is one indicator that the level of tourism is roughly static, although estimates of use vary (Duim and Caalders, 2004). However, significant changes are taking place in the types of holiday accommodation. Camping pitches are being replaced by holiday bungalows (which are occupied for a longer season), and bungalows are being bought as second homes, partly following the European trend towards property investment.

These factors provide the basis for an ongoing debate about the effects of tourism on the quality of life for islanders, evidenced by perceptions of crowded village streets, traffic jams (particularly queuing for the ferry at peak times), camping on farms and so on, which is all part of the love–hate relationship between Texel and tourism (Duim and Lengkeek, 2004).

The Development of the Texel 2030 Project

This case study examines the use of a particular participatory technique, the scenario process, as used in the Texel 2030 project. The use of scenarios is intended as a means of engaging stakeholders in a discussion of future alternatives and potential ways of deciding on a course of action. The thought process involves considering the influence of underlying social and economic trends, and thinking the unthinkable rather than assuming that the future is little more than an extension of the present situation. The participatory process is initially described and then analysed according to the criteria set out at the beginning of this chapter.

In the autumn of 1999 the Vereniging voor Vreemdelingen Verkeer Texel (VVV Texel, the Texel Tourist Information Board) initiated the Texel 2030 project.[1] The aims were to contribute to public debate and decision-making around the second tourism master plan of the municipality of Texel by developing a long-term integrated strategic vision for the year 2030. This would involve representatives from agriculture, fisheries, building companies, museums, nature conservation and village committees as well as the tourism industry (Philipsen, 2004).

VVV Texel contracted the project to consultants who specialized in organizational and policy advice. It was agreed that the project would be composed of four stages. The first preparatory stage consisted of desk research and a series of interviews conducted by the consultants. The second stage took the form of a 'search' conference that brought together 40 local and national experts, selected by VVV Texel and the consultants, in the fields of finance, construction, planning, design, farming, accommodation, retail, transport, conservation and marketing. Their task was to prepare a trend analysis and formulate the initial outlines of four scenarios for Texel in the year 2030. In the third stage, the preliminary results of the search conference were to be transformed into four tangible scenarios. The fourth stage was to be a series of conferences in which Texel inhabitants gave their opinions and voted on these scenarios (Philipsen, 2004).

The search conference took place in October 1999. The first day of the conference was spent in making an inventory of trends that were considered to have an important influence on the future of Texel. Initially, each expert identified the trends in his or her own field. Subsequently, the trends were compared and cross-examined, firstly in small groups and subsequently in plenary sessions. The experts were asked their opinions on the degree of certainty or uncertainty of the trends. Special attention was given to the identification of more fundamental driving forces. This operation was closely in line with Wack's (1985) idea that a scenario analysis should be primarily focused on the nature of the system and the forces that work within it, and not on the outcome of those processes. The second day was focused on the formulation of scenarios. The trend analysis was used to describe alternative situations in the year 2030, which could be used to analyse the implications of each situation for different interests on the island. The experts were encouraged to identify the extreme options for the future of Texel, rather than the most probable futures. The contrast between the scenarios was to be achieved by identifying the two most important elements of uncertainty and putting them on opposing axes spanning the range of uncertainty of that trend. The four scenarios were to be found in the quadrants between the two axes.

The experts agreed on likely demographic trends, such as an ageing population and smaller households, and the increasing influence of the EU. There was less agreement over the future of agriculture and tourism. Thus, one axis spanned the degree of soil salination and its implications for land use, while the other spanned the transfer of ownership of tourist accommodation from small family businesses to big firms and franchises. The experts were asked to formulate labels for the four scenarios (subsequently called Nature Island, Authentic Island, Eco-Island and Park Island) and to identify a range of developments that would fit into each scenario. The scenarios were published in local newspapers and presented on television (Philipsen, 2004).

In February 2000, three 'action' conferences were organized. Two were attended by a total of 120 adults and one by 30 secondary school children, all from Texel. Admission was by invitation only. However, it transpired that some inhabitants who complained that they had not received an invitation were allowed access (notably the members of Tien voor Texel), while others were not. Although VVV Texel and the consultants claimed a balanced representation of the Texel community, the precise selection procedure was not openly communicated and it was unclear what brokering went on behind the scenes.

The title given to these conferences was changed from 'action' to 'choice', and the exact objectives were unclear, so that there was some confusion over the task in hand. There was no proper explanation that the object was not to choose between the scenarios, but that they were meant as a starting point for discussion. On the one hand, the scenario project seemed to be focused on the creation of a shared understanding of processes of change and the implications for future development options. The reason for choosing extreme scenarios and the ample time spent on discussing them with participants were consistent with this objective. But on the other hand, the conferences seemed to be focused on getting agreement by voting on the options. This combination of tasks caused confusion, and some stakeholders objected to voting. Many participants felt that the scenarios were too extreme and that the timeframe of 30 years was too long. Others questioned the validity of the scenarios and subsequently the credibility of the experts at the previous conference. The initial and final voting results differed significantly. In the initial round, 46 per cent preferred Authentic Island, the most conservative and surprise-free scenario, but the support for this scenario dropped to 38 per cent in the final round. It seems that some participants became convinced of the negative consequences of this scenario compared to the unexpected positive consequences of other scenarios. The farmers even came up with their own scenario: Farmers' Island. The document they distributed started thus: 'The [consultants'] report is a vision of the future of Texel, seen through the lenses of negativists from the *overkant* that are sponsored by people from Texel with an interest in increasing recreation and tourism on Texel' (Philipsen et al, 2003).

In March 2000, VVV Texel presented a report to the municipality, which summarized the outcomes of the search and choice conferences and included a new scenario entitled Unique Island, although the need to draft a fifth scenario had not been foreseen. While the issues raised by the participants in the choice conference were also presented, it became obvious that VVV Texel was not confident that the municipality would adopt the outcome of the Texel 2030 process. Although VVV Texel claimed that the scenario project was an integrated endeavour and not just the vision of the recreation and tourism sector, Unique Island was clearly a compromise written by the consultants at the behest of VVV Texel, without consulting the other stakeholders.

Subsequently, two other stakeholder groups – the farmers and Tien voor Texel – made strong efforts to influence the process. The farmers' group presented its own report to the municipality, and Tien voor Texel commissioned Wageningen University to write a report on quality of life on the island, with the result that the municipality decided to consider both reports as well as the Unique Island scenario. The final process is summarized in Figure 8.2.

Assessment of Decision-making

Initiation

VVV Texel set the terms of reference and the agenda of Texel 2030. Although it purported to be an exercise in integration, it also aimed at putting tourism more firmly on the local political agenda. One direct consequence was that the farmers contested the legitimacy of Texel 2030, claiming that this plan was not the appropriate vehicle to debate the future of agriculture. As the most powerful landowners on the island, they were used to discussing such issues in private and were sensitive to external scrutiny. As they had been the cornerstone of Texel's political economy for so long, they did not want to admit publicly that their future was uncertain. For them, the discussions about the long-term agricultural prospects during the search conference were especially threatening. Their unease was increased by the enthusiastic way in which innovations in tourism and nature development were presented, and they increasingly felt that the future

Stages and representation	Format
First Stage	Preparatory desk research and interviews by the consultants
Second Stage: October 1999 *'Search' Conference*: involving 25 mainland and 15 local experts selected by VVV Texel and its consultant	• First day: Trend analysis identification of most uncertain trends • Second day: Formulation of outlines for prospective scenarios, processed into Nature Island, Authentic Island, Eco-Island and Park Island • Scenarios are published in local newspapers and presented on local radio and television
Third Stage: February 2000 *'Action' Conferences*: involving 120 adults and 30 school children from Texel, which prompted rival proposals from the young farmers and Tien voor Texel	• Initial presentation and voting • Discussion of scenarios in facilitated sub-groups • Plenary discussion • Final voting on scenarios Rival proposals • Farmers' Island • Quality of life report
Fourth Stage: March 2000 Preparation of a compromise scenario involving VVV Texel and its consultant	Drafting and presentation to the municipality of a fifth scenario – Texel: The Unique Island

Source: Philipsen, 2004.

Figure 8.2 *Summary of the Process of Preparing Texel 2030*

of agriculture was being written off. In this respect local experts and external experts had different standpoints. The local experts were also stakeholders who only wanted to talk about futures which did not threaten their interests, while the external experts took a more detached view. If a scenario appeared threatening, local experts immediately questioned its validity, whereas external experts would be prepared to discuss it as one of several options to be investigated at a later stage.

While the detail of whether the process followed its intended path is important, it only becomes of significance when the entire process is brought into question. This certainly occurred when major players – the farmers and Tien voor Texel – objected to an agenda and process being imposed upon them. VVV Texel and its consultants failed to recognize the value of obtaining shared ownership of both the agenda and process. By pressing on with their agenda they failed to allow time, for the farmers in particular, to adjust to ideas of potential change. The major omission, according to Tien voor Texel, was that the impacts of tourism on the local quality of life were ignored. Earlier involvement of this group could have ensured a broader coverage of issues that concerned the island community.

Inclusiveness

In the first stage of the Texel 2030 process, communities of interest were indirectly represented by local experts as well as experts from the *overkant*, who had been chosen by VVV Texel and its consultants. This allowed the farmers and Tien voor Texel to challenge the selection, claiming the representation between the interest groups was unbalanced and thereby casting doubt on the openness and legitimacy of the process. With hindsight, it is doubtful that the use of an apparently sophisticated technique, namely devising scenarios, was a wise choice. It tended to mystify the process rather than being a transparent and genuine aid to decision-making. Although 150 people participated in the second stage, again the method of selection was not clear and was hence disputed.

Tien voor Texel and the farmers were the most vociferous critics of both the process and results of Texel 2030. Generally speaking, Tien voor Texel keeps a critical eye on every new plan or development on the island. However, it is unclear whom this association represents, although it is supported by nearly 240 inhabitants, including 'genuine' Texel people and *overkanters* living on the island. The rival farmers' scenario (Farmers' Island) was in fact drawn up by a group of young farmers who claimed that they alone represented the future. However, the agricultural community is far more diverse than this, consisting of young and old, subsidized and non-subsidized, full-time and part-time farmers.

Information

By involving a wide range of experts from various disciplinary backgrounds in the first stage a wide range of issues was covered, ranging from the economic future of agriculture, the effects of global warming and the ageing population to trends in tourism and recreation. The local and national experts combined knowledge of global developments with local practices. However, as the farmers were not involved in the selection of experts, what was intended as an exercise in obtaining a wider range of information was not perceived as neutral. Tien voor Texel's concern about the omission of information about tourism impacts on the local quality of life was only rectified when it commissioned research to fill that gap (Lengkeek and Velden, 2000).

By placing details of the scenarios in the local media, VVV Texel attempted to inform the wider community. With hindsight, a more proactive method of involvement should have been used. One year later a household survey on Texel revealed that 17 per cent of the population of Texel believed that their voices were heard in the scenario project. Only two-thirds of this group (i.e., 12 per cent of the total) felt that their opinions had been taken into account (Duim et al, 2001). It appears that access to information was limited to those directly involved.

Influence

The political climate of Texel is not geared to cope with uncertainty, and the inter-dependence of the political parties, local administration, civil servants and the population possibly influences their integrity and objectivity. The close-knit community tends to focus on detail and to neglect long-term planning. Many locals complain about the lack of vigour within the municipality. As one of the locals argued: 'Texel is the archetype of the Dutch "polder-model", everybody talks with everybody, but no (radical) choices are made' (Duim and Caalders, 2004).

This political climate and lack of representation of the tourism sector in local politics probably guided the board of VVV Texel towards the instigation of the Texel 2030 process. The formal objective of the Texel 2030 scenario project was to make a contribution to the public debate and decision-making around Texel municipality's second tourism master plan. Therefore the project was designed to involve representatives from a broad range of sectors as well as tourism. Furthermore, VVV Texel wanted to make use of outside expertise which could contribute knowledge about future trends and creativity in finding innovative developments.

Meanwhile, local government played an ambivalent role within the Texel 2030 process. On the one hand, the municipality exercised a degree of control over the process of Texel 2030 by its funding of VVV Texel and by its membership of the VVV Texel board. On the other hand, the municipality, quite deliberately, did not commit itself in advance to be bound by the outcomes of the project. It did not publicly state whether it saw the process as an independent endeavour by the tourism sector, nor did it embed the process clearly in its statutory policy-making procedures. Thus it kept its options open and retained the ability to respond to subsequent challenges to the legitimacy of Texel 2030 by relegating its outcome to the status of just another sector plan. It could then claim to be even-handed in its treatment of this report and those of the farmers and Tien voor Texel. The municipality fully realized that it alone had the statutory responsibility to prepare the local spatial plan, and did not seem to welcome novel forms of participation, seeing them as too risky. As a result, in 2001 it hired another consultant to integrate the diverging sector plans. Eventually the municipality translated the results of the project into a new 'policy vision', Texel 2020 (published in 2002) and a policy document on recreation and tourism, published in 2003 (Duim and Lengkeek, 2004).

The analysis of participation in Texel 2030 summarized in Figure 8.3 is confined to the formal responsibilities of power, and does not recognize the realities of the informal decision-making processes on the island and the real distribution of power. Within the local community network, farmers have long had a special place, being as well represented in formal networks (local politics) as in informal ones, and being the largest group of landowners. Power operates at different levels with the local elite participating in decision-making on the island. For example, a group of 'invited' politicians, entrepreneurs and the directors of certain organizations meets informally

INITIATION
In setting the initial terms of reference for the project, VVV Texel failed to recognize the value of shared ownership of both the agenda and process. The attempt to cover local and global trends in agriculture alienated the younger farmers, while Tien voor Texel objected to the omission of impacts of tourism on local quality of life.

INCLUSIVENESS
Representation and openness: The selection of external experts to participate in a second stage 'search conference' was disputed and the representation at a third stage 'choice conference' challenged by those who felt excluded. The preparation of the final scenario involved only VVV Texel and its consultants. Later surveys revealed that few local inhabitants thought their views were taken into account by the 2030 project.

Accountability: It was unclear who the young farmers and Tien voor Texel were representing and whether they were accountable to their constituencies.

INFORMATION
VVV Texel publicized the four scenarios, but later surveys on the island revealed that few inhabitants were aware of the project. The lack of information on impacts of tourism on the local community was later rectified by Tien voor Texel commissioning its own research.

INFLUENCE
Although the local municipality is a member of the board of VVV Texel, it did not undertake to accept the results of the project. This non-committal position allowed it room to manoeuvre when making decisions on the statutory plan. However, Texel 2030 was successful in opening up a debate on the future of the island, discussions have continued and several projects on sustainable tourism have resulted.

Figure 8.3 *Texel 2030 – Assessment of Participation in Decision-making*

about four times a year. Named the 'Lindeboom Overleg' after the local restaurant where the group meets, major issues are discussed in an informal manner over lunch. Although no formal decisions are being taken, the group is nevertheless highly influential (Duim et al, 2001).

Texel Re-visited: Continuing Change and Uncertainty

Clearly the process of agricultural adaptation is slow, partly due to the emotional attachment that farming families have to the land and a reluctance to change to an unfamiliar enterprise. The options are: to intensify stock rearing; to 'extensify' by changing to a biological, organic form of production; to diversify by, for example, rearing horses, milking sheep or opening farms to tourism; or to manage the grazing of land owned by a nature conservation organization. All these adaptations, plus part-time working and farm amalgamation, are occurring on the island, with none dominating. Intensification is attracting criticism because of the intrusive scale of the new farm buildings that are required; they do not fit the image of 'rural authenticity'. The organic market is limited. The production of local products that can attract premium prices is more successful, whether marketed nationally via the Wadden label or in local restaurants and shops via the Texel brand (Duim and Caalders, 2004).

One notable example of tourism diversification, at De Noordkroon, has been open to paying visitors for ten years and has become a viable tourist and educational enterprise. It enables visitors to see the flock of milking sheep and goats and walk around the working farm before buying products, mostly made on the farm. But its success depends on the dynamism of the owner and her ability to put across the story of the farm to visitors, and the creation of individual products such as cheese and hand cream. This is not an easy enterprise to replicate. The opportunities to manage grassland for nature or landscape conservation are also limited by the conservation organizations' lack of resources to buy more land and bear the costs of maintenance. Yet there is a wide recognition of the inter-dependence of nature, landscape and traditional forms of agriculture, and the need to perpetuate the image of unspoilt rurality for the benefit of tourism on Texel.

Meanwhile there are concerns about tourism itself, such as economic overdependence, expressed by almost 70 per cent of the local population in a recent survey (Duim et al, 2001). Other concerns include worries that investment decisions are being taken by entrepreneurs who are not based on the island; problems in attracting seasonal labour; and discontent about impacts on the quality of life, as mentioned earlier (Duim and Caalders, 2004).

The Legacy of Texel 2030

Although some of the technical limitations of the planning exercise were highlighted in the earlier sections, and the impressions of local people were that the issues were too abstract, the scenarios too extreme and the timescale (2000–2030) too long (Duim and Caalders, 2004), several of the key informants who met on the 2004 study tour looked back almost nostalgically to the open public debate about the future. Such a debate is currently lacking. Yet dialogue between the previously rival sectors of agriculture, conservation and tourism is the most tangible legacy of Texel 2030 (Kuiper, 2004; Dros, 2004; Bos, 2004). It is occurring in at least three fora: VVV Texel; a proposed tourism forum; and most significantly, the Stichting Duurzaam Texel (the Foundation for Sustainable Texel).

A working group on sustainable tourism, formed in 1997, was re-constituted as the Foundation, with a wider remit and a membership that spans tourism and recreation, nature conservation, agriculture and the ferry company. Its current projects include renewable domestic energy generation and conservation schemes; environmental audits of tourism businesses; local Texel products; sustainable transport to reduce tourist dependence on cars; local information systems; and the problem of landscape management. The emphasis is on devising financially viable schemes and learning from experience. Each discussion starts broadly to ensure all the potential stakeholders are involved, before slimming down into a manageable project (Dros, 2004). This practical approach is in marked contrast to the lack of action at a more strategic level. Local criticism of the lack of policy focuses on a mistrust of the political process.

Nevertheless, some changes have occurred in local politics over the last four years. The predominance of agricultural representation in the municipality has declined, and there is some evidence that tourism is better represented within both the municipality and the informal networks. Over the years various alliances have formed between tourism, nature conservation and latterly agriculture, so that power is now more evenly balanced. However, the composition of the municipal council reflects the general move to the conservative parties which has occurred at the national level. This brings into question the depth of commitment to sustainability and is matched by a reluctance to take hard decisions, particularly those that have financial implications, such as supporting sustainable transport. Furthermore, the municipality of Texel seems likely to reduce its funding to VVV Texel, the Foundation for Sustainable Texel and Ecomare in the near future (Bos, 2004; Dros, 2004; Kuiper, 2004). The results of Texel 2030 were translated into a 'Structure Vision for Texel 2020 and Policy Document on Recreation and Tourism' by the municipality, but this document ducks many issues, such as the impacts of tourism on the quality of life. It focuses on small issues while neglecting long-term planning, and describes a desirable future situation but fails to formulate clear policies to reach it (Duim and Caalders, 2004; Eelman, 2004). This is partly attributed to the local political culture: the inter-dependence of politicians and officials, and the cosy network of personal contacts within a local elite where everybody is too close to everybody else. The municipality espouses participation, particularly via village development committees, although their operation is little known and the largest village, Den Burg, lacks a committee (Duim and Caalders, 2004).

Tien voor Texel stands apart as a protest group that is prepared to publicize and take legal action against the lack of enforcement of development control regulations by the authorities. For example, a procedure that allows permits to be issued for deviations from the zoning plan has been applied more frequently on Texel than in comparable municipalities in the rest of the Netherlands (Duim and Caalders, 2004).

Conclusions

The Texel 2030 scenario project initiated by VVV Texel was set up as a participatory planning process aimed at influencing local political decision-making. It definitely had its merits in opening up debate about the future of Texel. However, this analysis has also revealed some of the imperfections of the process. Its main shortcomings were the selective invitation of experts and participants, the lack of transparency in agreeing on scenarios, the formulation behind the scenes of the compromise scenario (Unique Island), and the lack of public information about and hence wider participation in the process. But the design was also influenced by two other important factors.

Firstly, VVV Texel, recognizing the economic dependence of the island on tourism, attempted to increase the influence of the recreation and tourism sector. Although its economic power was and still is relatively high, its political influence was relatively low when compared to agricultural and conservation organizations. But control of the scenario project did not bring about an immediate shift in power. VVV Texel failed to recognize the operation of the local island power structure, which relies on informal relationships and contacts. But gradually key figures in the tourism sector have gained influence at the expense of the agricultural sector.

Secondly, the municipality played an ambivalent role throughout. As a member of the board of VVV Texel, it was interested in reaching a balanced vision on the future of the island to be integrated into local planning. But the moment resistance from the farmers, and to a lesser extent Tien voor Texel, cropped up, the municipality failed to intervene and lend weight to the exercise. In effect, it disowned the Texel 2030 exercise. To reach a balanced view, the municipality should have initiated a fully participatory planning exercise from the start, uncompromised by the local power structure and the interests of the tourism sector.

However flawed in technical detail the process of Texel 2030 might have been, it was certainly successful in opening up a debate about the future. The relationships formed at that time have fostered elements of that debate, which continues under the auspices of the various fora including the Foundation for Sustainable Texel. The Foundation focuses on practical projects and builds consensus around them by casting the net widely to ensure that no stakeholders are excluded.

What the longer-term perspective on decision-making on the island illustrates is the intrinsic difficulty of maintaining community involvement in a debate about the future. What appears to be lacking is the leadership to develop a more systematic strategy. In part, this stems from the short-term nature of politics and the preoccupation of the most powerful players with maintaining their own interests through both formal representation in the municipality and the informal network of the local elite. Consultation exercises prevail over genuine involvement, with the result that trust is lacking between politicians and the community they are supposed to represent.

Key Points from the Case Study

- The importance of getting key stakeholders, such as the younger farmers and Tien voor Texel, involved in the design of the participation process so that they can share ownership both of the process and its outcome.
- The importance of getting a firm commitment from the final decision-maker (the municipality) to accept the results of the planning exercise.

- This lack of commitment is evident in other aspects of the municipality's policy-making, so that many elements of the community mistrust the political process.
- The significance of local negotiations within the informal power networks in determining policy.
- Although Texel 2030 appeared to have no immediate outcome, its longer-term legacy has been the continuing debate within a range of local fora about many of the issues it identified. This has resulted in a number of practical projects on sustainable living being developed by the Foundation for Sustainable Texel.

CASE STUDY 2: Preparing an Integrated Management Strategy for the Pentland Hills Regional Park

Context

The history of the PHRP and the controversy over its designation in 1983 were described in Chapter 2 and re-analysed in Chapter 3. Despite public consultation over the local plan produced in 1988, the underlying conflict (ostensibly over recreational access to privately owned grazing land) rumbled on. In fact, the conflict stemmed more from the manner in which regional park designation was introduced by Lothian Regional Council (LRC) and the inherent weakness in the legislation, which conferred few powers on the local authority and failed to provide significant resources to facilitate the public use of private land. Local government reorganization in 1996 resulted in the abolition of the LRC, while two government agencies – the Countryside Commission for Scotland (CCS) and the Nature Conservancy Council (Scotland) – had been merged to form Scottish Natural Heritage (SNH) in 1992. Thus a new partnership was formed to run the regional park, comprising the City of Edinburgh, Midlothian, and West Lothian councils together with SNH. The regional park currently comprises staff from each council under a park manager employed by the City of Edinburgh Council, which became the lead authority in 2004. This account of participation and partnership covers the period from 1999 onwards.

Review of Decision-making

Initiation

In 1999, the regional park recognized the need to replace the previous plan prepared in 1994 as part of the statutory planning system. It also recognized that the management of the park depended upon an active partnership between the local authorities and the local communities, which visit, live and work in and around the hills. Public involvement was to be increased so that local community ideas could be incorporated in the management strategy for the park covering the next five years. The regional park manager

1999	
November/ December	Rangers' and farmers' meetings

2000	
January	Participatory two-day events: Oxgangs, Pencuik, Balerno, Kirknewton
February/March	Meetings with advisory/management groups and joint committee
April/May	Report back to public (*Local Opinions and Ideas for the Future of the Pentland Hills Regional Park*), inputs from rangers
May/June	Development of policies and proposals
August	Preparation of *Caring for the Hills – Draft Management Strategy* for consultation
September/ October	Consultation period
October	Farmers' and open meeting (Balerno), advisory group meeting
November	Consideration by management group
December	Strategy approval by joint committee

Figure 8.4 *Summary of the Process of Preparing the Integrated Management Strategy for the Pentland Hills Regional Park*

therefore invited consultants to submit proposals to prepare an integrated management strategy which would be 'widely acceptable to the stakeholding communities'. The brief envisaged a conventional process whereby the consultant interviewed stakeholders and prepared proposals which were then put out to consultation (Pentland Hills Regional Park, 1999).

The proposal that was accepted took a different approach, and aimed to use participatory appraisal (PA) methods, which have been developed in response to the growing dissatisfaction with the traditional consultation process (Sidaway, 1999b).[2] The advantage of this approach was that it would enable a wider cross-section of people to share and exchange their knowledge and views on the hills and the future of the park.

The PA approach uses a range of tools according to the local situation and places particular emphasis on engaging local people with visual techniques, such as getting them to prepare maps or models. It also employs diagrams of seasonal and historical data as well as using semi-structured interviews with key informants so that the results can be verified by triangulation. But PA has been widely criticized for developing a long 'shopping list' of ideas which are not easily related to official decision-making. In this case the consultants aimed to overcome this by conducting a parallel process of interviews with local organizations and meeting with decision-makers. During the course of the project they held meetings with farmers and landowners, the regional park advisory group and regional park staff. The process of preparing the strategy is shown in Figure 8.4.

Enjoyment of the hills
- Welcome visitors to share in the enjoyment of the hills in a responsible way
- Promote the health advantages of peaceful recreation in the hills, including to those not currently participating
- Encourage appropriate forms of recreation in the park
- Provide information to raise public awareness of the opportunities to enjoy the hills in a responsible way
- Adopt sustainability as a key criterion in the provision of transport to the regional park

The economy of the hills
- Seek to ensure the viability of the local economy of the Pentland Hills
- Encourage the development of rural businesses of an appropriate nature and scale in and around the regional park

Landscape, natural and cultural heritage
- Protect the cultural heritage of the hills
- Protect and enhance the landscape character of the hills
- Increase the biodiversity of the hills

Public involvement and partnership
- Encourage wider participation by the public in caring for the hills
- Develop partnerships with individuals and organizations to further the objectives of the regional park

Source: Pentland Hills Regional Park, 2000.

Figure 8.5 *Adopted Policies of the Integrated Management Strategy*

In fact, there was a marked difference between the park users' and the farmers' agendas. The former focused on access for and information on recreation and transportation, a better trail network, access for disabled people, education programmes, planting native trees, and 'more meetings like this with feedback' (Oxgangs Green Group quoted in Hilton and Sidaway, 2000). Farmers were more concerned with securing more investment in farming, reducing recreation, educating park users, marketing produce locally, and even suggesting the regional park should 'buy the land off us'. The scope of the strategy is shown by the list of adopted policies in Figure 8.5.

Inclusiveness
In January 2000, a series of participatory events were held in four communities close to the hills: Oxgangs and Balerno, both in the City of Edinburgh; Penicuik in Midlothian; and Kirknewton in West Lothian. The choice of locations was determined by ensuring each of the contributory local authorities was represented and by the budget. The two-day PA events tried to stimulate participation by recognizing that few people attend public meetings, and by 'going to the people'. This entailed going to schools and day centres for older or disabled people, and meeting people

in the street or at the entrances of supermarkets. An open meeting was held each day at which people worked in facilitated groups to share their ideas.[3] The material obtained was then put on display so that ideas could be shared and further participation encouraged. In this way, over 600 people of all ages took part at one stage or another. Whilst the numbers participating represent a very small percentage of users, let alone the population of the neighbouring communities, they are appreciably higher than those that had responded to previous formal consultations (for example, there were 54 responses to the 1988 consultation on the draft subject local plan: see p31)

The study team asked people whether they used the hills for walking, cycling or riding, what they liked about the hills, what they disliked, and what changes, if any, they would like to take place over the next few years. A larger-scale map was the main feature of the group-work at the open meetings. Individuals were able to place their ideas on Post-it notes around the map and to trace the routes they used or would like to see developed, before engaging in group discussion. This was recorded in the form of an action plan covering the five most popular suggestions from the group. Thus the group went from gathering ideas to suggesting what should be done about the most important of them in the course of about two hours. Material gathered during the day and during the group-work was put on display and people were encouraged to study it and add comments. Priorities for action were selected by participants, who voted on their five favoured options. On the second day the process was repeated, with the material from the previous day being on display.

The material was incorporated into *Caring for the Hills – A Consultation Draft Management Strategy* (Sidaway, 2000), which summarized the wide range of comments that were received and showed how these influenced the preparation of a draft management strategy. It also showed how the policies and proposals were developed. Five hundred copies were distributed, attracting 22 written responses, with most new input at this stage coming from organizations. Two more events were held at this stage: a meeting for farmers (which attracted only five of them, compared to 18 who attended the earlier meeting), and a public workshop held in Balerno to review the proposals, which 31 people attended.

Information

Feedback to participants on the first stage was provided in the form of a full verbatim record (Hilton and Sidaway, 2000) which was placed in public libraries in Edinburgh as well as the regional park headquarters, where the original material was also deposited. Similarly, *Caring for the Hills – A Draft Management Strategy* (Sidaway, 2000), which traced how the public response was used, was widely circulated. Further feedback to the public has been limited to the circulation of the park's annual report and a quarterly newsletter, *The Pentlands Beacon*, about 4000 copies of which are distributed per year.

Influence

It was clear that people from all the local communities are deeply attached to the hills. They frequently commented on their accessibility and the sense of tranquillity, seclusion, freedom to roam and peace that being in the hills engenders. The study team received a wealth of suggestions for change, particularly on recreation in the hills, and these were grouped under the following broad headings: the enjoyment of the hills; the economy of the hills; landscape, natural and cultural heritage; and future public involvement and partnership. These were adopted as the policy topics of the management strategy.

Comments were made at some of the open meetings about the need to clarify the overall policy and set clear objectives about what the strategy was aiming to achieve. Thus a parallel process of policy development was set in train in a series of meetings between the study team and the park's staff, the Advisory Committee and the Joint Committee of Local Authorities. A range of options was considered within the context of the aims of the regional park that were agreed in 1989, namely:

- *To retain the essential character of the hills as a place for the peaceful enjoyment of the countryside.*
- *Caring for the hills, so that the landscape and the habitat is protected and enhanced.*
- *Within this caring framework, to encourage responsible public enjoyment of the hills.*
- *Co-ordination of these aims so that they co-exist with farming and other land uses within the park.* (Lothian Regional Council, 1989)

Any proposals had to take into account current trends and government policies which were likely to influence the economy and enjoyment of the hills, notably:

- changes in agricultural policy, which were considered unlikely to grant special status and higher levels of financial support to farming in the hills;
- population and economic growth in and around Edinburgh and the Lothians, combined with policy initiatives from both the Scottish Parliament (such as legislation for public access – see Case Study 2, Chapter 10) and local authorities (such as the promotion of policies for social inclusion, healthy lifestyles and integrated transport), which in total were likely to increase the importance of the hills for recreation; and
- bio-diversity action plans, prepared for species of concern, which could result in habitat creation and enhancement.

More crucially, any strategy options were limited by the policy and financial agendas of local authorities. Without active political support from the partners, it was questionable whether current levels of funding would be maintained, let alone increased to meet the expectations of the other stakeholders. Therefore any proposals had to be framed to accord with the local authority policies mentioned above.

Most discussions in these committee meetings concerned the range of options for recreation, set out as follows:

- nothing should be done to encourage visitors, and management should concentrate on minimizing the effects of recreational use (the de facto policy of the 1989 subject local plan); or
- more should be done to welcome visitors to share in the enjoyment of the hills, assuming this can be done without detriment to the environment, the local economy or existing users; or
- the park should be extended to the west to reduce visitor pressure.

The arguments over encouraging visitors were perceived to be finely balanced. It appeared that the effects of recreation on the hills, such as path deterioration, could be dealt with by good management, as long as adequate resources were made available. While many experienced users preferred things to stay the way they were, it was evident that many first-time or would-be users lacked the basic confidence and knowledge to get the most out of their visits. Their enjoyment would be improved largely by better information and relatively minor improvements to the path network. Thus, doing nothing was not considered to be a realistic option. The more radical options, like providing more facilities (e.g., toilets, picnic and play areas, refreshments), were also not favoured because of concerns about the risk of commercializing or over-developing the park. Recognizing the contribution that the park could make to healthy living and enjoyment, the Joint Committee came down in favour of the second option: welcoming the more responsible use of the hills.

Extension of the regional park was rejected by the Joint Committee 'until such time as the benefits of park management can be more clearly demonstrated to the local communities that would be most affected' (Pentland Hills Regional Park, 2000). This was a response to the continued scepticism about, if not outright hostility to, the regional park by a few landowners. Far greater consensus was evident on the other main themes, such as the need to develop the economy of the hills and increase the diversity of wildlife, whilst most people welcomed opportunities to be involved in park matters. The opportunity already existed to become a voluntary ranger and to help with conservation projects. One voluntary ranger in particular was instrumental in founding the Friends of the Pentlands Society in 2003. It aims to promote the conservation, protection and enhancement of the hills (Friends of the Pentlands Society, 2004).

Most of the suggestions from the participatory programme were included as 'priority proposals' in the draft strategy. Major elements have subsequently been incorporated in the Ranger Management Plan, the

INITIATION
The regional park manager was receptive to a proposal to substitute a proactive participatory approach to developing a strategy instead of the usual consultative model.

INCLUSIVENESS
The PA approach entailed a programme of events in four communities around the regional park and actively sought participation from local people in the street, schools and care centres as well as open evening meetings. Within the resource limitations of the study, this programme considerably widened participation across all age groups compared to previous consultations. Meetings were also held with regional park staff, farmers and landowners, as well as the existing advisory committee of representative organizations.

INFORMATION
A detailed record of contributions was made and deposited in local libraries. This provided the basis for the consultative document in the form of a draft management strategy, which was circulated in the four local communities.

INFLUENCE
The consultative document demonstrated how people's contributions were used in preparing the priority proposals of the draft management strategy. A parallel process of meetings with park staff, the Advisory and Joint Committees of partners developed an overall aim for the management strategy and ensured that its policy proposals were related to the policy framework of the financial sponsors to maintain the funding of the regional park.

Figure 8.6 *The Preparation of the Pentland Hills Regional Park Integrated Management Strategy – Assessment of Participation in Decision-making*

normal vehicle for implementation. Notable examples are the refinement of the core path network, the further development of Pentland Hills Produce, a woodland plan, research into cultural history involving the public, and the formation of the Friends of the Pentlands Society, which might be represented on the Advisory Group.

Meanwhile, there has been some uncertainty about funding and direction within the local authority partnership. In March 2002, Midlothian Council notified the other partners that it intended to withdraw from the Minute of Agreement which binds the partners and sets the level of funding contributions. Subsequent negotiations have resulted in the local authorities retaining their commitment to the regional park. The Minute of Agreement has been revised so that the City of Edinburgh Council has assumed the role of managing authority for the park, employing a reduced number of staff under service level agreements with the other partners (Pentland Hills Regional Park, 2003).

The analysis of participation in the preparation of the integrated management strategy is summarized in Figure 8.6.

Key Points from the Case Study

- The value of an internal advocate working at an influential level (the regional park manager) for an effective participation strategy rather than the conventional consultation approach. As well as advocating the acceptance of the submission and working with the study team, he was able to secure extensions to the timetable and augment the budget from internal resources as the programme developed and needs changed.
- The proactive participatory approach broadened the initial base of participation, but it proved hard to sustain this level of interest into subsequent stages. For example, ideally the process of further prioritizing the wide range of suggestions into a delivery programme would have had further stakeholder input.
- The frequent criticism of PA – that the large volume of material it generates is rarely linked into official decision-making – was met by devising a parallel process of framing the stakeholder agenda to match the partners' policy agendas.
- Initial scepticism on the part of park rangers ('We know what needs to be done. Why ask the public?') turned to enthusiasm in some cases. The facilitation of groups in the final open meeting was undertaken largely by rangers.
- An opportunity for further community involvement has been provided by the formation of the Friends of the Pentlands Society in 2003.

CASE STUDY 3: THE Morecambe Bay Partnership

Context: Integrated Coastal Zone and Estuary Management

The UK coast and estuaries are subject to a wide range of competing claims coupled with landward pressure for economic development (see Figure 8.7), and interest in their conservation was stimulated by the publication of a number of influential reports by non-governmental organizations (NGOs) in the late 1980s (e.g., Gubbay, 1990; Rothwell and Housden, 1990). But the first official recognition that the UK's coastal resources were not protected in an integrated or co-ordinated manner came in the second report of the House of Commons Environment Committee in 1992. The Committee came to the view that this stemmed from 'inadequacies of legislation, anomalies in the planning system, a lack of central guidance, and overlapping and conflicting policies and responsibilities (and in some cases a lack of action) among a host of bodies, with poor co-ordination between them' (House of Commons Environment Committee, 1992, x). The Committee listed 80 relevant acts and identified over 30 government departments and statutory national agencies concerned with the marine environment. The Committee recognized the need for government to develop an overall perspective and an integrated approach to coastal zone management and planning. The development of good working relationships between organizations would be critical to their

Competing claims on coastal resources	Institutional complexities
• Sea defences and coastal protection (compounded by climate change) • Mineral aggregate extraction local • Dock, port and harbour facilities • Bridges and tunnels • Recreational activities, and associated development (e.g., marinas) • Fisheries and marine aquaculture • Pollution and water quality • Nature conservation • Energy generation (easy access to cooling water, renewable sources)	• Multiple user and interest groups, with some activities which are difficult to co-ordinate or restrict (jet skiers, non-fishermen) • Numerous statutory bodies, some with overlapping responsibilities • No common co-ordinating body • No single resource owner but several interdependent 'commons' resources • Dynamic coastal processes

Source: based on Bleakley, 1994.

Figure 8.7 *Challenges of Coastal Management*

effectiveness. The government's response to the Committee's report did not accept that there was widespread duplication of responsibilities or poor co-ordination. However, it was minded to encourage the preparation of local management plans 'where these are needed' (Department of the Environment, 1992) and favoured English Nature's Estuaries Initiative as an example of its preferred approach.

Thus English Nature (EN) saw itself in an influential co-ordination role and issued advice accordingly in the form of *Estuary Management Plans: A Co-ordinator's Guide* (English Nature, 1993a). Its approach consisted of two elements: the establishment of a partnership and the preparation of a plan for integrated action. The guide placed considerable emphasis on organization, identifying management agencies, drawing up the project brief, identifying financial sponsors, and establishing a committee structure.

Herein lay the first point of tension: how estuary management groups would be structured, and more particularly how inclusive their memberships should be. In most cases, the initiative to form such groups came from a small number of national and local government bodies. As these bodies were the initial funding partners, the logic was that they should form a small steering group with executive powers, and only then consider involving a wider group of stakeholders in a wider forum, with a limited advisory or consultative role.

EN's advice followed this model and stressed the importance of executive committee members being fully committed to the project. The Executive Committee was given a commanding role at each stage of decision-making. At the first stage, it was to endorse a preparatory document before public consultation. 'In this way, the comments of the topic groups and interested public will be made on recommendations which have already been sanctioned, in principle, by the Executive Committee', and subsequently, the Committee would decide which of the earlier recommendations would be modified after consultation. Equally, the content of the management plan would be sanctioned by the Committee 'as it is important that management actions are agreed by organisations which are intended to discharge them' (English Nature, 1993a).

Yet running counter to the notion that relatively small numbers of agencies should hold the crucial responsibilities was the realization that many more interest groups were influential and might hold veto power. Given that these were voluntary and not statutory plans and that their success relied on cooperation, the agreement of all stakeholders was considered crucial during the successive stages of planning.

> *For such plans to be effective, it is necessary for all organisations who use and manage the estuary, both statutory and voluntary, to agree to the need for a plan and to commit themselves to work together to reach consensus on management policies and action.* (English Nature, 1993b, 12)

> *So far as possible, all policies should be agreed, not only by those implementing the policy and those directly affected by it, but by estuary users more generally.* (English Nature, 1993a, 14)

Nevertheless, these documents present a rather technocratic concept of conflict resolution, whereby the impacts of competing users are identified during data collection and presented in complex matrices, on the assumption that such conflicts can be resolved through information provision and regulation rather than by the development of consensus.

By 1995, EN had contributed to 27 management plans covering 31 estuaries, and instigated a review of its progress which once again highlighted the role of public involvement. Effective consultation should be early, continuous and targeted, with information presented clearly in plain English. Consensus would be achieved by identifying issues that were important to all consultees, with no one interest dominating. Commitment to the implementation of projects was seen to be dependent on obtaining and maintaining commitment to a common goal. The review identified several areas where improvements could be made, including:

- *ensuring a balanced representation of all interests on the management committee;*
- *encouraging industry to become involved with the projects at an early stage;*
- *improving consultation so that everyone has an opportunity to influence the project.* (Grabrovaz, 1995, 1)

In similar vein, a later review for the Scottish Executive of integrated coastal zone management (ICZM) projects in Scotland expressed concern that, in general, the lay public was largely unaware of the existence or activities of the partnerships and that the methods used to attract their attention were limited to passive involvement, such as websites and newsletters, rather than more active engagement (ITAD Ltd, BMT Cordah Ltd, 2002).

Thus the major themes that emerge from this brief review are:

- the need to co-ordinate the activities of a wide range of government organizations to secure common goals;
- the importance of the organizational structure of partnership, especially in engaging powerful players, such as industry and the utility companies;
- the extent to which a partnership operates on a consultative model or seeks active involvement in decision-making from all its stakeholders to secure wide ownership and effective implementation of its plans; and
- the extent to which the agenda is seen to be dominated by conservation issues, because most partnerships are initiated by conservation agencies or NGOs.

These issues are addressed in the following case study of the Morecambe Bay partnership.

The Geography of Morecambe Bay

Morecambe Bay covers nearly 34,000ha. It is the largest estuary in the UK, situated on the north-western coast of England between Fleetwood in the south and Isle of Walney in the north. Four main rivers – the Leven, the Kent, the Lune and the Wyre – drain into the bay, which at low tide has extensive areas of sand and mud flats and is surrounded by salt marshes, both of which attract large numbers of wading birds and wildfowl and contribute to its nature conservation value. Initially notified as a site of special scientific interest (SSSI), the bay is now managed as a European Marine Site. Barrow, Fleetwood and Heysham are the main industrial and commercial centres and there are fisheries based at Flookburgh, Ulverston, Morecambe and Fleetwood, but recreation and tourism are the most important contributors to the local economy.

Assessment of Decision-making

Initiation

The initiative for a coastal project came from the Morecambe Bay Conservation Group (MBCG), founded as an independent forum in 1992 because of concerns about pollution in the bay. The MBCG aimed to improve communication and debate, rather than act as a pressure group, and whilst it had no formal membership, it attracted a wide range of interests to its quarterly meetings. Its strengths as a network were seen to be providing personal contacts and access to information, which may have helped to prevent conflict. Its weaknesses were perceived by some of those involved to be its informal administration and its apparent domination by conservation and 'outside' interests. The latter views possibly stemmed from

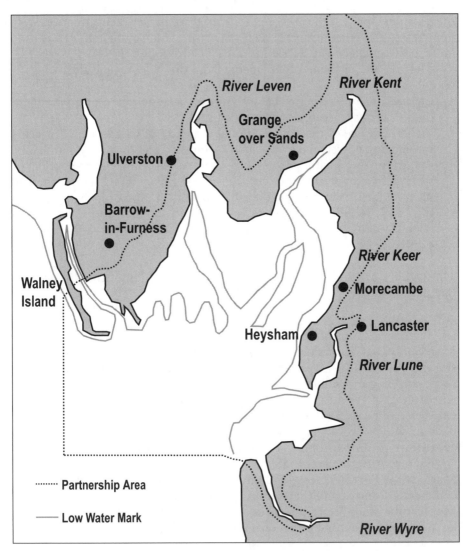

Figure 8.8 *Map of Morecambe Bay*

its origins, its association with the Estuaries Initiative and the active participation of conservation groups. Nevertheless, MBCG provided a vital driving force through its public meetings, and it instilled a sense of cooperation between usually opposing interests (Bleakley, 1994).

The Morecambe Bay Strategy was launched in 1993 by an initial steering committee formed between EN, the six local authorities and the Lake District National Park. Seven public meetings organized by the steering committee, each covering a different topic, were held in four towns in the south and east of the area. The material from these meetings was compiled into a draft Issues Report and debated by four working groups formed in

1994. Their findings were summarized in the Draft Strategy, which was widely circulated late in 1995 and contained proposals for a Management Group and a Standing Conference to be held twice a year. The result was the formation of the Morecambe Bay Partnership (hereinafter the Partnership) with the strategic aim:

> To build an economically prosperous and environmentally sustainable future for the communities, and the natural and man-made features which make the Bay distinctive.
> (Morecambe Bay Partnership, 1996, 8)

By 2001, the Partnership had obtained charitable company status to enable it to secure its long-term future by attracting funding from a wider range of sources. Major events in the development of the Partnership are recorded in Figure 8.9.

As noted earlier, the Estuaries Review envisaged wide participation being achieved through large numbers of official and non-statutory bodies being involved in management committees or topic groups to formulate policies on specific issues. The merits of this process were that no one interest would dominate and that everyone had an opportunity to influence the selection of issues, ensuring they shared ownership of the plan (Grabrovaz, 1995, 1, 11–14).

This structure was applied in the case of Morecambe Bay. Despite some of the early misgivings, the terms of reference and agenda appear to have been balanced and generally accepted through the process of meetings and consultation. Eight topics were identified in the 1993 Issues Report, and these became the main objectives of the strategy, namely: coastal defence; fisheries; heritage and landscape; industry, transport and development; land management; pollution; tourism and recreation; and wildlife. Examination of the working group reports and the final strategy shows that the recommendations of those groups which articulated clear policies were incorporated into the strategy verbatim. The other groups were less conclusive and the detailed policies had to be developed later. Nevertheless, the strength of this approach was that the agenda of issues was created locally.

Inclusiveness

The Scottish Review (ITAD Ltd, BMT Cordah Ltd, 2002) noted that projects often start with a small, practically-focused steering group whose members are chosen for their ability to manage and organize rather than be representative. From these beginnings, partnerships tend to have difficulties in reaching the lay public, with the result that engagement is through representative bodies, such as community councils, residents' associations, clubs and membership organizations, such as sailing clubs and youth groups. This is largely because of the time involved in attending meetings. It is also difficult to get representatives from utility companies, for example, who are only prepared to attend the larger regional partnerships.

Year	Event
1992	Formation of MBCG
	Agreement of preliminary management structure of steering group and working group by EN and local authorities
	Technical report prepared on scientific interest and design of participatory programme
1993	Launch of Morecambe Bay Strategy with initial public meetings
1994	Draft Issues Report published, publicized by newsletter and explained at public meeting of MBCG
	Formation of four topic [working] groups
1996	Publication of Morecambe Bay Strategy, which proposed:
	Establishment of the standing conference, management committee and working groups
	The appointment of a project officer
1997	2nd and 3rd standing conferences
1998	4th standing conference: Sustainability and Coastal Management in the North West
	(5th) seminar on public health issues
1999	6th conference: Agenda for Action
	(7th) seminar: Industry and Sustainable Development
2000	8th conference: Launch of Shoreline Management Plan
	9th conference: Launch of European Marine Site; change to charitable status, appointment of trustees
2001	10th conference on regeneration, annual election of trustees instituted
	11th conference on interpretation
2002	Launch of open (free) membership
	Annual general meeting and 12th conference on wind energy proposals
2003	13th conference covering beach care, the Wyre Code of Conduct, and cockling in the bay

Figure 8.9 *The Development of the Morecambe Partnership*

In the case of Morecambe Bay, initial concerns were expressed from those interests that were not represented on the steering group. However, a wider range of interest groups and individuals were brought into the working groups, whose membership was unrestricted, and representatives of the major interests are present in the Management Committee (see Figure 8.10). The initial board of trustees was appointed from the original steering group and industry, and (unlike the Scottish experience) the Partnership has been successful in attracting the membership of utility companies.

The communities around the bay were invited to become involved in the strategy from its inception. The agenda of issues was developed from the 1993 public meetings 'starting with exploratory questions which attracted interest and local curiosity' (Bleakley, 1994, 55) and developed through topic groups during 1994, with consultation on the intermediate documents and the draft strategy in 1995. The strategy itself was endorsed at the conference in 1996 and progress has subsequently been reviewed through

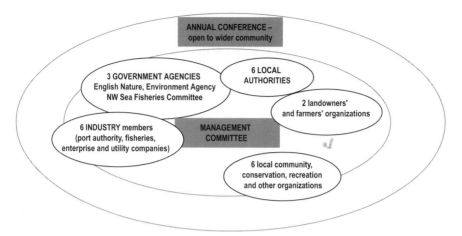

Figure 8.10 *Representation within the Committee Structure of the Morecambe Bay Partnership in 2002*

the medium of the annual conferences. Indeed, the conferences have been a major feature of the Partnership, providing an opportunity for wider participation.

The Partnership has also been successful in engaging with the sports and recreation community by establishing a Sport and Recreation User Group, whose meetings have attracted (in the words of the Project Director) 'blokes with beards [who] go out in boats but don't necessarily like conferences' (Bleakley, 2003). The group was founded in 1999 and meets two or three times a year. It aims to provide a collective view within the Partnership from the wide range of sport and recreation bodies using the bay. It has been successful in reducing conflict among these users and with other activities by promoting responsible use and codes of practice (Morecambe Bay Partnership, 2003).

More recently, involvement has been further extended by the production of a guide for teachers which takes an exploratory approach to environmental education around the bay. The aim is to encourage children's critical thinking and raise deeper philosophical questions about relationships with the coastal environment. The teacher's role becomes one of encouraging questioning and creativity in seeking a variety of outcomes rather than a pre-ordained 'correct' answer. This approach to environmental education encourages communities to consider their impact on the environment and to alter their activities which deplete natural resources and threaten sustainable livelihoods (Rowley and Lewis, 2003).

Information

Although there were early concerns about greater awareness and information being more available on the south and east sides of the bay than on the north, this may have been due to the venues of the first meetings.

Since then, information on the Partnership's activities has been more widely available with the circulation of draft documents and the distribution of the *Baywatch* newsletters, which target particular topics of interest, such as water quality and wind farm proposals, and have a circulation of between 5000 and 8000.

Influence

Concerns were expressed in Chapter 7 about the risk of participatory projects being tokenistic, with the less powerful stakeholders having little influence on events. One way to assess this is to consider the extent to which an agreed strategy influenced the action of those partners with executive responsibility, either in addressing hitherto neglected issues or taking action sooner than might have otherwise been the case. The practical difficulty with the approach is that of assessing added value or 'additionality', i.e., knowing what action can be attributed to participation in the partnership per se. But as these are not controlled experiments, it is hard to judge what might have happened anyway, particularly when there are also external interventions, such as new national or European legislation.

The Scottish review of ICZM partnerships recommended that 'The partnerships need to be more effective in influencing the plans, policies and behaviour of stakeholders' (ITAD Ltd, BMT Cordah Ltd, 2002, iii). It also noted that as participation in the plans was voluntary, and partners were not formally required to commit themselves to adopting plan prescriptions, recommendations were taken on board as partners saw fit. More significantly, it reported criticisms that 'economically significant developments in the coastal zone [such as port developments] do not pass across the tables of the partnerships, but rather resort directly to the statutory bodies' (ITAD et al, 2002, 19). This is attributed to the desire to maintain consensus by not embracing difficult issues or challenging other partners. Fisheries are cited as an example of a contentious issue which the projects have tip-toed around (ITAD et al, 2002, 38).

As the Morecambe Bay Strategy was a voluntary and not a statutory plan, it was accepted that policies were more likely to be implemented 'if they are practical and popular, proposals that lack support will founder' (Morecambe Bay Partnership, 1996, 4). Thus it is crucial to understand that it is the partners, rather than the Partnership, that have statutory functions and are accountable for fulfilling them. The implementation of policies and programmes is the responsibility of the partners. While it is difficult to assess the extent to which the strategy has influenced partners' programmes, there is little doubt that the Partnership has engendered a spirit of cooperation. The greatest success of the Partnership has probably been in building trust between the partners through networking and the personal contacts that develop.

The Partnership can play two roles. Firstly, by taking initiatives on issues where there is no clear lead agency. One example is the leading role its project team has played in the Beach Care project, getting local communities to remove litter from their part of the bay. Secondly, the Partnership can provide an opportunity for informed debate, without taking a stand on any particular issue, as it is neither a decision-making body nor a lobby group. An example of this second role is the discussion of proposals for wind farms off Walney Island, which were influential in getting the developers to talk with local communities at an early stage, so there was real understanding on both sides and the developers knew how best to accommodate local concerns (Bleakley, 2004, personal communication).

Another way of gauging the influence of the Partnership is to review progress against the Agenda for Action, a plan covering the 76 policies from the strategy and agreed at the annual conference in 1997. Six working groups were established the following year and progress was reviewed at the subsequent conference. The last comprehensive review, presented to the 1998 conference, showed that substantial progress had been made both in terms of the initial set of actions and a number agreed subsequently; 104 out of 112 and 11 out of 24, respectively. This does not of course answer the additionality question, which would be necessary in a full evaluation of the project. Nor does it entirely address the difference a community-based partnership made on the level of commitment of the major players.

The issues of commitment and influence are illustrated by considering probably the most controversial set of issues within the strategy, namely pollution, which has featured prominently in the Partnership's programme, not necessarily to the satisfaction of all the concerned individuals. Certainly, the Partnership has not tip-toed around the topic. The criticism levelled at some aspects of the ICZM project is illustrated in the following example, which summarizes the way the Partnership has covered pollution issues.

The analysis of participation in the Morecambe Partnership is summarized in Figure 8.11.

Key Points from the Case Study

- From its initiation, the Partnership has sought the active involvement of its stakeholders in the preparation of its strategy and this has continued into a range of community projects.
- The initial concerns that the agenda was dominated by conservation issues have been assuaged.
- The Partnership has developed a clear role in taking initiatives on issues where there is no clear lead agency and has provided an opportunity for informed debate.
- The Partnership has been successful in engaging powerful players, such as industry and the utility companies, and in attracting a significant proportion of its funding from them – approximately one-third of its funding has come from the private sector for a number of years.
- Continuity of staff and representation from the partners has built up local commitment to the Partnership. The Partnership is particularly fortunate in having had greater staff continuity than many other ICZM

Box 8.1 Continuing Concerns about Marine Pollution

Pollution in Morecambe Bay was one of the initial concerns which led to the formation of the MBCG and eventually the Partnership. The strategy noted 'widespread concern about pollution from sewage and radioactive sources, shipping and the risk of pollution from the oil and gas industries. Worries about pollution and its effects were raised more frequently than any other issue' (Morecambe Bay Partnership, 1996, p5). Whilst all these topics were considered in the strategy, the policies concentrate on water quality (policies 1, 2, 6, 7, 8, 9), waste disposal (policies 3 and 4) and noise (Policy 5).

In part, the disparity between public perceptions and scientific 'reality' is one of communication. Indeed, the topic was the subject of much vocal criticism from community groups in the early conferences. Yet water quality in the bay was higher, according to Environmental Agency classifications, than was publicly perceived, while exposure to radioactivity from industrial sources was well within government limits. The strategy recognized that public concerns arise from low awareness, 'largely because much of the data describing water quality is technical, inaccessible and unintelligible' (Morecambe Bay Partnership, 1996, p43). The answer to the problem was seen to lie in openness and dialogue to be implemented by Strategy Policy 6, which states: 'Regulatory authorities and operators should work together to raise awareness of the water quality of the bay.'

The outcome was a series of events which focused on different aspects of the problems. The issues got a thorough airing at the 1998 Public Health Seminar, which started with a series of presentations from community groups that spanned concerns about the incidence of asthma in local children, disposal of toxic waste and landfill sites, contamination of seafood, traffic emissions, safe drinking water and radioactivity. Later speakers addressed public and environmental health perspectives and public perceptions of risk, while workshops debated perceptions and the management of risks to health. The main value of the event was that it provided an opportunity for the open discussion of complex and contentious issues.

The seminar was followed by a joint initiative between the regulator (the Environment Agency) and the utility company (North West Water, now United Utilities) to produce and deliver water quality standards for the bay and address the sources of organic pollution. New sewage treatment plants have been constructed at Fleetwood, Morecambe, Barrow and Ulverston, together with additional stages at Lancaster, at a cost of £660 million since 1994. Work proceeded on treatment systems for smaller communities and monitoring the quality of bathing water at beaches around the bay (Morecambe Bay Partnership, 2001). This work was publicized in a series of local events – the Sewerage Roadshow – and a Beach Care project is working with local communities to remove litter from the coast. As a result, much of the concern about water quality in the bay has subsided (Chester, 2003).

Less progress has been made with the concerns about radioactivity from discharges from Heysham nuclear power station, the construction of nuclear powered submarines at Barrow shipyards and the Sellafield plant, despite discussions between Nuclear Electric and local groups. The major outstanding concerns are about Sellafield, which is the subject of national debate and beyond the influence of the Partnership (*The Guardian*, 19 February 2000; *Herald*, 24 June 2003).

INITIATION
Although the initiative for a coastal project came from a conservation group, an initial consultation exercise identified a wide range of issues which was debated in working groups. The objectives of the Morecambe Bay Strategy were derived from the working group reports with related policies and an action programme developed to address this agenda.

INCLUSIVENESS
The Partnership has operated in an inclusive way following the tradition of open membership established by the MBCG. While the membership of the steering group and later the Management Committee and trustees was drawn largely from the financial sponsors, a wide range of interests was involved in the working groups. This policy of inclusion has continued with the annual standing conference, which has attracted a broad following of organizations and individuals. Other groups, such as the Sport and Recreation User Group, have been established to meet the needs of specialist interests. A number of educational projects have attracted involvement from schools.

INFORMATION
During the early consultations, information was widely circulated via newsletters and this has continued with the regular *Baywatch* newsletters on topical themes.

INFLUENCE
The partnership has been influential in taking initiatives on issues where there is no clear lead agency by developing coastal management projects with local communities. It has also provided opportunities for informed debate, without taking a stand on any particular issue, as it is neither a decision-making body nor a lobby group. Substantial progress has been made in implementing the 76 policies of the management strategy. The partnership has increased liaison between the statutory bodies, but the extent of influence on the implementation of their programmes is hard to gauge.

Figure 8.11 *Morecambe Bay Partnership – Assessment of Participation in Decision-making*

projects. This has enabled the Project Director to provide leadership (from the early days when the Partnership was unclear about its aims) in developing and implementing the strategy and, crucially for an NGO, in obtaining core and project funding.

CASE STUDY 4: The Upper Deeside Access Trust

Context

The upper catchment of the River Dee lies to the south and east of the Grampian mountain range in north-east Scotland, an area that has attracted many conservation designations on account of its exceptional scenic beauty and nature conservation interest. Scenically, Upper Deeside is a mixture of lowland glens containing native birch and pinewoods backed by the wild

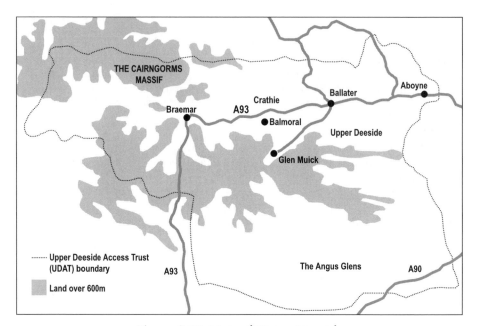

Figure 8.12 *Map of Upper Deeside*

terrain of the mountain peaks of Lochnagar, Mount Keen, the Cairnwell Hills, the Cairngorm massif and Morven. The core of the area was designated as the Lochnagar and Deeside National Scenic Area in 1981. It now contains several Natura 2000 sites of European significance, and since September 2003, the Cairngorms, including much of Upper Deeside, have been designated as Scotland's second national park. Most of the area is owned by a few large estates, notably the royal estate of Balmoral, and the private estates of Invercauld, Glen Tanar and Glen Muick, some of which contain designated historic landscapes and are visitor attractions in their own right. Balmoral attracts about 100,000 visitors a year as it lies on a main highland route which is popular with coach tour operators using hotels in the largest settlements on Upper Deeside: Aboyne, Ballater and Braemar. Thus the local economy has benefited both from tourism and the prosperity of Aberdeen, the centre of support for the North Sea oil fields.

Glen Muick and Lochnagar are major attractions within this area largely because of their accessibility from Ballater, which was enhanced by the construction of the car park at the Spittal of Glen Muick in the early 1970s to provide a counter-attraction to Balmoral as the main gateway to Lochnagar and the East Grampian Hills. This move proved so successful that visitor numbers have steadily increased in the glen and on the surrounding hills. Loch Muick has proved to be a favourite destination for holiday-makers and day visitors from Aberdeen, particularly since the paths have been improved to allow families to make a relatively easy circuit of the loch. It has been estimated that between 100,000 and 120,000 visitors reached Glen Muick by car in 1995 (Mather, 1996). But the car park at the end of road (the Spittal) is also the main access point for Lochnagar, which attracts walkers and climbers all year round. Winter use is boosted by the attractions of snow and ice climbing when daylight hours are short, plus the fact that the East Grampian Hills often have clear weather when the central tops are covered in low cloud.

Although Scottish peaks are relatively low in European terms, their vegetation is classified as Arctic-Alpine because of their severe exposure. These habitats are fragile, sensitive to disturbance and slow to recover from damage, which could be caused by trampling from walking and climbing. This risk lies at the heart of concerns about the potential impact of recreation on the hills and the management of upland access.

Assessment of Decision-making

Initiation

The Balmoral Estate held informal consultations with the local authority and user groups about the situation at Glen Muick for several years (Environmental Resources Management/Sidaway, 1997). The general impression was that the car park at the Spittal was over-stretched, with cars often being parked on the road verges leading to the car park. This, combined with concerns about the possible environmental impacts of visitor use plus the financial burden on landowners of maintenance, led to the formation of the Lochnagar Advisory Committee by the Balmoral estate in May 1995. The committee provided a way of involving the key public agencies, local community and user interests in discussions about how to manage the pressures from increased numbers of visitors. This and subsequent events are set out in Figure 8.13.

In September 1996 the advisory committee commissioned consultants to undertake a study 'to establish a widely supported programme to address current and projected visitor management pressures at Glen Muick, Lochnagar and the Ballater area' (Environmental Resources Management/ Sidaway, 1997). The study drew together existing information, consulted 150 stakeholders (including workshops in Ballater), identified key issues and defined key objectives for a strategy. While the responses from the interviews provided a more representative view and the two workshops (held on the same day) attracted only 31 people, the response from the workshops encouraged the consultants to write:

> *Given the potential sensitivity of the local community and the regular users to the introduction of management measures in the study area, we note the study aim of reaching consensus and recognise certain practical arguments for increasing public involvement, which would allay any outstanding suspicion on the aims of motives of the new management measures. Although we would make no claims that the Ballater workshops were representative of the interest groups, we*

1960s	Initial consultations by Balmoral Estate on the creation of a car park at Glen Muick
1972	Construction of car park at Spittal of Glen Muick by Aberdeenshire Council
1995	Lochnagar Advisory Committee formed by the Balmoral Estate
1996	Environmental Resources Management and Roger Sidaway commissioned to prepare visitor strategy for Glen Muick, Lochnagar and Ballater area
1997	Study recommends formation of partnership trust, appointment of project manager and objectives of strategy. Working group formed of key funding partners to establish aims, constitution and membership of the trust
1998	UDAT formed as a limited company with charitable status. Directors and project managers appointed
	Initial £72,000 EU funding programme secured as a pilot project with match funding from the partners
1999	UDAT invites local organizations and individuals to become affiliate members
	Initial project work: low level paths and publicity, initial work on mountain paths
	Consultation paper on traffic management in Glen Muick (December)
	More substantial £461,000 EU funding secured for a further three years with match funding from the partners
2000	Workshop on traffic management held in Ballater (February), circulation of results (April), application for planning permission for car park alterations (August), progress report to stakeholders (October)
	Further project work on low-level path development and mountain path repairs
2001	Workshop on mountain paths restoration held in Ballater. Completion of car park at Glen Muick, car park charges raise £28,000 for path repair. Eastward expansion of trust area
	Consolidated three-year business plan and £700,000 funding programme agreed by the partners including a commitment to wider exploration of funding from other sources and income generation. Expanded programme of activity across Upper Deeside
2002	10km of mountain paths improved and 27km of lowland path network improved and publicized since 1998. Car park revenue of £30,000. Wider landscape scheme implemented at the Spittal of Glen Muick. New visitor website developed providing information about access opportunities to the area
	Development of a substantial funding bid to EU and HLF for a combined £2.4 million programme across Upper Deeside and the Angus Glens

Source: Upper Deeside Access Trust, 1999; 2002; 2003.

Figure 8.13 *The Development of the Upper Deeside Access Trust*

> *detected the potential to reach consensus given wider representation and adequate time.* (Environmental Resources Management/Sidaway, 1997, 45)

The topics that were identified for further discussions were vehicle access and transport, visitor pressures, natural heritage, estate management and visitor management. The most significant of these was undoubtedly vehicle access. The irony was that the car park and facilities established at the Spittal of Glen Muick were victims of their own success, providing easy access to the mountains by road and acting as a magnet in an area where few such facilities existed. The combination of the narrow approach road and the relatively small car park (60 spaces) meant that parking capacity was exceeded on 85 out of 214 days in the seven-month period from April to October with, on some occasions, up to 260 parked cars being counted on the road verges leading to the car park (Environmental Resources Management/Sidaway, 1997, 49). The problems were further compounded by the numbers of coaches using the glen.

The consultants' report set out a wide range of options, rejecting some of the most radical (such as road closure) and recommending others for further consideration (such as parking charges and restrictions on roadside parking). Other recommendations covered raising visitor awareness, improving visitor facilities, path maintenance and monitoring. However, the key recommendation was the formation of a partnership trust to develop the role of the advisory committee, which would appoint a project officer with a budget to be provided by the public agencies as a means of tackling the issues. The trust would be in a strong position to attract European funding.

The Upper Deeside Access Trust (UDAT) was formed in 1998. Its aims were closely modelled on those suggested in the consultants' report, but it operates more widely on a range of visitor management and access issues across the whole of Upper Deeside, rather than focusing solely on those identified in Glen Muick. This broader model provided a platform that the relevant public bodies could sign up to, namely 'to help maintain and assist public access and enjoyment of the area and promote its sensitive use, by developing and undertaking a strategy for managing access within Upper Deeside which balances recreational use with the natural heritage, land management and other interests' (Upper Deeside Access Trust, 1999, p3).

The aims and agenda of UDAT were developed out of the consultations of the Glen Muick study and brokered through the advisory committee. Given the establishment of a common agenda, the main public agencies and the private landowners were able to put aside any differences and realized the benefits of working in partnership. It was realized that no one agency could tackle the issues on its own, and that a partnership approach would enable them to pool resources, draw in external funding and work together across a range of common policy objectives. The early days of UDAT were certainly helped by the active involvement of key individuals within the public agencies in Aberdeenshire who were used to working together, and the lack of a truly divisive issue, such as ski area development, which has plagued working relationships in other parts of the Cairngorms.

While there were individual concerns about some proposals, most stakeholders were well aware of the problems, understood the issues involved and were happy to support an initiative that would attract new resources and get things done. Once UDAT had appointed its directors and project manager it worked openly with local interests, involving them in the detailed development and implementation of projects. The charitable status of UDAT and its perceived relative independence may also have helped maintain support for its work (Coleman, 2001).

Inclusiveness
The inclusive approach developed by the advisory committee at the outset was continued by offering a wide range of local organizations affiliate membership of UDAT. Membership of the board of UDAT has been limited to the funding partners with an independent chair. The board meets four times a year and is supported by an advisory management group of representative officers from each of the main public agencies, and its project manager and support staff. Some thought has been given to widening representation on the board, but this has presented both technical and practical difficulties. Membership of the board would require an individual to be legally responsible as an executive director of a limited company, which most outside bodies would resist. There is also no simple mechanism for finding a few knowledgeable individuals to genuinely and effectively represent and report back to a wider constituency of interests, without an election process and a more costly briefing and reporting system. The board has thus opted to remain small on the grounds of reducing bureaucracy and costs, and gaining efficiency in decision-making (Coleman, 2004, personal communication). This tendency towards exclusiveness is countered by establishing an affiliate membership and openness in decision-making. Representation within UDAT and its wider membership is shown in Figure 8.14.

The affiliate membership provides both wider representation from land managers, recreation users, the local communities and others in the area, and a degree of accountability, as affiliate members are automatically invited to UDAT's annual general meetings at which there is open discussion of its activities. Representation has been sought wherever possible from individuals who are familiar with local access issues. Where a national body has been invited to join, it has been encouraged to put forward a local member with knowledge of the area. It is hard to judge how accountable representatives are to the organization they represent. 'How effectively they communicate back to their own group depends upon these individuals, and there is no pattern to this' (Coleman, 2001, 45).

Information
UDAT has been particularly effective in communicating with its stakeholders. It has followed the sound practice of explaining the reasons

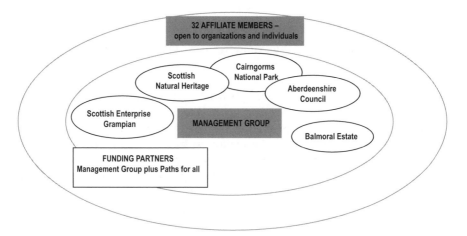

Figure 8.14 *Representation within Upper Deeside Access Trust and Associated Groups 2002*

why it has adopted certain policies, such as car park charges at the Spittal car park and, just as importantly, giving reasons why other policies were not viable.

The good working relationships built up among the UDAT partners and with the affiliate members have allowed the parties to handle uncertainty. Where there were unanswered questions, research has been undertaken either internally by the project manager or externally by independently commissioned studies. The findings of these studies have been used to support decision-making and in some cases wider consultation. One example was the commissioning of an Upland Paths Condition Survey, which was presented at the Ballater workshop in 2001, proving to any sceptical walkers present that there was clear evidence that path repairs were needed, and providing the opportunity to participate in a process to agree what should be done.

Influence

Whilst the wider interests were consulted at the outset, they were not directly involved in negotiations about the management structure. Nevertheless, there has been close cooperation on the detailed implementation of policy and respect for different viewpoints when it came to making difficult decisions. The responsibility for decisions ultimately lies within the UDAT board (four members and an independent chairman). Voting powers have never been exercised, and in practice the board takes advice from the management group and responds openly to public opinion and the views of its affiliate membership. The main agents bring varying resources and influence to the partnership but generally put the interests of UDAT above those of individual agencies (Coleman, 2001).

UDAT has so far developed four main streams of activity, reflecting its interpretation of the above broad aims and in direct response to the recommendations of the Environmental Resources Management/Sidaway study (1997). These are:

1   The development of low-level path networks around settlements and places of interest to improve low ground facilities for visitors to the area.
2   The development and provision of various visitor information and interpretation boards about public access and related matters.
3   Various visitor management activities, notably traffic management to ease congestion at the key access points, visitor monitoring and research and survey work relating to the above activities.
4   A mountain path repair programme to tackle the environmental impacts of path erosion.

By giving initial priority to the first two of these tasks, UDAT was able to build credibility with key constituents: local landowners and the communities of Braemar and Ballater. This showed that UDAT could deliver and was not just a talking shop, and then enabled it to move onto the more complex and potentially controversial tasks with confidence. The visible evidence of projects being implemented helped to raise confidence that the process was working.

The consultative process that began with the establishment of the advisory committee and was continued by the Environmental Resources Management/Sidaway study (1997) led to a series of recommendations that have been gradually put into effect by UDAT. Since then, it has brokered proposals with its wider group of stakeholders via the affiliate membership, the annual meeting and special events such as the participatory workshops on traffic management at Glen Muick in 2000 and upland path management in 2001.

The first of these workshops attracted 45 knowledgeable participants who worked in small groups through the main issues considered in an earlier consultation paper. The groups showed a remarkable degree of consensus on what had been hitherto controversial measures, particularly the introduction of car park charges, which previously had been opposed on principle by the mountaineering community. Participants made it clear that charging was only acceptable if the proceeds were dedicated to upland path repair. UDAT's degree of independence from its sponsors allowed it to give an undertaking that funds would only be used in this way.

It was also agreed that there should be a small extension to the car park with the proviso that no other facilities should be provided. Access should be retained for a limited number of coaches but no agreement was reached on the method of collecting charges or landscaping of the area. The extent of agreement could partly be explained by the advanced circulation of an explanatory consultation paper to a wider audience, and the presentation of these views which helped to clarify UDAT's thinking. This set out the reasons why UDAT favoured some options over others. There was also a feeling that it was time to bite the bullet and take a decision, and relationships had steadily improved.[4]

There are strong feelings in the mountaineering community about path erosion, its causes and remedies.

> *The largest single footpath issue about which we received evidence was erosion, particularly in upland regions. Some eroded paths are extremely unsightly, some were impassable and in a few cases the erosion was spreading outwards over a very wide area. According to the evidence we were given, the causes are complex... We saw various solutions in operation. We regret to say that some of them appear inappropriate or ineffective... In other cases, very substantial physical work has been undertaken which has changed the nature of the path from hillside track to a paved way not unlike an urban footpath. In these cases the cure is worse than the disease.* (House of Commons Environment Committee, 1995, xlii)

This is the context behind the second workshop when, for the first time in Scotland, climbing clubs and mountaineering organizations were invited to set priorities for a programme of upland path restoration, having been provided with survey information on path conditions on Upper Deeside. The exchange of views proved very productive and is guiding UDAT's programme, which has completed 10km of upland and 28km of lowland path restoration to date (Upper Deeside Access Trust, 2003).

The analysis of participation in the UDAT is summarized in Figure 8.15.

Key Points from the Case Study

- The openness of UDAT in its working, as evidenced by representation, affiliate membership, annual meetings and its preparedness to involve stakeholders in the discussion of things that mattered to them (e.g., the workshops on traffic management and footpath restoration).
- The delegation of responsibility for projects to a dedicated team by the partners, notably the landowners who could see the benefits of work being done on their land for which they did not have the resources, project staff or experienced supervision. This started early in the life of UDAT, so that it gained local credibility and has regularly met its annual targets (Upper Deeside Access Trust, 2002; 2003).
- A notable factor has been the presence of team players among the agency representatives who are committed to making the process work.

INITIATION

The need for collaborative management on Upper Deeside was identified by an advisory committee established by the Balmoral Estate. It commissioned a consultative study which identified the major issues of concern to the local and mountaineering communities and recommended the formation of the UDAT.

INCLUSIVENESS

Whilst membership of the trust and its management committees is limited to funding sponsors, the establishment of an open affiliate membership has proved to be an effective way of involving local organizations and individuals. Participatory workshops have been used to engage with particular interest groups on potentially contentious topics.

INFORMATION

The UDAT has taken care to explain the reasoning behind its policy proposals and, in particular, why certain options were not favoured. It communicates regularly through its website, its annual reports and open annual meetings.

INFLUENCE

The sponsoring partners have delegated certain local responsibilities to the trust and funded and supported bids for project funding. The emphasis on programmes of concern to its stakeholders has given considerable credibility to the trust.

Figure 8.15 *Upper Deeside Access Trust – Assessment of Participation in Decision-making*

CONCLUSIONS

The conclusions drawn from these case studies focus on those factors which contribute to effective participation in planning, and consider how these factors apply in the development of partnerships which build trust between agencies and local communities. The case studies illustrate the importance of engaging both agencies with statutory responsibilities and a wide range of interested stakeholders in partnership to achieve sustainable management of natural resources. This usually results in a two-tier structure: a grouping of agencies in steering or management committees and regular events to engage the wider community. The success of such arrangements depends on the credibility of the upper tier and the trust that it develops with other stakeholders from a consistent practice of open governance.

Initiation

While the Texel 2030 project failed to get a number of influential stakeholders involved at the outset, the Morecambe Bay Partnership had the advantage of reaching broad agreement on its purpose through an initial consultation exercise. It subsequently developed a management strategy for the bay which met the issues and concerns identified during early meetings with the local communities. On Upper Deeside, wide consultation led to the formation of UDAT, which gained local credibility by carrying out practical improvements to recreational access within its first year.

Inclusiveness

Both the Morecambe Bay Partnership and UDAT have continued to operate in an inclusive way. This is reflected both in their open governance and in the range of consultations, working parties, workshops and annual conferences or annual meetings which have attracted a broad following of organizations and individuals. This approach has certainly enabled UDAT to reach consensus on proposals that might have provoked conflict a few years earlier. The Morecambe Bay Partnership has engaged major industries in its work and attracts a significant proportion of its funding from them. A proactive participatory approach to preparing the management strategy for the PHRP was successful in broadening the initial base of participation. An opportunity for further community involvement has been provided by the formation of the Friends of the Pentlands Society.

Information

The wide circulation of information during the early consultations, continuing with regular newsletters on topical themes, has been a feature of the successful partnerships. This can be seen in most of the case studies, with good channels of communication being established between members of the partnerships. In the case of Texel, a formal partnership does not exist and informal contacts are the rule.

Influence

Whether a partnership has influence and progresses towards its targets depends largely on the degree of commitment of the decision-making bodies, which takes various forms depending on the role that the partnership performs. At Morecambe Bay, the commitment to community involvement over a ten-year period has enabled national agencies and local government to develop a programme of ICZM with community support. In Upper Deeside, the partners have delegated clear responsibility to a project team, which has been of particular benefit to the landowners who lacked the resources, project staff and experienced supervision to undertake this work. The longer-term legacy of Texel 2030 has been a continuing debate of many of the issues it identified within a range of local fora. As a result, several practical projects on sustainable living are being developed by the Foundation for Sustainable Texel. The Foundation ensures that all stakeholders have the opportunity to contribute to project development. In the PHRP, the formal partnership is limited to the local authorities and a government agency, but most project work is undertaken on private land with the agreement of the landowners. Reflecting on the effectiveness of independent partnerships with charitable status and their success in attracting funding from a wide range of sources, serious thought should be given to establishing such a body for the Pentland Hills.

Commitment and Trust

Partnerships depend heavily on the effort and commitment of the people involved and continuity in both project teams and the representatives of organizations. Such commitment and continuity and the willingness to delegate are crucial to the development of trust between partners and with local communities. This can be seen in the Morecambe Bay Partnership, with its staff continuity and the long-term involvement of many representatives of the partners. The case of UDAT is similar; the commitment of team players among the agency representatives ensures the partnership works, and the agencies have had the confidence to delegate some of their local responsibilities to UDAT. Staff continuity has been more difficult to sustain in the PHRP. Nevertheless, the commitment of the local authorities to the regional park has been maintained in the face of a critical political environment. Thus the development of successful partnerships is dependent in large measure on the prevailing political climate. The Texel case illustrates the reluctance or inability of local political decision-makers to enter into long-term commitments. In part this stems from the short-term nature of politics and the constraints of the electoral cycle. Commitments entered into by one party may not be recognized by its successors. The insights these case studies provide into power and politics pave the way for the following section of this book, which considers consensus, power and the political process.

Part 3

The Realities of Power

Chapter 9

Organizations, Power and Conflict

There is a certain tendency among humans to identify power with the capacity for victory, that is, overcoming some other person, will or institution (Boulding, 1990, 16)

SYNOPSIS

This chapter reviews the relationships between government, organizations and people and relates these to the earlier themes of negotiation, conflict resolution, participation and empowerment, and then examines the power relationships of organizations. This chapter also traces the contribution of power in triggering conflict and its role in conflict resolution. It elaborates on the proposition presented in earlier chapters, based on social action theory, that the distribution of power determines the outcome of conflict. Thus changes towards more participatory decision-making do not in themselves produce fair and just outcomes. The relationships in some of the earlier case studies will be reviewed using the tools of power analysis before two additional case studies are presented, illustrating the impact of state intervention and the consequences in terms of the balance of power.

POWER AND CONFLICT

Power has been a continuing theme throughout the earlier parts of this book, arguably starting with the definition of environmental and public policy conflicts given in Chapter 1. Indeed, this definition was qualified thus: 'typically, one group is attempting to control the action of others and limit their access to a natural resource,' i.e., exercise power over competing interest groups. The context of such conflicts includes social and political change arising from competing and changing values and the belief of each participant that they alone truly represent the public interest. In Chapter 3, conflicts were typified by the adversarial approach taken by the parties, who were out to win at almost all costs, used information as power and had little direct contact with their opponents. The contrasting situation of cooperation was all about building relationships based on trust by respecting differences and being prepared to set aside power differentials and share resources, notwithstanding any initial differences in positions or values.

Stakeholder analysis is frequently used as a diagnostic tool by mediators and others, who define stakeholders in terms of the types of power they hold. For example, stakeholders have an interest in what happens, can bring about, influence or stop change, and will be affected by the outcome. Alternatively, they may be recognized by the skills, money or resources they can contribute and whether they ultimately decide what happens (Wilcox, 1994).

Chapter 3 also drew on Weber's social action theory, which highlighted the fundamental role of power in society and observed that power was unevenly distributed, that the social structure represented the interests of the powerful and that they opposed change. Whilst the powerful seek to convince others that their use of power is legitimate, individuals seek power to pursue their self-interest (Weber, 1948). Thus the active phase of conflict is frequently portrayed as a power struggle, whose outcome is determined by the balance of power between the competing interests and the prevailing form of decision-making (Coser, 1956). In observing conflicts between groups, Coser contrasted 'flexible' social structures, which allowed adjustments in the balance of power through multiple small conflicts, with 'rigid' social structures, where conflict was suppressed with a high risk of subsequent catastrophe.

Chapter 4 contrasted adversarial and consensual forms of decision-making, which displayed similar features to the earlier analysis of conflict and cooperation. Compared to many conventional types of decision-making, such as voting (which relies on the exercise of power by the majority), building consensus depends upon sharing power. Where consensual approaches work within a formal decision-making structure, a key factor is the delegation of authority by the ultimate decision-makers or acceptance that the deliberations of the groups (or community) will have real influence. Failure to recognize this as a prerequisite of genuine public involvement frequently leads to community disillusion with consultation exercises (Chapter 7).

Mediation was seen to be one form of dispute resolution that attempted to reconcile underlying interests, rather than depended on adversarial process and the exercise of power (Chapter 5). Nevertheless, power is an important consideration in determining when mediation is likely to be effective. For example, such mediated negotiations may be prompted by such factors as external pressure on the opposing parties to settle, the fact that other means of dispute resolution have been tried but resulted in stalemate, and whether each party has some leverage. Part of the mediator's initial assessment will consider whether there are adequate safeguards against manipulation of the weak by the powerful. Indeed, the mediator's dilemma is whether he or she could or should attempt to balance power during the negotiations. One school of thought argues that the role of the mediator is to assist the weak and thereby help to deliver justice by controlling the process. The alternative line of argument is that the mediator's role should be truly neutral, that negotiation implies power sharing, that the powerless gain influence during the process of negotiation and only the parties can decide what constitutes an acceptable agreement.

Power is an important theme throughout the participation and development literature. It is explicit in the definitions of participation (given in Chapter 7), whether phrased in radical re-distributive terms ('the redistribution of power that enables the have-not citizens ... to be deliberately included in future'; Arnstein, 1969, 71–72) or more cautious managerial ones ('a process through which stakeholders influence and share control over development decisions'; World Bank, 1996, xi). But the commitment of the World Bank to participatory development has also been questioned in a critical review of this field. Too often, the authors claim, development agencies are preoccupied with satisfying their financial sponsors at the risk of not understanding the power structures within local communities, to the detriment of the powerless (Cooke and Kothari, 2001).

Agency commitment to participation may be no more than empty rhetoric hindered by the competition between agencies, which are sometimes forced to work in partnership. In these circumstances, it is perhaps unsurprising that agencies are unwilling to clarify the basis or purposes of their cooperation and that the partners are unwilling to delegate authority. Hence the observation that organizational behaviour is too often determined by internal preoccupations with individual needs, rivalries and risk aversion (Brown, 1993).

Lack of trust between decision-making agencies and the communities they serve was a continuing theme throughout Chapter 7. Indeed, powerful decision-makers may be just as ambivalent about working in partnership with other organizations as they were about public involvement in decision-making. The problems of commitment, apathy and mistrust were seen to be basically political and hinged on the distribution and use of power.

> *Perhaps there is also an underlying concern that increased public participation will result in a reduction of power and prestige for the planner, administrator or the politician.* (Sewell and Coppock, 1977, 6)

To fully understand this response, it is important to understand the perspective of the office bearers and the constraints under which they operate. Indeed, many chose to work in the public service as a way of furthering the public interest and contributing to society.

> *Agency missions embody values – packages of views on how the world ought to be [which service] some segment of society's values.* (Delli Priscoli, 1980, 12)

Constitutionally, they are accountable to their political masters to execute a limited set of activities; to operate outside this remit would be *ultra vires* and this is not always appreciated by pressure groups. The power of office carries with it *authority* (the ability to exercise delegated power), but it also confers *responsibility* (the ability to take rational decisions without supervision). It is this latter aspect – the ability to act without supervision – that gives job satisfaction, yet may lead to the arrogance of power and the neglect or avoidance of accountability. These characteristics of office combined with conflicting mandates, political pressures to deliver and the limited accountability of government agencies make them reluctant to negotiate with local communities or enter into genuine partnerships. Those seeking influence (or power without responsibility) may challenge officialdom and be seen as a threat to its authority. Thus it seems that organizational culture tends to view participation and mediation as threatening, with the risk of loss of control.

Organizations respond to challenges to power in a number of ways, notably by excluding or incorporating challengers to compromise their effectiveness and suppress conflict (Weber, 1948; Van Til and Van Til, 1970). Once inside the circle, subtle pressures can be applied. Organizational tactics within planning organizations were studied by Forester (1989), who demonstrated that organizational culture uses its power to manage decision-making by managing representation (e.g., excluding dissenters from committees), information (thereby dictating the comprehension of problems) and consent (by controlling how decisions were made). Classically, organizations are concerned with economy, efficiency, performance and productivity, so that conflict may be seen as an error to be corrected. From this perspective, the resolution of conflict must be speedy; yet, as demonstrated in Chapter 3, conflicts are complex and speedy resolution may be neither feasible nor desirable.

The Influence of Decision-making and the Paradox of Power

The analysis in Chapter 3 suggested that local environmental conflicts have to be seen within a broader perspective of social change. From this perspective, the nature and causes of environmental conflict are partly explained by understanding the role of conflict in mediating change, and partly by seeing it as a dynamic process passing through a series of phases which are liable to continue in a repeating pattern. The distribution and control of resources between the competing interests is central to environmental conflicts, and the allocation process is important to the interest groups because it confers power. In Chapter 3, a dynamic framework was used to set out in schematic form the inter-relationships between the competing parties. This helped to explain why groups acted and responded as they did to the action of others during a conflict episode. The tactics of the competing parties, the balance of power between them and the form of decision-making was seen to influence the outcome of the episode.

Identifying and measuring changes in the balance of power between the parties appears to be the key to predicting the outcomes of conflict, and herein lies what Coser (1956) called the 'paradox of power'. He examined the proposition that conflict establishes and maintains the balance of power:

> *The paradox derives from the fact that conflicts, as distinct from other forms of interaction, always involve power and that it is difficult to appraise the relative power of the contenders before a conflict has settled the issue ... it would seem that without actual exercise [of power], only some types of power can be measured with any degree of accuracy.* (Coser, 1956, 134–135)

He gave as an example financial power, which may be measurable in terms of money, but concludes by reformulating the proposition in the following way:

> *Conflict consists in a test of power between antagonistic parties. Accommodation between them is possible only if each is aware of the relative strength of both parties. However, paradoxical as it may seem, such knowledge can most frequently be attained only through conflict, since other mechanisms for testing the respective strength of antagonists may be unavailable.* (Coser, 1956, 135)

Ideology may be used to advance arguments of principle and thus to improve the legitimacy and social standing of interest groups, since legitimacy is the key to increased power. Political organization and lobbying in the corridors of power are therefore of critical importance to interest groups in their attempts to influence the balance of power in their favour. To further increase their power, such groups may build coalitions with other interest groups or may seek national affiliations. Coser further suggests that it is the combination of ideological cohesiveness within a close-knit group and the group's political organization that makes a highly politicized and politically effective force. This suggests the possibility that politicization and group cohesion might be used as proxy measures for power in an attempt to predict the outcome of a conflict.

Synthesis: Decision-making and Disparities of Power

Coser's theory of the social function of conflict also suggests how social institutions develop to deal with change; once again, legitimacy is a key concept. Both the constitution of the institution and the decisions it makes are only accepted within society when they are seen to be legitimate. Reference has been made to that part of Coser's analysis which suggested that it is the rigidity or flexibility of decision-making structures which influences the outcome of a dispute (see p194). Within a rigid social structure, established groups exercise power to maintain the status quo. Power is only transferred to a challenging group after a power struggle. Within a flexible social structure, the outcome of a power struggle might be a concession by established groups following negotiations which could also produce a new order based on consensus and a degree of power sharing.

Chapter 4 examined participatory decision-making, and the preconditions of initiation, involvement, information and influence for reaching consensus were set out in Figure 4.4. This framework has been used to examine decision-making in the case studies presented in subsequent chapters of this book. There are clearly parallels between Coser's concepts of rigidity and flexibility and the adversarial and participatory processes of decision-making, albeit that Coser was describing the total system of decision-making in society rather than the more local situations in these case studies.

Accepting the arguments about the centrality of power, any further analysis needs to consider the influence of both decision-making and the distribution of power on the outcome of a (potential) dispute. By treating disparities in power and decision-making as independent dimensions, it is possible to represent the outcomes of (potential) disputes in one diagram. In Figure 9.1, the extent to which decision-making is participatory is set on the vertical axis. In any given situation this can be approximated using the preconditions of participatory decision-making. As power cannot be measured in absolute terms, it is assessed relatively. The horizontal axis conveys the power relationships between the interest groups, using politicization and group cohesion as proxy measures to assess, not the absolute level, but the relative balance of power; whether there is parity or disparity of power between the parties.

This diagram contrasts the following alternatives:

- disparity of power with a non-participatory (adversarial) system of decision-making (south-west quadrant);
- disparity of power with a participatory system of decision-making (north-west quadrant);
- parity of power with a non-participatory (adversarial) system of decision-making (south-east quadrant); and
- parity of power with a participatory system of decision-making (north-east quadrant). In this situation, negotiation and participation allow the parties to cooperate.

Arguably, all outcomes on the right-hand side of the diagram (north-east and south-east quadrants) are stable as long as the parity of power between the parties is maintained, while outcomes on the left-hand side of the diagram are potentially unstable, because of the disparities of power. Thus conflict resolution is only achieved within a participatory form of decision-making and depends on the maintenance of the balance of power.

In the south-west quadrant of Figure 9.1, disparity allows the powerful to exercise or consolidate their power, and they are assisted by the

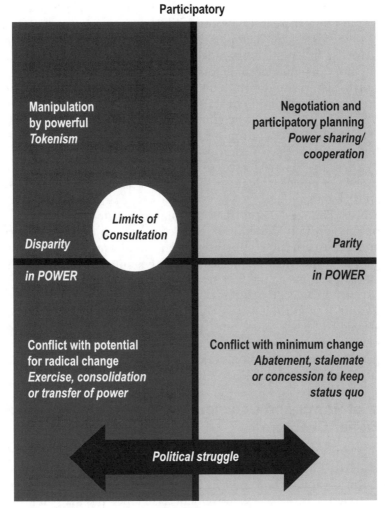

Participatory

Manipulation
by powerful
Tokenism

Negotiation and
participatory planning
*Power sharing/
cooperation*

*Limits of
Consultation*

Disparity

Parity

in POWER

in POWER

Conflict with potential
for radical change
*Exercise, consolidation
or transfer of power*

Conflict with minimum change
*Abatement, stalemate
or concession to keep
status quo*

Political struggle

Non-participatory

Source: based on Sidaway, 1996.

Figure 9.1 *Power and Decision making*

adversarial non-participatory system of decision-making. But the injustices resulting from the disparity of power mean that, eventually, opposing groups will emerge and there is the potential for radical change through the transfer of power. During the course of the power struggle, disparities in power may be reduced and the conflict moves towards the south-eastern quadrant. Concessions may be made to maintain the status quo, the conflict may subside (abatement), or stalemate may be reached, and the conflict remains in the south-eastern quadrant.

At the point of stalemate, the prospect of negotiating becomes more attractive, and thus there is an opportunity to change the system of decision-making. If this is taken, it is possible to collaborate. Thus, with power balanced (or the differential suspended) the options of mediated negotiations or participatory planning become feasible. Conflict gives way to cooperation in the north-eastern quadrant. This sequence of events lends support to Amy's argument that a period of stalemate is necessary before negotiation is feasible. In his words, 'Only when the politics of power have been exhausted can the politics of co-operation become a viable possibility' (Amy, 1987, 92). This diagnosis that mediation or negotiation only become viable options when the parties have reached a state of mutual frustration following a long power struggle appears to be borne out by the case studies later in this chapter.

However, changes in the decision-making system to make it more participatory without the equalization of power allow the powerful to manipulate the situation (north-western quadrant), as they are not committed to respond to the needs and wishes of other participants. The powerful may see this as the best strategy for maintaining their power, but the injustice perceived by the powerless may act as a stimulus for their politicization. It is in these situations that consultative planning exercises are perceived to be tokenistic and, as was suggested in Chapter 4, one of Amy's (1987) criticisms of environmental mediation – that it (or any other participatory form of decision-making) might be used to advantage by powerful economic interests – becomes valid.

Review of Power and Decision-making in the Case Studies from Earlier Chapters

Successive episodes of the long-standing conflict over access to the countryside in England and Wales and attempts at its resolution were described in Chapters 2, 3 and 5. There have been successive phases of political struggles as the access movement has gained popular support. Each attempt to obtain access legislation has depended on the Labour Party gaining political power. While there have been parliamentary majorities for legislation in 1939, 1949–1951 and from 1997 to the current date (2005), the final form it has taken has failed to deliver the outcome sought by the access lobby because it could not match the political clout of the landowners in the House of Lords. Attempts at negotiated solutions have been of only local significance and have not set a precedent for a legislative solution at the national level. Nevertheless, the negotiations in the Peak District National Park have been successful at reaching consensus solutions, initially through the Access Consultative Group in 1993 and more recently concerning the management of the Stanage Estate, owned by the National Park Authority. These shifts in power and modifications in decision-making are plotted in Figure 9.2. A rather different course of events has occurred in Scotland, and this is described in Chapter 10.

DECISION-MAKING

Participatory

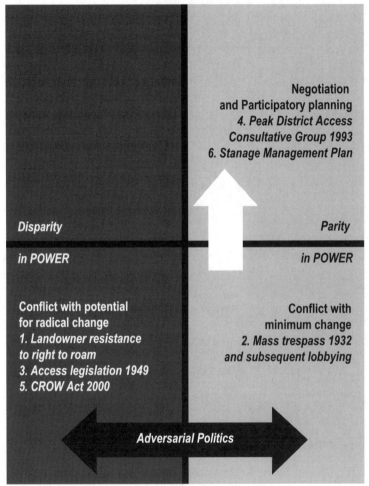

Negotiation
and Participatory planning
4. Peak District Access
Consultative Group 1993
6. Stanage Management Plan

Disparity

Parity

in POWER

in POWER

Conflict with potential
for radical change
*1. Landowner resistance
to right to roam
3. Access legislation 1949
5. CROW Act 2000*

Conflict with
minimum change
*2. Mass trespass 1932
and subsequent lobbying*

Adversarial Politics

Non-participatory

Figure **9.2** *Changes in Power and Decision-making: Access in England and Wales*

The economic power of the pulp mill owners in Rumford, Maine was sufficient to resist investigation of local concerns about the incidence of cancer until a campaign by activists questioned the integrity of the regulatory authorities (see Chapter 6). Forced to intervene, the Environmental Protection Agency (EPA) and the Maine Department of Environmental Protection (DEP) sponsored the mediated negotiations of North Oxford County Coalition (NOCC). Thus the power of the mill had

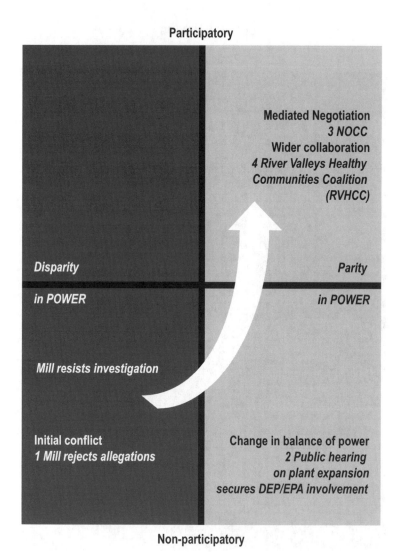

Figure 9.3 *Changes in Power and Decision-making: NOCC*

been matched by the environmental agencies and the adversarial conflict was replaced by collaboration between local interests. This sequence of events is charted in Figure 9.3.

A somewhat similar series of events can be traced in Texel (described in detail in Chapter 8), where the traditional source of power, in this case the farming community, has been challenged by the instigation of a collaborative planning exercise (Texel 2030). The shifts in the power and form of decision-making can be seen in Figure 9.4, which also recognizes that the latest policy for recreation and tourism, initiated by the municipality, was based on consultation not participation.

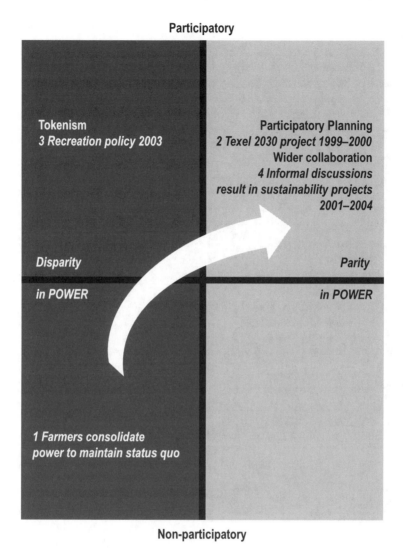

Figure 9.4 *Changes in Power and Decision-making: Texel*

Overt power struggles have played a lesser role in the history of the Pentland Hills Regional Park (PHRP), covered in Chapters 2, 3 and 8. While the intervention of the Lothian Regional Council (LRC) provoked the conflict over designation, the power of the local landowners resulted in modifications to the park boundary. Central government, in the form of the Scottish Office, arbitrated in 1983, not between the interests in the conflict but on the appropriateness of the area for regional park status. This judgement left the farming community with a sense of injustice which has persisted to the present day, largely because the park authority is not funded

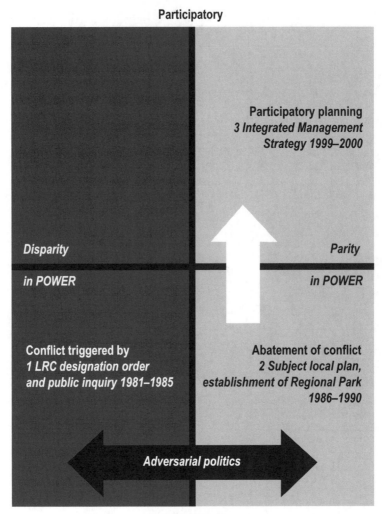

Figure 9.5 *Changes in Power and Decision-making:*
Pentland Hills Regional Park

to ameliorate the effects of public recreation on the farm economy. A more recent attempt to develop a collaborative plan resulted in a management strategy, but the local authorities have yet to develop a strong partnership with the local communities. These events are set out in Figure 9.5.

One of the lessons from the Pentlands was that conflict may be triggered by the actions of competing government agencies as they strive to develop and implement an aspect of public policy within their mandate. Their interventions can alter the balance of power considerably. Two further case studies are presented here to illustrate these processes.

CASE STUDY 1: The Designation of the Skomer Marine Nature Reserve[1]

Skomer is the largest of a complex of islands which lies off the coast of Pembrokeshire. It covers nearly 300ha, including its off-shore rocks. It has a fairly flat plateau rising to 75m, with a series of rock outcrops that forms ridges running east to west, and a striking feature in the narrow isthmus, only 4m wide, which connects the main part of the island to the 'Neck'. The climate is extremely mild and the annual rainfall is little more than 75cm. The wildlife interest and literary associations, particularly the works of R. M. Lockley who lived on, observed and wrote vividly about the neighbouring island of Skokholm in the 1940s (Lockley, 1947), make the islands of West Wales something of a shrine to naturalists. They began to visit the island to observe its birdlife in the early 1900s. Scientific interest grew, and in 1946 the West Wales Field Society made a detailed biological survey. The site of special scientific interest (SSSI) was first formally notified in 1954. In 1959, the island was acquired as a national nature reserve (NNR) by the then Nature Conservancy (NC), with help from the West Wales Naturalists' Trust. The Trust managed the reserve on behalf of the NC, having a warden in residence from March to October, and operating a daily boat service for visitors during the summer months. The islands lie within the Pembrokeshire Coast National Park. Further protection was given to the NNR by its designation in August 1982 as a Special Protection Area under the terms of the European Community Directive 70/409/EEC on the Conservation of Wild Birds. The sequence of events which led to the designation of a statutory marine nature reserve (MNR) are set out in the following sections and summarized in Figure 9.6.

The accessibility of the island, the often clear water during summer months, the spectacular underwater scenery and marine life, and the wreck of a Dutch freighter (the *Lucy*) make the waters of the Skomer particularly attractive to divers. The numbers of divers visiting Skomer increased considerably during the 1980s. In 1987, it was estimated that 1264 divers (118 groups) made 2727 'diver visits' between 21 March and 20 September. Nearly half of the dives around Skomer were made to the wreck of the *Lucy*; there have been occasions when as many as 20 diving boats were around the wreck at the same time (Bullimore, 1987, 14).

The Voluntary Marine Reserve

The idea of a marine reserve was first proposed in 1971 by local naturalists and biologists. In 1974 a steering committee was set up representing the following bodies: the British Sub-Aqua Club (BSAC), the Field Studies Council, the Nature Conservancy Council (NCC), the Pembrokeshire Coast National Park Authority, the South Wales Sea Fisheries Committee, the Welsh Association of Sub-Aqua Clubs and the West Wales Naturalists'

Early 1900s	Initial interest shown in island by ornithologists
1944	Detailed biological survey by West Wales Field Society
1954	Island notified as SSSI by NC
1959	Island acquired as NNR by NC and West Wales Naturalists' Trust
1971	Local proposal for marine reserve
1974	Steering committee for marine reserve established
1976	Management plan for marine reserve prepared and management committee formed
1981	Wildlife and Countryside Act provided powers to designate MNRs
1982	Skomer designated as a Special Protection Area for wild birds
1986	Nature Conservancy Council (NCC) circulated proposals for MNR in draft consultation document
1987	Appointment of liaison officer for MNR, first collation of data on diving and potential disturbance
	Secretary of State for Wales requires NCC to undertake further consultations after representations from British Sub-Aqua Club (BSAC) and Sports Council for Wales on proposed by-laws
1989	Revised consultation document accepted by Secretary of State
1990	Designation of MNR confirmed by Secretary of State
1991	First meeting of advisory committee to MNR. Marine conservation officer for MNR appointed
1993	Agreed management policy issued by Countryside Council for Wales

Source: Sidaway, 1996

Figure 9.6 *Historical Summary of Skomer Marine Nature Reserve*

Trust. The steering committee published a management plan in August 1976, and this was followed by the formation of a management committee. As well as those bodies represented on the steering committee, membership was extended to include representatives from the local communities, anglers, boat owners, harbour users and the water authority (see Figure 9.7).

The functions of the committee were:

- *to co-ordinate the implementation of the management plan by the users;*
- *to promote and, to a limited extent, implement the management plan;*
- *to provide a forum for the discussion of relevant subjects as they arise, including the revision of the management plan as necessary;*
- *to seek finance to implement the management plan, largely on behalf of the users;*
- *to seek legislation where appropriate.* (Skomer Marine Reserve Steering Committee, 1976, 12)

The voluntary reserve covered the seabed around Skomer Island, Middleholm and the Marloes Peninsular. It extended from the level of mean

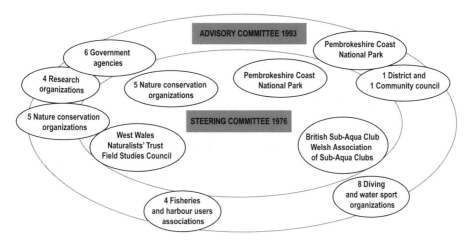

Source: Sidaway, 1988; Countryside Council for Wales, 1993.

Figure 9.7 *Representation on the Management Committees for the Marine Reserve at Skomer*

low water at ordinary tide to 0.5km off-shore, with a straight line from High Point to Gateholm Stack forming the eastern boundary. It enclosed a sea surface area of about 1000ha.

Proposals for a Statutory Reserve

Some ten years after the establishment of the voluntary reserve and armed with the new powers granted by the 1981 act, the NCC made the first move towards the designation of a statutory MNR for Skomer. The NCC was keen that this process should pass smoothly, its successful conclusion being a valuable precedent to be applied elsewhere.

A proposal was also being developed for the island of Lundy in the Bristol Channel, and there was some internal rivalry over which order would be confirmed first. Both cases had the advantage of being based on voluntary reserves of over ten years' standing. The Skomer proposals were closely modelled on the 1976 management plan and the voluntary code of practice that had been agreed and publicized by the management committee, and appeared to be well observed. The management plan included conduct guidelines which had been publicized in a number of ways. A brief *Divers' Guide* had been published which gave information on conservation and the suggested code of behaviour, as well as details of tides and currents around the island and useful advice on safety. The NCC had published a leaflet giving details of areas in which the voluntary restrictions applied, while the national park published a waterproof version of this information.

In July 1986, the NCC circulated its draft proposals in the form of a consultation document. The scientific evidence was presented in a separate annex. These documents attempted to address the issues that had been identified in the management plan and had been subsequently deliberated by the management committee. The seaward boundaries of the reserve were extended slightly to the north and south, but the major proposals which attracted much controversy were contained in the draft by-laws included in the consultation document. The proposed introduction of legally enforceable by-laws raised an important matter of principle. Entering certain areas at certain times would now require the written permission of the NCC instead of the previous voluntary code of practice. In particular, the BSAC took a stand on grounds of principle, although most of its arguments focused on the detail of the proposed by-laws. These were concerned with disturbance to nesting seabird colonies and seals during their breeding seasons, underwater damage and fishing (see Box 9.1).

This diving issue received so much attention that it aroused the suspicion that the object of the proposed MNR designation might be to enhance the status of the island for the nesting seabird colonies. The essence of the legislation is concerned with the environment below water, and not the adjacent land. Furthermore, the 1981 act precluded the NCC from making by-laws to control activities which were within the jurisdiction of other statutory authorities. The NCC was keen to secure the acceptance of the statutory reserve by the local communities, and was bound under Section 37 of the Countryside Act of 1968 to 'pay due regard to the economic and social interests of rural areas'. But in-shore fishing was regulated by the South Wales Sea Fisheries Committee, and the NCC, which was not represented on this committee, could only request that controls on in-shore fishing be made where there was good evidence that this was having a deleterious effect on the marine reserve.

Communication and Future Management

The impression created by the consultation document was of discrimination against divers. The majority of examples given to justify restrictions involved diving, although divers were not the only recreational users of the waters around Skomer. The area had become increasingly popular with canoeists, and their activities close to the cliffs could be equally disturbing to seabirds. Furthermore, in-shore fishing would not be affected by the proposed by-laws.

As a result, the proposed by-laws attracted a spirited response from the BSAC, which initially claimed that they affected 60 per cent of the area used for diving (British Sub-Aqua Club, 1986). The BSAC also suggested that a blanket speed limit of 8 knots should be adequate to reduce any 'frightening behaviour'. Divers considered that they had been singled out for restriction without justification, as another proposed by-law exempted fishing boats from the proposed exclusion zones. The Sports Council for Wales supported the divers' arguments and, like them, questioned the evidence presented by the NCC which purported to show the harmful effects of disturbance over

BOX 9.1 THE ISSUES IN CONTENTION

The impacts of disturbance to nesting seabird colonies and seals during their breeding season

The causes of the concern about nesting seabirds were occasional observations by reserve wardens of fast-moving boats, usually thought to be divers' support vessels, coming in too closely to the sea-cliffs. This had the effect of startling the nesting auks (razorbills and guillemots) so that eggs were dislodged and fell from the narrow rock ledges, or predatory gulls moved in to rob eggs or chicks. Similarly, boats moving in too closely to the sheltered coves on the southern coast of the island might cause parent seals to abandon their pups. This latter form of disturbance is thought to be particularly disruptive to the formation of a mother–pup bond. To mitigate these effects, the voluntary code had requested that all boats keep at least 100m out to sea when in the vicinity of the bird colonies or the seal breeding areas, during March to July and September to October respectively.

The proposed by-laws had been modelled on the voluntary code but were more specific. To protect the auks, five zones were prescribed around the island, and to protect the seals, two coves on the mainland peninsular and three areas around the island were identified as 'haul-out and pupping sites' (see Figure 9.8). Entry into or movement within these areas was prohibited unless written permission had been received from the NCC. These restrictions were to apply from 1 March to 31 July for the seabird colonies and 1 September to 28 February for the seal sites. The general speed limit of 8 knots was to apply between 1 March and 15 November throughout the reserve, while a restriction on boat movement and mooring was to apply for an area within North Haven to protect an unusual eelgrass (Zostera) bed.

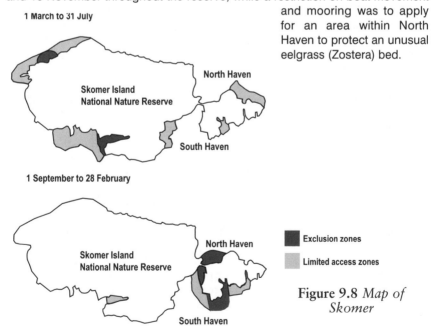

Figure 9.8 *Map of Skomer*

Underwater damage

The NCC was successful in demonstrating the need to control scallop dredging within the reserve. Although not well-documented at the time, it was widely suggested that divers had taken large numbers of scallops around Skomer in the early 1970s. Concerned about the effects of commercial dredging, whereby a large metal harrow was dragged across the seabed, the NCC organized a demonstration of the technique in 1985. The resulting video gave evidence of widespread and indiscriminate damage and this evidence was sufficient to persuade the South Wales Sea Fisheries Committee to prepare a by-law prohibiting this activity within the reserve. However, it horrified some marine conservationists that the NCC could contemplate such a destructive operation within a reserve, albeit on a trial basis.

Meanwhile, divers were explicitly prohibited from taking sea fish or shell fish under a proposed NCC by-law. As sea angling was to be exempt from this restriction, the divers felt they were being unfairly singled out yet again. To make matters worse, the NCC had considered, but rejected, proposals to ban the use of tangle nets or the virtually invisible filamentous gill nets, which imperil the safety of divers but were not used at Skomer. Spear fishing was to be totally prohibited and as it had not been observed at Skomer since the 1970s, the divers' organizations described this proposal as a ban on non-existent activity. Although it could equally be argued that this was the continuity of a restriction that had been widely agreed under the voluntary code, it added fuel to the debate.

Collecting marine organisms had been restricted by the voluntary code. Divers were asked to replace rather than invert boulders, to photograph rather than collect specimens and to restrict any collection to single specimens of moving species (e.g., sea urchins) while taking none of the sedentary animals (e.g., corals and sea-fans). Later editions of the code suggested that nothing should be taken. This was because more information was becoming available from underwater monitoring which revealed that, for example, sea-fans grow at the rate of approximately 3mm per year, which would make some specimens 50–100 years old. Many of the corals are particularly attractive and tempting to collectors, but are extremely fragile and rarely survive being taken out of the water. With little known about the rates of recovery and re-colonization, the NCC opted for a ban on collection without its written permission.

There was also mounting concern about accidental damage to fragile organisms. When underwater and wearing a mask, a diver's vision is very restricted. He or she may be unaware that flipper movements have damaged sensitive sea creatures if he or she is concentrating on observing some particular feature ahead. The term 'trampling' was used in the consultative document and proved to be a particularly unfortunate choice of word. In ecological circles it has accepted connotations, usually relating to the wear and tear on vegetation from trampling feet. It was intended that the term might cover a range of underwater activities, such as the release of air and its formation of pockets in under-hanging cliffs or within wrecks, which can also have harmful effects on sea creatures. The use of the term probably suggested to recreational divers that they lacked skill and agility, and it provoked an emotional response.

the years. While no one argued that the seabirds and the seals had not been disturbed occasionally, there was no evidence to show that these sporadic events had any long-term effects on the breeding success of the colonies. There was also the complicated legal argument about whether the seabirds and their colonies could be held to be part of the marine reserve and covered by the legislation.

The divers were not alone in detecting discrimination. They gained support from the marine biologists undertaking research in the area and from the Marine Conservation Society. The scientists were sceptical about the arguments for sustaining traditional local fishing when they knew that most of the lobster pots around Skomer were being set by newcomers to the trade who sited their pots quite irresponsibly. With the evidence on disturbance and damage being open to interpretation, and conservationists being seen to be in disagreement about the approach to be taken, the good relations between conservationists and divers were seriously undermined. An atmosphere of mistrust was created so that other aspects of the proposals were seen in a different light.

In the NCC's proposals, the role of the management committee was to change. Although the management powers of the voluntary reserve committee were virtually non-existent, particularly as it had no funds at its disposal, its autonomy under an independent chairman was valued. Under the proposals, the NCC would manage the reserve (as it was bound to under the provisions of the 1981 Act) and the committee, to be chaired by an officer of the NCC, would be relegated to an advisory role.

The transition from voluntary to statutory scheme was questioned. It was suggested that as a voluntary scheme had worked reasonably well for ten years, the NCC should be content to leave it at that. Weaknesses in the voluntary code were glossed over in the debate and although public references were made to occasional irresponsible behaviour, it was suggested that divers frequently entered the restricted areas knowing that they could not be detected. One major advantage of the statutory reserve, that its management could be adequately funded by the NCC, was overlooked.

Underlying all of this was the basic clash of principles, notably on the proposed change from a voluntary code to enforced regulation, as the NCC was now seeking enforceable powers to license and control access underwater. The BSAC clearly saw this as a stand of principle, and the proposals ran contrary to its ideology that divers can go when and where they like underwater: '...the very idea of citizens being required to obtain written permission to enter the waters surrounding the United Kingdom is objectionable' (British Sub-Aqua Club, 1987).

As in many other sports, the enforcement of codes of conduct was not universally popular. But with the principle of 'controlled access' becoming more widely accepted in sporting and recreational circles, it would be appropriate if the onus to self-regulate their membership were to be placed on diving organizations. In other situations in South Wales (e.g., caving), the NCC had been prepared to delegate the responsibility for operating a permit system to the user body. It would have been preferable if this degree of active involvement of the diving clubs in management had been part of the original proposals.

Indeed, when the powers to establish MNRs were discussed during the parliamentary debate of the Wildlife and Countryside Bill, the then Secretary of State made it clear that cooperation among all interests was essential.

> *We are anxious to see that such a marine nature reserve goes forward with the widest possible support. It will not work if it does not. For all the by-laws there may be, if people are determined to defeat and frustrate such a scheme, it will not work. It will depend on the agreement of all the bodies concerned. There will not be any fishing by-laws unless the sea fisheries committee decides to make them. That is what we mean by the consent of all the bodies concerned ... If this provision is to succeed, it will need a large measure of good will.* (Hansard, 13 July 1981, 937)

These were prophetic words, and the anomalies created by the ability of separate powers to make by-laws were highlighted in the Skomer case. In its desire to carry the sea fishery interests, the NCC created the impression of discriminating against divers. Inadvertently the NCC lost much of the advantage gained during the ten years of the voluntary reserve. It was difficult to determine just how and why communication broke down. It may well be that the NCC did not anticipate the BSAC's stand on principle, presumably unaware that the BSAC had been recently involved in successful parliamentary negotiations to amend the Military Remains Bill, which had originally proposed a blanket restriction on divers' access to a vast number of wrecks.

However, not all the failures of communication lay within the NCC. While a good rapport was established in the Skomer Voluntary Marine Reserve Management Committee over the years, it may be that representatives of the diving organizations either failed to represent national views or did not fully report on the policies being developed in the management committee. What also seemed doubtful was whether the BSAC could maintain the principle of resisting controlled access under increasing pressure from conservation-minded divers that they should be pioneering the management of underwater access.

In April 1988, the Secretary of State for Wales requested that the NCC undertake further consultations to resolve objections to the proposals. Subsequent discussions took place with the World Wide Fund for Nature, the Marine Conservation Society, the Sports Council for Wales, the BSAC and the Royal Yachting Association. These resulted in the proposals for exclusion zones enforced by by-laws around the reserve to be deferred in favour of voluntary agreements for a trial period. The designation of an MNR was confirmed by the Secretary of State in 1990, and an advisory committee was formed in the following year by the successor agency the

Countryside Council for Wales, with an enlarged membership to include a wide range of stakeholders (see Figure 9.7).

The employment of a liaison officer (who crucially was a diver) in the summer of 1987 helped to secure a better understanding among divers and other water users of the proposals for the statutory marine reserve and the underlying conservation issues, and led to a permanent appointment of a marine conservation officer.

Assessment of Participation in Decision-making

The operations of the voluntary reserve and the proposals for a statutory reserve are assessed in Figure 9.9. Both of the contending parties, the nature conservationists and the divers, proved to be well organized, and their tactics during the course of the dispute were confrontational. Information became a major element of the dispute. Its coverage was uneven, giving more attention to the disputed effects of disturbance to cliff-nesting birds than the possible impacts of diving within the marine reserve. The objectivity of information put forward by conservation organizations was challenged. By changing the decision-making process to a formal one of consultation on unilateral proposals, the situation became more polarized rather than less. In this dispute, the politicization of the recreational interests and the resulting power they could exercise at a national level proved crucial. As a result, the initial proposals by the NCC were significantly modified by the Secretary of State for Wales before designation could be confirmed.

Prior to the designation of the Skomer Marine Nature Reserve, the balance of power was equally distributed within the management committee of the voluntary nature reserve, on which both nature conservation and diving organizations were represented. This power balance, combined with a participative form of decision-making, should have led to a development of consensus and negotiated settlement over the management of a reserve. However, a potentially sound process was affected by the decision of the NCC to designate a statutory reserve. This would have allowed the NCC to control underwater access by legally enforceable by-laws, in direct challenge to the national policy agenda of the BSAC, which had the recent experience of successfully resisting national legislation to restrict access to military wrecks. Thus the evenly balanced situation in the local committee was disrupted by national pressure (from the NCC) but later restored (by the response from the BSAC). The changes in power and decision-making are mapped in Figure 9.10.

Key Points from the case study

- The conflict was triggered by the proposed move from a voluntary self-regulating scheme of management to one of enforced management by a national agency. This ran counter to the spirit of cooperation that had developed between the stakeholders serving on the management committee of the voluntary reserve.

- The proposed restrictions also elevated the argument into a clash of basic principles, as the diving organizations invoked the ethos of freedom, while some conservationists argued for the primacy of environmental values.
- Underlying these arguments was the lack of clear evidence about the incidence and seriousness of disturbance to cliff-nesting birds and underwater damage. Better information on the conditions of the marine environment and of human impacts upon it was needed to convince both divers and in-shore fishermen of the need for conservation and restrictions on their activities.

INITIATION
The terms of reference for the voluntary reserve were set out in the management plan to include all relevant subjects. Although the management committee's coverage was included in the consultation document for the proposed statutory reserve, NCC concentrated on the potential impacts of diving, ignoring the impacts of fisheries which were not within its remit. The interests of divers were largely ignored.

INCLUSIVENESS
Representation: There was broad representation of national and local interests within the management committee for the voluntary reserve with an independent chair. NCC proposed to relegate the committee to an advisory role and take the chair.

Accountability: The management committee operated without formal ground rules so that, for example, the diving representative failed to report back and obtain feedback from BASC.

Openness of and involvement in decision-making: Involvement in decision-making changed from dialogue with the management committee for the voluntary reserve to formal consultation on the proposals for the statutory reserve. Communication was restored with the appointment of a liaison officer.

INFORMATION
A voluntary code of practice had been agreed and publicized by the management committee, and the management plan included conduct guidelines which had been publicized in a brief *Divers' Guide* which gave information on conservation and advice on safety. Both the NCC and the national park had published versions of this information. Information on the impacts of diving became a major element of the dispute. Its coverage was uneven, giving more attention to the disputed effects of disturbance to cliff-nesting birds than the possible impacts of diving within the marine reserve. The objectivity of information put forward by conservation organizations was challenged.

INFLUENCE
The management committee for the voluntary reserve had been responsible for reserve management. NCC had proposed to relegate the committee to an advisory role.

Figure 9.9 *Skomer Marine Nature Reserve – Assessment of Participation in Decision-making*

- The intervention of the national diving organization, allied with the Sports Council for Wales, restored the balance of power that had existed in the management of the voluntary reserve. This highlights the value of political organization when seeking to gain influence in the corridors of power.
- The employment of a liaison officer for the reserve, who as a diver himself had credibility with other divers, was crucial in securing a better understanding among divers and other water users of the proposals for the statutory marine reserve and the underlying conservation issues.

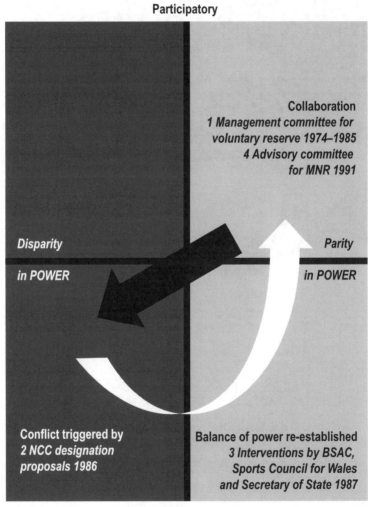

Participatory

Collaboration
1 Management committee for voluntary reserve 1974–1985
4 Advisory committee for MNR 1991

Disparity

in POWER

Parity

in POWER

Conflict triggered by
2 NCC designation proposals 1986

Balance of power re-established
3 Interventions by BSAC, Sports Council for Wales and Secretary of State 1987

Non-participatory

Figure 9.10 *Changes in Power and Decision-making: Skomer*

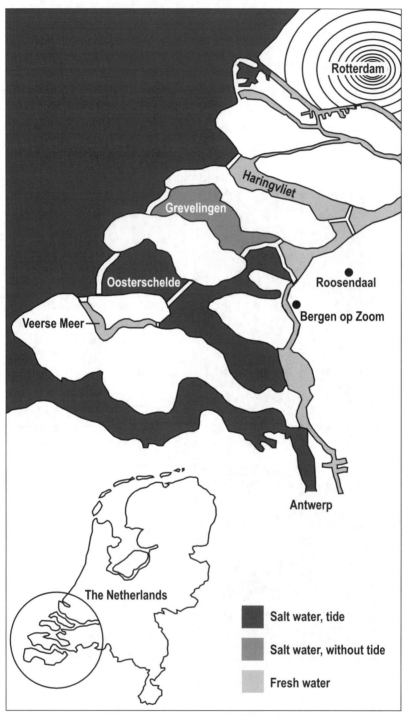

Figure 9.11 *Map of the Rhine Delta*

Case Study 2: Planning in the Rhine Delta[2]

Outline Description of the Rhine Delta Scheme

Following the catastrophic floods of 1953, the Dutch government enacted the Delta Plan to protect communities in Zeeland, Noord Brabant and Zuid-Holland. This entailed building a series of dams across four of the six tributaries of the delta, starting with the enclosure of the Veerse Meer, which was completed in 1961 (see Figure 9.11).

In the late 1960s, it was intended that the Grevelingen – a lake formed by the closure of part of the estuary – would provide a drinking water reservoir, which would be crossed by a railway and connected by a canal to the Haringvliet to the north. Major reclamation and afforestation were also intended, whilst recreation developments would be given priority over the creation of relatively small nature reserves. Following the oil crisis in the mid-1970s, it was realized that future industrial needs no longer justified the canal, the railway crossing and the reservoir; it was decided to concentrate recreation provision near the two dams at each end of the Grevelingen. In the 1980s, a major nature reserve was created on the northern margins of the lake and plans to create further islands solely for recreational use were shelved, partly reflecting changes in policy as population projections for the Netherlands were revised downwards and environmental concerns increased. Thus, over the years, planning has been responsive to changing needs and the balance between recreation and conservation adjusted via several revisions of the management plan. The chronological order of dam construction in the delta and subsequent events is set out in Figure 9.12.[3]

In the second half of the 1960s, plans to dam the Oosterschelde were opposed by both conservation and commercial fishery interests. The nature conservation opposition to the building of the dams centred on the potential loss of inter-tidal habitats, which had become relatively rare in the Netherlands following various reclamation schemes and the enclosure of other parts of the delta. These habitats are important to marine life and support large populations of migratory wading birds. These representations eventually resulted in the construction of a barrage which allows the passage of normal tidal flows. It is only necessary to close the sluices about two or three times a year to prevent storm damage. Construction started on the barrage in 1980 and was finished in 1986. The conservation significance of the Oosterschelde was recognized in 1987, when it was designated as a wetland of international importance under the terms of the Ramsar Agreement, followed by special conservation status under the European Union (EU) Bird Directive in 1989.

In 1990, the inter-tidal areas and salt marshes of the Oosterschelde were designated as state nature reserves, which meant that permits were required for development, earth removal, reclamation or other activities affecting water quality. Although certain forms of recreation were considered

1953	Disastrous flooding of 150,000ha. 72,000 people evacuated, 1835 lost their lives.
1958	Establishment of Delta Commission to examine feasibility of closing the estuary by dams and/or raising and reinforcing the sea dykes, which reported in 1955.
	Delta Act.
1961	Enclosure of Veerse Meer by completion of Veerse Gat Dam (1961). Zeeland Society of Science conference initiated formal opposition to closure of Oosterschelde.
1967	Enclosure of Grevelingen with completion of Brouwers Dam.
1971	Agreement to build tidal barrier on the Oosterschelde.
1976	Establishment of the Stuurgroep Oosterschelde (Oosterschelde Steering Group).
1977	Publication of policy plan by the Oosterschelde Steering Group.
1982	Completion of Oosterschelde barrier, Philips Dam and Oesterdam.
1986	Designation of inter-tidal areas of Oosterschelde as Ramsar reserve.
1989	Designation of inter-tidal and inland areas of Oosterschelde as (State) Nature Reserve based on the Nature Conservation Law.
1990	Protest rally by Recreatie Overleg Oosterschelde (Action Group of Recreation Interests).
	Preparation of Plan Tureluur for nature development on the coastline of the Ooesterschelde.
1992	Publication of the draft report Evaluation Policy Plan Oosterschelde (Evaluatie Beleidsplan Oosterschelde) and approval by the Stuurgroep Oosterschelde.
	Zoning regulations introduced for the Oosterschelde nature reserve.
	Request for research on effects of recreation, tourism and fisheries on ecosystem.
1994	Establishment of Breed Overleg Waterrecreatie (BOW), national lobby of water sport organizations, with regional chapter for the Delta.
	Draft Beleidsplan Oosterschelde published by steering group.
	ANWB and other organizations make representations on the draft plan.
	Chair of steering group proposes national park designation for Oosterschelde and executive meets Voorlopige Commissie Nationale Parken (VCNP) (national park commission).
1995	Interest groups invited to join the steering group in an advisory role.
	Beleidsplan Oosterschelde approved by the province of Zeeland and published by the steering group.
	Consultation on feasibility of establishment of a national park.
	Publication of research on recreation behaviour.
1996	Establishment of Breed Overleg Deltawateren (BOD) – recreation pressure group for the Delta.
	BOD and ANWB criticize zoning regulations for diving.
	Publication of further recreation research and assessment of access regulations by steering group.
1997	Publication of national park proposal in concept.
1998	Publication of detailed proposals for the establishment of the national park, its main goals and organization.
1999	Establishment of the Overlegorgaan (governing body) of the Oosterschelde National Park.
2000	Abolition of the steering group.
2001	Consultation on and adoption of the management plan (Beheers en inrichtingsplan Oosterchelde).

Source: Ministry of Transport and Public Works, 1989; Provincie Zeeland, 1988; Stuurgroep Oosterschelde, 1992; Glasbergen, 1991; BOW-Bulletin, 1992; Bosma, 1992; interviews by R. Sidaway and H. van der Voet, 1991, 1992, 2001, 2003.

Figure 9.12 *Summary of Events in the Rhine Delta Leading to the Establishment of the Oosterschelde National Park, 1953–2003*

acceptable within the nature reserve, a number of restrictions proved controversial, namely:

- access regulations to the water area, sandbanks, marshes and mud flats which limited water recreation, commercial activities like bait-digging, and the traditional gathering of seafood by the local inhabitants; and
- the closure of a crucial channel (the Oliegeul) to vessels because of the potential disturbance to the establishment of a seal colony on nearby sandbanks. This had the effect of restricting the popular tour boat that operated from Zierikzee, and also affected the use of the small harbour at Schlephoek for cruising and sports fishing.

Although the restrictions on bait-digging and the tour boat were subsequently eased, the immediate effect was the formation of a federation of the water sports and fishing organizations (Recreatie Overleg Oosterschelde). A rally was held on 27 May 1990, which attracted 3000 supporters in boats and 2000 on the dykes.

Assessment of Decision-making in the Oosterschelde and the Grevelingen, 1977–1997

In September 1977, the province of Zeeland established a steering group for the Oosterschelde (Stuurgroep Oosterschelde), whose terms of reference were initially very broad: to formulate strategic policy for the development and management of the area. The steering group supervised the preparation of a policy plan which was published in 1982, and which was subsequently given legal status by the national, provincial and local authorities when they signed a declaration of intent and delegated their development control powers to the steering group. Generally, municipalities resist binding agreements of this kind as they wish to protect their freedom to undertake developments which will benefit their communities.

Following the decision to construct the tidal barrage across the Oosterschelde, primacy has consistently been given to nature conservation. Thus, the agenda has inevitably been constrained, with only a limited discussion of recreational issues. This contrasts with the balancing of needs in different stages of planning in the Grevelingen. Thus, the main objective of the 1982 Oosterschelde policy plan was:

> *the conservation and if possible enhancement of the existing natural values (of the area), taking into account the basic conditions for the satisfactory social functioning of the area, in particular in regard to fishing.* (Anon, 1989)

Reserve management focused on protecting the international status of the estuary for the populations of migratory and breeding birds. It also aimed to establish a breeding population of seals on sandbanks in the estuary. The approach was to eliminate the risk of disturbance by following the precautionary principle, unlike the evaluation of risks in different areas in the Grevelingen.

The steering group of the Oosterschelde was responsible for preparing and implementing the policy plan and was chaired by an elected deputy of the provincial council. Its membership consisted of representatives of five government departments,[4] the province of Zeeland, the municipalities surrounding the Oosterschelde and the regional water boards. The executive committee of the steering group had only seven members: two from the province of Zeeland, two officials from the Ministries of Agriculture, Nature Management and Fisheries (Ministerie van Landbouw, Natuurbeheer en Visserij – LNV) and Traffic and Public Works, and three representatives from the municipalities and the regional water boards. Non-governmental organizations (NGOs) and interest groups were not represented on these bodies.

In many ways, the governance of the Grevelingen was very similar. A joint management board comprised representatives from national government and the provinces as well as the ten municipalities and the regional water boards, but no NGOs were directly represented. The executive was supported by a technical group comprising advisors from national agencies and representatives from the provinces of Zeeland and Zuid-Holland. However, during the early planning phases, another national agency – the Development Authority for the IJsselmeer Polders (Rijksdienst IJsselmeer Polders – RIJP) played a crucial role. It provided technical expertise, such as research and monitoring on potential recreation impacts, and also ensured that the needs of the different interest groups were met. The results of its research were freely available, and this information was regarded as objective as it had been gathered independently and its coverage was balanced.

Glasbergen's (1991) evaluation of several policy plans, including that of the Oosterschelde, drew attention to the lack of representation of NGOs. He pointed out that the omission of these groups led to delays in implementing the scheme and that interest groups, local residents and recreational users carried no responsibilities for any decisions made during the planning process. He also noted that some attempt to get over this problem was made by regular consultation with some of the organizations and the holding of evening meetings for users.

Both the recreation and nature conservation groups were recognized as having legitimate interests in the Grevelingen from the outset. This resulted in a more open process of planning, with full consultation so that recreation and conservation issues did not attract the same level of controversy as in other parts of the delta. Although the board encouraged the involvement of interest groups by holding regular annual meetings for representatives of organizations and interested individuals, the interest groups were not directly involved in management. They were consulted on the periodic revisions of the management plan and kept informed on management proposals by annual liaison meetings.

In drawing up the nature reserve regulations for the Oosterschelde, there was no attempt to involve interest groups in any formal way, even though the municipalities had advised against the closure of a crucial channel (the Oliegeul) to vessels, and the steering group was divided on the issue. However, it was suggested that advisory members should be appointed to the steering group to represent each of the three sectors: recreational users, fisheries and nature conservation (Stuurgroep Oosterschelde, 1992).

Subsequently, the power became more concentrated within the steering group and at national level. By incorporating the Oosterschelde policy plan within its regional plan the province of Zeeland delegated planning powers to the steering group, which in effect meant its executive board (Glasbergen, 1991). Following the designation of the state nature reserve, all development and land use permits were decided at the national level by LNV.

The information coverage of the impacts of various recreational and commercial activities on wildlife in the Oosterschelde was a matter of some contention. Glasbergen commented that the initial policy plan was dominated by the conflict between recreation and nature conservation (Glasbergen, 1991). When examining the use made of information during the earlier stages of plan preparation, Van Amstel et al (1988) concluded that decisions were based as much on political considerations as on the objective use of scientific information, and that data on impacts were used to legitimize the introduction of regulations.

This emphasis is maintained in the formal evaluation of the original plan for the Oosterschelde. The analysis concentrated on increasing recreational pressures and highlights the potential risks of recreational disturbance to birds. However, the seriousness of these effects was contested by recreational interests. Rightly or wrongly, they questioned the objectivity of such information because of the close association, in their eyes, between conservation interests and biological scientists. Meanwhile, the effects of commercial fishing on food supplies were not evaluated, which could be having more significant effects on the bird populations than the possible effects of recreational disturbance.

Any interest group involvement was limited to the formal consultations that took place on the reports prepared by the steering group, yet the access regulations on bait-digging on the Oosterschelde were handled in a different way. Many traditional areas used by bait-diggers were to have been closed under the nature reserve regulations. Following an initiative by the sport fishing organizations, a working group was established to advise the LNV on the supply of fishing bait and the access regulations. Both sport fishing organizations and nature conservation officers were represented on the working group, which then devised arrangements for bait-digging acceptable to all parties.

Participation in decision-making in the Grevelingen and the Oosterschelde is contrasted in Figure 9.13, and a further comparison can be made with the more participatory procedures used in the designation of national parks in the Netherlands, as set out in Figure 9.14. The national

Planning and Management of the Grevelingen
INITIATION
There was a conscious attempt to balance the interests of recreation and nature conservation in the planning and management of the Grevelingen, despite a change in policy from provision for intensive recreation to nature conservation.

INCLUSIVENESS
The management board had a broad representation of interests and although non-governmental organizations were not directly represented, a balance was achieved by taking impartial technical expertise.

Participation in planning followed a consultation model although the board encouraged some involvement of interest groups by holding regular annual meetings for representatives of organizations and interested individuals.

INFORMATION
Research and monitoring work was undertaken independently and the findings were freely available to the board. This information was regarded as objective and information coverage was balanced as the evaluation programme was determined by the board.

INFLUENCE
Ultimate responsibility for decision-making was held by the management board and the authorities, who provided its financial support, but detailed management functions were delegated to the director.

Planning in the Oosterschelde
INITIATION
The terms of reference and agenda for policy development in the Oosterschelde were constrained by the decision to give nature conservation primacy in the area.

INCLUSIVENESS
Representation within the steering group was confined to government organizations. Public consultation in the policy development process was limited to the later stages of planning.

INFORMATION
Availability of information was limited by restricted representation. The information on which the evaluation was based was not seen as objective by recreation interests as it was gathered by scientific experts who had closer links with conservation interests. Considerable prominence was given to the conflicts between recreation and nature conservation, far less to considering the impacts of commercial fishing in the estuary.

INFLUENCE
With increasing power being delegated to the steering group, accountability was reduced.

Figure 9.13 *Rhine Delta 1977–1997 – Assessment of Participation in Decision-making*

INITIATION

The criteria for selecting national parks reflect multiple aims, starting with the conservation of nature but including environmental education and recreation. There is a range of objectives, with priority being given to nature conservation. Potential national parks are considered for designation when:

- they contain characteristic ecosystems and can form core areas of the national ecological infrastructure;
- large parts of the areas are controlled and managed by government authorities, such as the national forest and landscape service (Staatsbosbeheer – SBB), Natuurmonumenten and the provincial conservation organizations; and
- there is local political support for the proposal and both the provincial and municipal authorities are willing to cooperate with the scheme.

INCLUSIVENESS

Designation is supervised by a national standing commission – the VCNP – which is an independent advisory body reporting to the Secretary of State of LNV. The members of VCNP are either experts or members of nature conservation or recreational organizations drawn from different levels of government and non-government organizations. The commission has an independent chair and a small secretariat within LNV.

Once a park has moved to the preparatory phase of designation, a local management committee (Overlegorgaan) is formed. This committee has wide representation both from different levels of government, together with representatives of landowners and managers, and the local community. It is chaired by an independent person.

Extensive consultation begins before a decision in principle is taken about designation and continues at each subsequent stage. There is a strenuous attempt to involve all local interests in the management board and/or its committees and working parties.

INFORMATION

During the extensive consultations prior to designation, information is widely circulated among interested parties and local householders.

INFLUENCE

The management of participating owners is influenced by the park management plan prepared in consultation with local committees and ad-hoc working parties. Land managers are required to sign a formal agreement to obtain the full financial benefits from designation.

Source: Sidaway and van der Voet, 1993.

Figure 9.14 *The Designation of Dutch National Parks – Assessment of Participation in Decision-making*

parks have multiple aims: they are primarily concerned with the conservation of nature, but are also concerned with environmental education and informal 'nature-oriented' recreation. Thus national parks in the Netherlands have a range of objectives with a degree of balance between them, although nature conservation is given priority. The next section of this case study traces how participation has changed since the designation of the Oosterschelde as a national park in 1999.

The Establishment of the Oosterschelde National Park

The previous controversy in the 1990s left a legacy of resentment and lack of trust, which reflects on the way in which the state nature reserve restrictions on commercial fisheries and water recreation were introduced as much as their practical implications. As in many other conflicts described elsewhere in this book, interest groups are resistant to change at the best of times, but particularly when it has been imposed rather than brokered, and participation has been limited to formal processes of consultation.

However, the designation of the national park in the Oosterschelde some ten years later has brought about significant changes, and these have been made in a changed political climate. In particular there have been moves to improve relationships and build trust, the most notable being the inclusion of interest groups in the Overlegorgaan, which replaced the Oosterschelde steering group in 2000. The interest groups – concerned with fisheries, nature conservation and recreation – that latterly had been advisors to the steering group have now been made full voting members of the Overlegorgaan, and are also represented on the executive board, which oversees the day-to-day operation of the national park. Whilst this may seem to be a long-awaited reform, it raises issues of public accountability. The interest group representatives do not carry the same legal responsibilities as the government agency, provincial and local government members.

Even more contentious, as far as the interest groups were concerned, was that their membership of the Overlegorgaan was made conditional on their agreement that the 1995 policy plan would be the basis of the national park management plan. This ensured that primacy is given to nature conservation, in line with national legislation and EU environmental directives. The interest groups had to accept that the principle of collective responsibility would apply with full membership of Overlegorgaan. On the one hand, the logic was clear; this was no more than the continuation of a policy established in 1982. On the other hand, it is in marked contrast to the established process for all other national parks in the Netherlands. Normally, the Overlegorgaan collectively develops an agreed management plan as part of the designation process, subject to approval from the Secretary of State. Thus, by full participation in its preparation, the Overlegorgaan takes ownership of the national park plan. Limited involvement in planning for the Oosterschelde allows the interest groups to stand back and criticize park policies.

Nevertheless, the aims of the Oosterschelde National Park have been endorsed by all members of the Overlegorgaan, following a lengthy consultation process orchestrated by the park's independent chairman and the secretariat provided by the province of Zeeland. The choice of chairman has been widely supported. He formerly worked locally as an educationalist, before becoming a member of parliament. He hails from, and still lives in, the area. With experience of chairing the international co-ordinating committee for the Schelde, he has certainly risen to the demands of the post, and has been prepared to listen and take time to reach decisions: 'If you have to vote, you have a problem.'

The outstanding saga of navigation through the Oliegeul was a case in point, and had become of almost symbolic significance for the recreation sector and tour boat operators. The national park commissioned an independent assessment of research on potential disturbance to breeding seals, while the recreation sector obtained a second opinion before the policy was discussed at length within the Overlegorgaan. In the event, a vote was taken with 20–18 members in favour of the policy of restricted access. Although the recreation representatives were outvoted, their votes were on the record and they agreed to abide by the majority decision and present a united recommendation to the minister.

These detailed changes in procedure and the diplomatic style of the chairman, who has encouraged full and frank discussions, help to explain the improved relations within the Oosterschelde since the designation of the national park. Allied with this have been other tangible benefits of working in partnership with public landowners and with commercial recreation enterprises. The national park recognizes the economic importance of tourism in the area, and is contributing to the marketing of tourist accommodation by providing information on the natural qualities of the area, tailored to the needs of each site. It aims to encourage appropriate use rather than stress the need for regulation, illustrated by attractively produced codes of practice for divers, sports fishing, walkers and cyclists prepared in partnerships with them. The park is also using its independent status to raise money for education and interpretation projects, such as a major visitor centre to be built in an unused pillar of the tidal barrage.

The Changing Political Climate in the Netherlands

While procedural changes within the national park modus operandi have been important, changes within the political climate leading to closer cooperation between the interest groups will probably prove to be of greater long-term significance. The interviews conducted by the author in 2001–2003 with some of the key players from nature conservation and recreation interests indicated a number of changes in the political climate, which are bringing these previously opposing interests together.

Nature conservation used to be marginalized but has become a central interest in Dutch society, making it easier to discuss the environmental effects of agriculture, new seaports and recreation. Meanwhile, the conservation and recreation sectors have been growing in confidence and their attitudes towards each other have changed. Nature conservation interests have achieved a great deal at the national level, including the Green Structure Plan, and locally, such as the construction of the barrage across the Oosterschelde. The agreement in the Oosterschelde national park plan that primacy should be given to nature adds to their confidence.

The threat of further recreation developments in the dunes has receded, and views within the recreation sector have changed also. Commercial recreation organizations had tended to take a very parochial view, limited to the prospects for their own hotels or campsites. Now their marketing recognizes the value of accentuating the individual characteristics of certain areas, such as the peaceful open landscapes of Zeeland.

But in marked contrast to the undoubted organization and political strength of the conservation movement, the recreation sector lacked organization. The water sports coalition (Breed Overleg Deltawateren – BOD) was weak, and it took several years of internal development to gain professional knowledge and influence. Despite the decentralization and deregulation of government implemented about ten years ago, recreation is not well represented in or by local authorities, the provinces and the LNV. (This echoes the situation regarding tourism in Texel, as described in Chapter 8, p156.)

Although there is a range of views about the value of cooperation between nature conservation interests and recreation interests, the benefits of a collaborative approach are generally recognized. Projects which have been agreed in this way are welcomed by local and provincial politicians as the work has already been done for them. The only opposition has come from the agricultural sector (as in Texel – see Chapter 8). The new strategy for the Veerse Meer region in Zeeland (Veerse Meer 2030) is an example of successful joint working. It was produced by a wide range of groups, including the Staatsbosbeheer (SBB),[5] Natuurmonumenten and the Zeeland environmental lobby group as the main conservation interests, with representatives from the recreation industry, water sports groups and the regional tourism bureau from the recreation sector. The initiative for a series of working group meetings and excursions came from the provincial level, and resulted in agreement on a vision for the region as a whole. In the original plan for the Veerse Meer, prepared in the 1970s, recreation dominated, whereas the new scheme is based on multiple use objectives. There is greater provision for nature conservation, while the landscape setting for recreation activities will be improved.

Overview

This case study follows the changing pattern of cooperation and conflict over a period of more than 20 years during the successive phases of planning the Rhine Delta scheme in the Netherlands. It demonstrates how the outcome at different stages was influenced by changing national priorities between recreation, tourism and nature conservation. Early projects, such as the Veerse Meer, concentrated on providing opportunities for water recreation, but environmental concerns grew as the formerly remote areas of Zeeland became readily accessible for mass tourism. The planning process was adjusted to balance these competing needs, so that some parts of the Grevelingen were set aside for nature reserves, while others were set aside for water recreation. Subsequently, planning gave primacy to nature conservation in the Oosterschelde. While its designation as a nature reserve attracted initial public support, the subsequent detailed regulations, which planned to reduce recreational access, precipitated a degree of conflict. These outcomes can be traced back to crucial changes in planning procedure and are in marked contrast with the more participatory process used in designating Dutch national parks. A balance has now been restored, with significant moves towards cooperation and multiple use since the Oosterschelde has been designated as a national park.

This analysis has demonstrated that relatively subtle changes in decision-making during different phases of the Delta scheme, albeit aimed at implementing national policy, led at some stages to increased conflict, as the goal of balancing the rival claims of recreation and conservation was abandoned. But in most respects, a new era of cooperation has dawned in the Rhine Delta, as the new governance of the Oosterschelde National Park meets the criteria for consensus building. These shifts in participation and power can be followed in Figure 9.15, which plots the changes in the balance of power and decision-making.

This power imbalance reflects the extent to which the nature conservation and water sports lobbies have become more politicized. The conservationists have long been well organized with a strong unifying ideological base, whilst local interests maintained good lines of communication with their national counterpart organizations and networked effectively with regional and national government. Water sports interests have lacked this degree of organization, they had little local presence, and their diffuse national organization was unskilled in political activity.

Key Points from the Case Study

- Centralized planning in the Rhine Delta has reflected the current priorities of national policy, as power and influence has been concentrated in key planning teams of officials from central government. The lack of interest group representation within the management structure meant that change was not mediated at the local level. Whilst there was general support for the broad aims of conservation, the detailed proposals for implementation attracted public criticism and controversy as participation was delayed into the late stages of planning.
- Decision-making in the earlier planning for Oosterschelde showed a marked contrast to that in the Grevelingen. The fact that consensus and balance have been maintained in the Grevelingen has been due to the neutral facilitating role played initially by the RIJP and latterly the

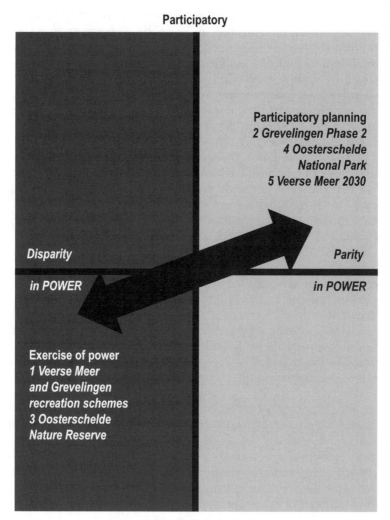

Figure 9.15 *Changes in Power and Decision-making in the Rhine Delta*

board's staff.

- During the earlier period, non-governmental and voluntary organizations could only gain influence by effective lobbying. The nature conservation interests were more effective in this respect than the recreation interests, which at that stage were not politically organized.

- This contrasts with the greater emphasis given to interest group involvement in the early stages of decision-making in the Dutch national parks. Successive rounds of consultation explain and clarify the implications of national park designation and are designed to secure the commitment of interest groups to national park objectives. But public participation also informs local households as well as the relevant interest groups, and the latter are subsequently involved in park management by their membership of specialist working parties. This model has now been adopted in the Oosterschelde.

CONCLUSIONS

Building on the proposition, presented in earlier chapters, that the distribution of power determines the outcome of conflict, the argument has been further developed that changes to more participatory decision-making do not in themselves produce fair and just outcomes. To pursue this argument, a device was developed to assess the relationship between power and decision-making (Figure 9.1). Accepting that power cannot be measured in absolute terms, the degrees of politicization and group cohesion are used as indicators to assess, not the absolute level, but the relative balance of power between interest groups. This formed the horizontal axis in Figure 9.1, with the extent to which decision-making is participatory set on the vertical axis. In any given situation the latter can be approximated using the preconditions of participatory decision-making.

The earlier case studies were then re-examined to chart the changes in decision-making and the balance of power over time. These illustrated:

- how power has shifted within the adversarial system of politics during successive episodes of the long-standing conflict over access to the countryside in England and Wales (Figure 9.2);
- the dominance of the economic power of the pulp mill owners in Rumford, Maine until the environmental agencies intervened and sponsored the mediated negotiations of the NOCC (Figure 9.3);
- the challenge to the power of the farming community posed by the instigation of a collaborative planning exercise (Texel 2030) and subsequent shifts in power and the form of decision-making (Figure 9.4); and
- the controversy over the PHRP, which was triggered by the intervention of the LRC in seeking park status for the hills. The more recent attempt to develop a collaborative plan resulted in a management strategy, but the local authorities have yet to develop a strong partnership (Figure 9.5).

One of the lessons from the Pentlands was that conflict may be triggered by government striving to implement an aspect of public policy within its mandate. Such interventions can alter the balance of power considerably. Two further case studies illustrated these processes.

- Prior to the designation of a statutory marine nature reserve, the nature conservation and diving organizations collaborated within the management committee of the voluntary nature reserve for Skomer. The regulations which the NCC proposed prompted the intervention of the BSAC, supported by the Sports Council for Wales. Thus both the balance of power and collaborative management were restored (Figure 9.10).

- Successive interventions by Dutch government agencies have secured the changing goals of national policy. Priority for water recreation was reflected in the plans for the Veerse Meer and then the Grevelingen, in the latter case subsequently modified to include major provision for nature conservation. This balanced solution was facilitated by a government planning agency (the RIJP). As the balance of power and national policy priorities swung to nature conservation, the Oosterschelde was designated a state nature reserve with controversial restrictions on water recreation. In recent years, more collaborative decision-making has found favour, demonstrated by both designation of the Oosterschelde as a national park and the development of multiple use strategies for the Veerse Meer (Figure 9.15).

- Although this last analysis treats each development as an episode in a continuing conflict, arguably they are not. A succession of negotiated settlements in the Grevelingen has produced a stable situation there. Elsewhere, it is the external political context which has produced significant pressures. The growth of tourism in Zeeland led to an initially defensive response from nature conservation interests, which resulted in the designation of the Oosterschelde as a nature reserve. Subsequently, formerly rival interests groups are now gaining the benefits of collaboration both in the Oosterschelde National Park and in the Veerse Meer.

These interventions by government agencies and their effects are summarized in Figure 9.16. Interventions by interested parties may create a disparity of power and trigger conflict (Skomer phase two, Oosterschelde phase one and Pentlands phase one), or they may have the effect of achieving balance and furthering collaboration by participation in planning and decision-making (as in Skomer phase three, Grevelingen, the Dutch national parks, the UDAT and the NOCC). Changes in decision-making may be partial to achieve policy aims, and while such interventions may terminate that particular episode, they do not resolve the conflict (as in Skomer phase four, Oosterschelde phase two and Pentland phase two). Interventions as a facilitator to secure the participation of stakeholders are more successful in achieving balance and contributing to conflict resolution (as in the designation of the Oosterschelde as a national park, the integrated management strategy for the PHRP, the planning and management of the Grevelingen, the UDAT and the Peak District Access Consultative Group – PDACG).

This shows how government can act in either a partisan or impartial way, and suggests that within an adversarial system of politics, the former is more likely to be the case. Chapter 10 presents two case studies which consider attempts to introduce consensus building into the political process.

Initial distribution of power	Interventions as interested party which create a DISPARITY in the balance of power	Interventions as interested party which achieve or strengthen a BALANCE of power	Interventions in decision-making	
			PARTIAL to achieve policy	IMPARTIAL as facilitator
PARITY	SKOMER (phase two) – Designation proposal by NCC OOSTERSCHELDE (phase one) – Designation proposals by LNV/NBLF	SKOMER (phase three) – Representations by Sports Council for Wales	SKOMER (phase four) – Welsh Office confirmed suitability as reserve but upheld access for divers OOSTERSCHELDE (phase two) – Executive power used to implement policy	OOSTERSCHELDE (phase three) – Designation as national park
INITIAL BALANCE UNCLEAR	PENTLAND (phase one) – Designation proposal by LRC/Countryside Commission for Scotland (CCS)	Agency representation GREVELINGEN, DUTCH NATIONAL PARKS, UDAT – Establishment of Trust by agencies	PENTLAND (phase two) – Public inquiry into designation confirmed suitability of hills as Regional Park	PENTLAND (phase three) – Preparation of integrated management strategy Participative planning GREVELINGEN, DUTCH NATIONAL PARKS, UDAT – Delegation of management to trust PEAK – Park authority employed neutral facilitator for access consultative group
DISPARITY		NOCC – US EPA and Maine DEP sponsorship of mediation		
EFFECTS OF INTERVENTIONS	Interventions TRIGGER conflict episode	Countervailing interventions achieve BALANCE	Interventions terminate episode but may not resolve conflict	Interventions achieve BALANCE AND RESOLUTION

Figure 9.16 *Government Interventions which Affect the Distribution of Power between the Parties and the Outcomes of Disputes*

Chapter 10

Consensus and the Political Process

In a progressive country change is constant; and the question is not whether you should resist change which is inevitable, but whether that change should be carried out in deference to the manners, the customs, the laws and the traditions of a people, or whether it should be carried out in deference to abstract principles, and arbitrary and general doctrines. (Benjamin Disraeli's Edinburgh *ober dictum* quoted in Cole, 1992)

SYNOPSIS

The background to the following case studies is that there are alternative systems of public discourse. In contrast to adversarial politics, consensus building provides a reasonable, rational and ideologically sound alternative. Sadly, when consensus does appear in the vocabulary of political decision-making it is rarely in a favourable light. In the political world, consensus is synonymous with compromise, fudge, concession or (possibly) informed consent.[1] But then the political usage of consensus does not follow the stricter definition used in Chapter 3.

Both the theory and procedures of consensus building differ markedly from the process of voting. While voting can break the log jam of getting nowhere and allow life to move on, its consequences may deliver victory for the majority but leave an aggrieved and resentful minority – outcomes that do not resolve conflict. Yet to combine the two systems appears to offer the best of both worlds. The advantage should be that, with all the spade-work done, the legislative process will be swift and smooth. But that relies on the supposition that politicians and their advisors will readily endorse broadly based agreements. In reality, marrying consensus and politics may seem like Little Red Riding Hood meeting the Big Bad Wolf. This chapter explores the main characteristics of the political process, before presenting two case studies which illustrate what can happen when consensus building and politics are combined.

UNDERSTANDING POLITICAL PROCESSES

Organization and Influence

In the world of politics, individuals rarely act alone. More characteristically, they organize themselves into local groups which may or may not have links into a wider political network. The nomenclature of such groups is confused, and Richardson (1993) identified over 20 terms for basically the same kind of organization. He preferred the term 'pressure group', which he defined as '...any group which articulates demands that the political authorities ... should make an authoritative allocation'. This assumes that, unlike a political party, these groups do not seek to occupy the position of authority (Richardson, 1993, 1). For the sake of consistency with earlier chapters, the term 'interest group' is preferred here.

Richardson's definition is consistent with the concept of influence as seeking power without responsibility, which may be gained from expertise and personal ability such as the skills of persuasion and the ability to negotiate. Alternatively, influence may stem from wealth and the economic and social status that it confers, a moral stance, or membership of an organization. McCormick (1991) notes that the influence that groups have with government varies according to their size, strengths and resources, but also their standing in public opinion. Environmental groups have traditionally had less influence on government than economic interest groups, although in the assessment of Alan Mattingly (a former director of the Ramblers' Association – RA) the influence of environmental groups increased in the UK in the 1990s (McCormick, 1991). However, such assessments are relative and have to be set in the context of continuing government reluctance to embark on environmental reform.

Why Organize? Who Benefits?

Lowe and Goyder's (1983) survey of voluntary conservation organizations revealed that people join these organizations to register support for a group's aims, to get actively involved in its activities so as to influence its direction, to obtain the benefits of membership, and to make social contact. They bring a number of benefits to the organization, providing new ideas, information on local developments (in the case of a national organization), voluntary assistance, income, and – particularly as an organization grows – legitimacy in dealing with government (consistent with Weber's concepts, noted in Chapter 3). Their enthusiasm and contacts help to spread the message and are vital in lobbying.

Lowe and Goyder describe the organizational styles of the conservation groups in their study. They make a distinction between participatory organizations – where elected representatives seek the views of their members and are directly accountable to them – and those that operate under a more authoritative leadership that promotes the organization's aims without consulting the members. Some groups, with their origins in participatory campaigns, nevertheless remain firmly in the latter category. The loosely structured, non-hierarchical 'new social movements' are a case in point. They may opt for decentralization so that they can be responsive to their members and supporters by involving them in local groups. Others operate quite openly on corporate lines, where truly democratic structures are deliberately avoided (Jordan and Maloney, 1997).

There is an inherent conflict between maintaining autonomy and survival, and it centres on the sources of an organization's funding. Greater autonomy and financial stability can be gained from membership subscriptions and, in the case of prestigious organizations like the National Trust, from endowments and gifts, which provide major sources of investment income. Jordan and Maloney's study cited Friends of the Earth and Amnesty International as examples of campaigning groups in the 'protest business' which used direct mailing to supporters to raise funds. This additional source of funding provides autonomy while relieving supporters of the obligations of membership. This avoids dependence on sponsorship from independent trusts, government or private companies, which restricts autonomy. But the problem for so many of the smaller voluntary organizations is getting sufficient core funding to survive. Sponsors can more easily be found for projects that attract favourable publicity than for administration or fund-raising.

Political Tactics

Campaigning organizations use different lobbying tactics, perhaps alternating between different modes as the situation demands; they are veritable 'chameleons', to use Pross's word (1993). Two styles can be identified. There is the radical/activist style of taking unconventional action and being uncompromising and confrontational, with the result that the group plays the role of critical outsider and is never consulted by government. In contrast, insider groups ensure that they are consulted, perhaps only informally, because of their moderate conventional tactics. Such groups are prepared to engage in dialogue and use established procedures to compromise and cooperate to gain influence on decision-makers. The distinction between 'insiders' and 'outsiders' was made by Grant (1978) and is now widely accepted (McCormick, 1991; Young, 1993). Young charts the course of the principal conservation groups in the UK during the 1980s, and how the tactics of many groups changed as they became better established and arguably more influential. McCormick (1991) gives the example of Friends of the Earth switching tactics, from confrontation (in the form of a threatened public ban on aerosols) to an insider role of giving advice to the construction industry by commissioning a technical report on the industrial use of chlorofluorocarbons. The elements of this debate over choice of tactics within the RA will be familiar from Chapter 2 (see p24).

Relationships with Government

To be successful, the lobbying organization needs to know where and how decisions are made, and this varies according to both the type of issue and the legislative system. There are emotive, value-laden issues, such as abortion or the introduction of genetically modified crops, which are topics of both public protest and continuing debate in the public and parliamentary arenas. Issues of a more arcane nature, such as taxation, tend to be kept out of the public arena and are the subject of internal negotiations between bureaucrats and experts. Where decisions are made and who is influential in decision-making varies according to the political system in each country. For example, the legislatures of federal and state government in the USA and their committees play a more direct role than in some European systems, where many, if not most, decisions are effectively made by officials. This is particularly true in the UK, where civil servants provide continuity between elections (McCormick, 1991; Richardson, 1993). Furthermore, it is often difficult to know who is responsible for environmental policy. The issues are complex and not fully understood, and the scientific evidence is hotly contested, whilst the delineation of departmental responsibilities is often difficult to follow. It is hardly surprising that policy-making does not follow a rational course but a process of 'disjointed incrementalism' (McCormick, 1991). This leads to calls for integration, as in the case of integrated coastal zone management (ICZM) described in Chapter 8 (see p168).

Caught in the political crossfire, the departmental official, schooled to respond to the powerful or the potentially powerful and in need of advice, naturally turns to the insiders rather than the activists. Decision-making is then routinely based on selective consultation with powerful affected interests (McCormick, 1991). Agriculture is one such closed area of policy-making (Richardson, 1993). The process is not without its problems: policies are negotiated like peace treaties, and 'like all peace treaties which have been difficult to negotiate, there is a marked reluctance to renegotiate them once they have been agreed' (Richardson, 1993, 88).

Thus the relationship between interest groups and government becomes symbiotic, one of shared needs. It also becomes institutionalized, as groups seeking influence are co-opted to serve the needs of government (Richardson 1993). This has been described as a 'policy community' of departmental officials dependent for technical advice on the professionals in the interest group. The community is likely to span the insiders from both sides of the fence. It meets in different guises: in the corridors of power, the lobby of the legislature or, more formally, within the advisory committees of government. Just as important is the neutral territory of the conference, when officials can take informal 'soundings' of professional, academic or political opinion (Jordan and Richardson, 1987; Pross, 1993).

The Transformation of Voluntary Organizations

However, some organizations find themselves involved in conflict when their initial motives were far from political. This is true of most people who pursue recreational interests, and organize themselves into clubs to meet their common needs for mooring boats or obtaining insurance for equipment or risky activities. Hence the comment in the Morecambe Bay Partnership case study that 'blokes with beards go out in boats but don't necessarily like conferences' (see p175). For organizations that are formed in this way yet become involved in lobbying or other political activity, it is possible to trace their evolution through (essentially) four stages as they are transformed into more professional bodies (see Figure 10.1).

Stage 1: The voluntary club
- A voluntary organization forms around common need
- The membership provides ideas, energy, skills and money
- The club is serviced by honorary officers elected from its membership

Stage 2: Easing the burden of administration
- The voluntary organization lobbies government through the personal contacts of office bearers
- Administrative assistance is obtained to support the honorary officers
- The members provide energy and money

Stage 3: The national body
- The organization lobbies government through the political process – the size of its membership provides legitimation
- Professionals are employed to provide membership services, technical expertise and representation
- They advise a policy group (the board or national council) elected by the members with regional representation

Stage 4: The non-governmental organization
- The non-governmental organization (NGO) advises government
- Specialized professionals are responsible for policy backed by the expertise of research colleagues
- Legitimation for the professional staff comes from fellow professionals in a national network or policy community
- There is little corporate accountability to the membership, which still provides a source of funding and political legitimacy
- The organization may be funded directly by government or indirectly through sponsored projects or services

---

Figure 10.1 *The Transformation of Voluntary Organizations*

This sequence traces the development of professionalism as the initial sources of dynamism and resources from the membership wane, depending on the internal ethos of the organization – its commitment to a democratically accountable structure and desire to remain autonomous and be able to speak its mind. By Stage Four in this life and death of voluntary organizations, legitimation stems from fellow professionals in the policy network.

Several key concepts emerge from this brief review of environmental politics. Voluntary organizations may start life naïvely, only to realize that to be politically effective they need to adapt and work in coalition. They are confronted with the tactical choice of gaining influence as political insiders or remaining true to their founding principles by acting as uncompromising outsiders. The merits of both approaches are illustrated in the following case studies.

CASE STUDY 1: Striving for Sustainability in the Northern Maine Woods

Context

The future of the Northern Woods[2] in New England, USA has been in the balance since the mid-1980s. During this time there have been underlying concerns about the rate of timber harvesting, which has exceeded the regrowth of the forest, and the sale of forest land for housing, which restricts traditional local access to lakes and forests for recreation. There have been successive attempts to build a consensus on each of these issues; few have led to a clear conclusion. As environmental activists in Maine grew impatient, they gained sufficient public support to initiate a state referendum on a clear-cutting ban in 1996. In response, more comprehensive and conciliatory counter-proposals were drawn up by the 'sensible centre', a group of moderates from the forest industry and the environmental organizations attached to the state. This coalition reached agreement on a document (the 1996 Forest Compact) which attempted to cover all aspects of the forestry problem and provide a blueprint for sustainable forestry in the state. Although the Compact gained widespread support in the subsequent referendum, it narrowly failed to gain a majority due to voters' suspicions of a proposition negotiated behind closed doors.

The Compact negotiations have to be seen in the context of a dispute of long standing. The Northern Maine Woods contain over half (15 million out of 26 million acres) of the wild land remaining in the eastern USA and are of major economic, social and symbolic value to urban New England, with its population of 70 million people. The status quo ante, which had existed for decades, was generally thought to be benign. A few large, locally-based landowners, with a primary interest in timber production, generally acted paternalistically by providing much-needed livelihoods in remote areas and by tolerating traditional forms of unrestricted recreational access. As the dominant employers, they wielded considerable power and political influence in the state yet, on balance, the forest appeared to be in good hands. In short, the 'working forest' provided jobs and recreation, and its ecological value appeared to be maintained without outside interference from conservation organizations or federal government.

> ...*all the good feeling between many conservationists and the forest industry in northern New England rested on the irrefutable assumption that keeping the forest working was a far better fate than hacking it up for development.* (Boucher, 1989, 36)

Threats to the Status Quo

This situation held until the mid-1980s, when things changed dramatically in the face of a series of destabilizing threats, notably:

- the scale of apparent devastation in the forest, initiated by the ravages of spruce budworm and subsequent salvage harvesting, which led to extensive clear-cutting becoming the standard practice;
- large-scale purchases of forest land by owners who had no direct interest in forestry or timber production, initiated by the speculative purchases of a UK financier in northern New England in 1981. These introduced the prospect of asset stripping (selling prime development sites for an enhanced value). More recent large-scale purchases by financial institutions based outside the state have renewed these fears;
- threats of loss of traditional access to lake shores brought about by sub-division and the development of private residences or second homes; and
- the lack of effective conflict resolution methods. The traditional response of state legislation and/or federal research failed to provide sufficient remedy. For example, the Maine Forest Practices Act of 1989 was paralleled by the US Forest Service's Northern Forest Lands Study (NFLS) covering the states of Maine, New Hampshire and Vermont and upstate New York. There were major collaborative elements to both exercises but, as adequate responses to multi-faceted problems, their outcomes fell short of expectations.

What changed the course of political events in the mid-1990s was the uncompromising intervention of the more radical Forest Ecology Network (FEN) led by Jonathan Carter. This campaign concentrated on the all too evident effects of clear-cutting, and this visual evidence struck a chord with the lay public, who care about 'their woods'. The public attributed the major changes that had occurred in the forested landscape in the 1980s to the harvesting practices of the powerful lumber companies, and ignored the contribution of budworm infestations and fire.

Carter's political tactics were novel, and took advantage of a little-known provision in the constitution of the state of Maine. This allows citizens to require a proposition to be put to a state ballot if enough registered voters sign a petition requiring a referendum. It requires a number of signatures equal to 10 per cent of votes cast in the last gubernatorial election, which amounted to 52,000 signatures in 1995. This provision had rarely been used until FEN successfully petitioned for a referendum on a ban on clear-cutting in that year.

The Negotiation of the Forest Compact

Governor King had established a council on sustainable forestry, one of a succession of initiatives, which followed the NFLS. But its painstaking efforts were sidelined by the crisis posed by Carter's referendum. King hastily set up another more exclusive group drawn from moderate opinion within the forest industry and the environmental organizations to devise alternative proposals. These intensive negotiations had to conclude within the timetable imposed by the impending referendum, and they resulted in the Forest Compact. The Compact proposed an intricate series of measures covering the regulation of tree harvesting, a voluntary audit of forest practices by forest owners, the control of liquidation harvesting (clear-cutting on small wood lots to enable development) and increasing the area of protected land in public or non-profit ownership.

Whilst the Compact failed, in the sense that it lacked sufficient public support to obtain the necessary majority in a state-wide referendum, it fell short of the required majority by only three percentage points (see Figure 10.2). Ostensibly, it failed because it lacked sufficient credibility when attacked by opposite ends of the political spectrum. Whilst Jonathan Carter portrayed it as the creature of powerful industrial interests, the exponents of private property rights, led by Mary Adams, saw its proposed regulations as an attack on their fundamental beliefs as enshrined in the US constitution. Admittedly, the Compact was designed to address the problems of extensive forestry in the largely uninhabited northern part of the state. Its impact on small-scale holdings in the south had not been considered.

Technically, one obvious weakness was the insistence on negotiating the Compact behind closed doors without a parallel educational programme to inform the public of the progress of the negotiations. The exercise failed to gain public trust, and suspicions that it was being manipulated by the powerful forest industry were fuelled by its US\$5-million public relations campaign.

November 1996: Turnout 65%	November 1997: Turnout 37%
Propositions:	Propositions:
A: 29.3% for Clear-cutting ban	47.5% for Forest Compact
B: 47.2% for Forest Compact	52.5% for No change
C: 23.5% for No change in forest practices	

Source: Rolde, 2001.

Figure 10.2 *Voting in Maine Forestry Referenda*

Secondly, because it was dealing with all aspects of a multi-faceted problem, the very complexity of the agreement made it difficult to understand compared to the simple messages and sound bites emanating from Carter (who employed the deceptively simple slogan 'Ban clear-cutting') and Adams ('Stop the backroom deal'). The reasonable approach presented by the Compact had fallen foul of the rough and tumble of adversarial politics, with its emphasis on 'spin'.

Assessment of Decision-making

Further evaluation of the Compact negotiations reveals that it meets most of the consensus building criteria in terms of a balanced agenda, accountability, influence and information (Figure 10.3). Representation was deliberately limited to the moderate middle ground, although it is unlikely that Carter would have joined the negotiations or that this would have been acceptable to the forest industry.

INITIATION
The terms of reference spanned key elements of the forestry and ecological debate: timber harvesting and the auditing of forest practice and the extension of protected ownership for conservation purposes.

INCLUSIVENESS
Representation was deliberately limited to the middle ground to ease decision-making with the exclusion of some key interests, such as the environmental activists.

Accountability: The negotiations followed consensus building conventions with representatives reporting back and obtaining feedback from their constituencies.

Openness of and involvement in decision-making: Meetings were not open to the public to facilitate negotiation. The tight timetable set by the impending referendum proved to be a major constraint. The lack of a public information programme during the course of the negotiations led to widespread mistrust in the credibility of the exercise.

INFORMATION
Supporting information was provided by the Maine Forest Service, although the state forester was not directly involved in the discussions.

INFLUENCE
The negotiations were initiated by the state governor, with the intention of their outcome forming the basis of state legislation.

Figure 10.3 *The Maine Forest Compact – Assessment of Participation in Decision-making*

However, the Forest Compact has to be set in a wider context. Analysis over a longer period reveals other important considerations. Earlier attempts to reform forest practice, such as the NFLS, were constrained by the power of the forest industry. Environmental critics have identified the following limitations of the NFLS agenda, and claimed that many relevant issues were excluded under pressure from the Maine Forest Products Council (see Figure 10.4).

- Administrative action by any federal agency, i.e. national parks or extensions to national forests, public acquisitions or green line parks, regional (i.e., wider than state action)
- Forest management practices, such as harvesting
- Replacement of traditional uses of the land – regulation of land use
- Forest health (use of herbicides) and biodiversity
- Recreational development

Source: Boulton, 1990; Reidel, 2000.

Figure 10.4 *Contemporary Issues Excluded from Consideration by the Northern Forest Lands Study*

The Compact was unusual in trying to span both the forestry and ecological agendas. The focus of most initiatives has been on one element or the other, neglecting an associated socioeconomic agenda. The 1989 Maine Forest Practices Act (Milliken, 1990) and the Biodiversity Plan (McMahon, 1998), which identified ecologically sensitive areas, are cases in point. Many environmental initiatives have centred on a particular solution (such as national park designation) and on short-term tactics, rather than longer-term strategy. Thus there has been no measured discussion based on a detailed problem analysis, and therefore no (opportunity for) agreement on long-term goals or the priority that should be given to the various issues within the three agendas. As a result, some issues on the socioeconomic agenda have been largely ignored, notably the threat posed by sub-division for housing, and the fragmentation of the resource with the consequent loss of public access. Activist initiatives have been based on the assumption that the simpler the concept, the easier it is to get general public support, no matter how relevant it may be to a more measured analysis. Moreover, some of the 'single-issue' solutions, e.g., national park or wildland reserve proposals which advocate federal involvement, seem very unlikely to gain much popular or political support in the state, not least because they are perceived as originating outside the state.

The Legacy of the Compact

It is tempting to conclude that the last decade of political infighting has achieved little more than stalemate and that in theory, at least, a more inclusive process (inclusive in terms of both issues and constituencies) might have produced a more successful conclusion. Perhaps process design (as described in Chapter 5) would have helped individual stages of the negotiations, although it is questionable that it would have got a better outcome in the case of the Compact. Certainly, in that instance, a more open process could have gained greater public legitimacy and trust. But applying the principles of process design across the full range of issues and stakeholders would itself require a lengthy process of negotiation. The political world rarely stands still to allow such things to happen. More likely, the task is beyond process design and it is a political strategy that is needed.

This case study illustrates the influence that can be exerted by an insider network or 'policy community' in which a consistent group of moderate organizations (drawn from landowning, industry and environmental organizations) has played a prominent role in advancing the agenda for sustainable forestry. Certain individuals have become key players, often because of their multiple and/or changing roles and inside knowledge, as they move between organizations. Taken individually, their repeated attempts at consensus building have had limited success, but over a long period of collaboration the coalition has had major influence and is yielding practical results.

Conservation organizations have made substantial purchases, either of land or development rights (easements). Initially these were small scale and opportunistic, but increasingly a more systematic approach is being taken to purchasing areas for their ecological value, influenced by the Biodiversity Plan. Many of the purchases are now being financed through the Land for Maine's Future Board, which is in turn funded by a bond issue from the state legislature backed by widespread political support from the Maine electorate. Meanwhile, the introduction of forest certification has meant that another of the key elements of the Compact is being implemented, albeit gradually and complicated by the existence of two rival schemes. The Sustainable Forestry Initiative is the forest industry's preferred form of self-regulation, but it lacks a full independent audit. However, some companies and the state forests are now certified by the Forestry Stewardship Council scheme, which operates world-wide and is independently audited. While there is no comprehensive plan, local planning exercises are being facilitated by the Northern Forest Alliance. These plans form the basis of local negotiation between the community and the timber companies. Thus substantial, albeit incremental, progress has been made towards saving the Northern Forest. Pieces of the jigsaw are being put in place.

In the real world of politics, there is a role for both coalitions and political activists. Indeed, it can be argued that the sensible centre would not have achieved so much without the intervention of activists like Jonathan Carter. FEN's challenges to the system have been highly influential in moving the centre of gravity in their direction. Items that were once off the agenda gradually became mainstream thinking, despite continuing resistance from the powerful forest industry.

> *It is important to note, however, that the pressure exerted on Maine's forest products industry by forest protection advocates – through agency rule makings, legislative initiatives (including*

Latent phase	Escalation	Active phase	Aftermath	
>1990 *Adversarial system of decision-making*	1996 *Negotiation of Forest Compact*	1996 *Referendum voting* Turnout 65%	1997 *Referendum voting* Turnout 37%	2003 *Collaboration: de facto implementation of Forest Compact*
Forest industry defends status quo and resists regulation		Status quo 24%		

Moderate
environmental
groups press for
regulation
	Moderates within
	the forest
	industry and the
	environmental
	groups negotiate
	a 25 point
	Compact
		Compact 47%	Compact 48%	• Forest
				  certification
				• Land
				  purchase for
				  conservation
				• Local
				  planning

Growing support for radical environmental groups	Radicals campaign for clear-cutting ban	Clear-cutting ban 29%	Against 52% Radicals join forces with property rights groups	Influence of radical agenda

Figure 10.5 *Process of Decision-making in the Northern Maine Woods*

citizen-initiated referenda), and the promotion of third party 'green certification' – has led some of Maine's large landowners to make significant progress towards sustainable forest management. In less than a decade, we have seen tighter regulation of clearcuts (the annual acreage of which has been reduced by half), increased awareness of the need to protect riparian zones and critical habitat, an enthusiastic embracing of green certification by Maine's largest landowner.

We have still a long way to go before Maine can lay claim to truly widespread sustainable forest management. Much of the industry continues to resist reform, and spends about $400,000 per year on 'image-related education' designed to affect public perception of its practices. (Natural Resources Council of Maine, 2001, 2)

The shifts in power and changes in decision-making during the different phases of the conflict are set out in Figure 10.6. The forest industry in Maine has long been a dominant power, with strong connections within the legislature. It exercised this power by resisting legislation on major changes

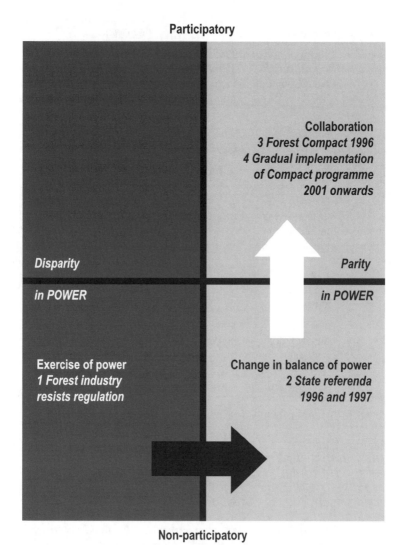

Figure 10.6 *Northern Maine Woods – Changes in Power and Decision-making*

to forest practice throughout the 1980s. This situation is represented in the south-western quadrant of the diagram. The negotiations that produced the Forest Compact depended on parity of power between the parties and collaboration, and are represented in the north-eastern quadrant. Arguably, the interventions of the FEN during the referenda campaigns resulted in a shift in power, but the outcome of that political struggle amounted to stalemate (south-eastern quadrant) with no clear immediate outcome. The present situation, in which many of the elements of the compact are being implemented, is the result of long-term collaboration (north-eastern quadrant).

Key Points from the Case Study

- The Forest Compact negotiations were prompted by the FEN campaign for a state referendum on a clear-cutting ban.
- Although the referenda did not result in a majority for either the ban or the Compact, public awareness of sustainable forest practices was heightened and power shifted away from the forest industry.
- Nevertheless, the Compact has had a lasting effect as most of its proposals are being implemented without legislation.

CASE STUDY 2: Countryside Access in Scotland – The Work of the Scottish Access Forum

Context

The long struggle to gain access to the countryside was described in Chapter 2, but apart from recording James Bryce's repeated attempts to get legislation to provide a right of access to the mountains in Scotland, that case study concentrated on England and Wales. One of the key issues that surfaced at various times during that debate was when to enter voluntary negotiations as opposed to campaigning for legislation to secure more general rights of access. This has echoes of the continuing discussion of the effectiveness of insider versus outsider tactics. But in general the access campaigners have sought to negotiate from positions of strength, after they have secured rights through legislation. The recent history of access in Scotland contains both elements: negotiations within the Scottish Access Forum and a parliamentary campaign which culminated in the provisions for public access contained in the Land Reform (Scotland) Act 2003.[3]

In Scotland there had been a long tradition of 'freedom to roam' on the hills, but some uncertainty over whether this constituted a de facto right and whether there was a law of trespass. In practice, access to the uplands of Scotland was largely unrestricted, and the more significant problem was the lack of a path network in the Lowlands close to the main centres of population. Nevertheless the debate about access continued, fuelled from time to time by reports of incidents between hill walkers and deer stalking parties (McOwan, 1993). So whilst the government agency with formal responsibilities for countryside recreation (the Countryside Commission for Scotland – CCS) reported that 'there is no doubt that this freedom to roam is seen by most Scottish walkers as a moral imperative' (CCS, 1988, 28), legislation was a non-starter, given the political clout of the landowners. Various campaigners for land reform (notably McEwan, 1977; Callander, 1987; Cramb, 1996; and Wightman, 1996) drew attention to the concentration of ownership in a few hands, and the large number of estates with absentee foreign landowners seeking the kudos of being a Highland laird. The issue of ownership, linked to previous injustices such as the

Highland Clearances, provided an emotionally charged context to the debate. It certainly overshadowed cooperation at a practical level, in the form of information on periods of restriction and preferred routes on shooting estates being jointly published by the Scottish Landowners' Federation (SLF) and the Mountaineering Council of Scotland (MCofS) from 1972 onwards (SLF and MCofS, 1984)

The annual reports of the CCS for 1986, 1987 and 1988 noted the ambiguities of the legal situation on access (CCS, 1987; 1988; 1989). In 1989 it began a more formal review of access, concentrating initially on rights of way and path maintenance, before commissioning a programme of research, including a study of legislation in selected European countries (Scott, 1992). This work was considered by a technical working party established in 1991 with representation from landowning and recreation interests and public bodies, culminating in a consultation paper on access published by the CCS's successor, Scottish Natural Heritage (SNH), which broached the issue of possible legislation (SNH, 1992).

The Attempt to Build Consensus via the Access Forum

A further stimulus came from a local agreement, the Letterewe Accord, made in 1993 between the Dutch landowner of the Letterewe estate in north-west Scotland and recreation interests. This provided public access that had previously been discouraged by the estate and had been a matter of some controversy. The accord proved that agreement between these competing interests was possible despite earlier antagonisms. But as government policy at that time favoured voluntary agreements over legislation, SNH concluded that a change in the law to create a right of access to open hill land was not required. However, it established the Access Forum, one of whose tasks was to prepare a national concordat on access to the hills based on the principle of mutual responsibilities (SNH, 1994).[4] The breakthrough in these discussions came with the signing of a concordat on access to Scotland's hills and mountains in 1996 (SNH, 1996a). The concordat set out a series of general principles respecting the interests of both landowners and recreational users of the hills, and was accompanied by an advisory booklet (*Care for the Hills*, SNH, 1996b) and information on a hill phone service to reduce conflict between shooting and walking.

The political climate changed radically with devolution and the establishment of the Scottish Parliament in 1997, not least because as a devolved issue, such legislation did not need the approval of the House of Lords with its predominance of landowning interests. Furthermore, access legislation was a manifesto pledge of the incoming coalition government. The new administration sought the advice of SNH on the form legislation should take, and SNH in turn involved the Access Forum. In 1998, the Forum agreed the principle of establishing a public right of recreational access to the Scottish countryside in general (not just hill land) as long as that right was responsibly exercised. The advice was to base the legislation on the principles of a general right of access covering all land and water, to be exercised responsibly, while safeguarding the right of privacy near dwellings. The details of implementation were to be covered in a Scottish Outdoor Activities Code.[5]

Entering the Political Process

It might have been expected that the Forum's recommendations would be easily transposed into legislation by the Scottish Parliament in 2001. In fact the process proved more tortuous, demonstrating the power of both the landowning and access lobbies and the crumbling consensus obtained by the Forum. Under parliamentary procedures, proposals are contained in a draft bill which is published for consultation before being examined by the relevant parliamentary committees. The committees can take evidence from the interests and amendments can be tabled, possibly as a result of lobbying officials of the administration (the Scottish Executive) or 'friendly' Members of the Scottish Parliament.

Given the heightened political climate of land reform it was not surprising that the consensus built up in the Forum did not hold. The complexities of the bill extended its timetable, and gave time for the landowners in particular to compare their position with their colleagues south of the border. In England and Wales, the new access provisions were only to apply to:

- 'permitted activities' (cycling and horse riding are excluded);
- defined areas of 'open country' (excluding woodland, cultivated land, the coast and riversides, as opposed to all land and inland water in Scotland); and
- access could be further restricted in England and Wales on grounds of nature conservation and land management, i.e., landowners have the right to restrict access for any reason for up to 28 days a year and to apply to the local authority for further temporary restrictions.

How any restrictions for conservation and land management might apply in Scotland and the matters of safety around farm buildings and privacy around dwellings were details to be left to the Code of Practice. The membership of the landowning organizations grew suspicious that their representatives had not fully protected their interests.

The day the draft bill was published in February 2001, the National Farmers' Union of Scotland (NFUS) withdrew from membership of the Forum, with the effect that it ceased to function. It appeared that the NFUS had successfully lobbied the Scottish Executive and secured new sections in the draft bill. Of these, Section 9, which would give land managers the power to suspend temporarily the right of access over a defined area, was extremely controversial, not least because it was contrary to the previous advice of the Forum. During the subsequent period of public consultation, a wide range of organizations voiced their objections and the RA urged its members to write in protest at the offending sections. Faced with 3500 responses to the consultation, 85 per cent of them on access, the parliamentary committees took further evidence and eventually recommended the reinstatement of the principles of freedom to roam. The bill was enacted in January 2003, when the ruling coalition of Labour and the Liberal Democrats supported by the Scottish National Party was happy to defeat one of their traditional opponents, the landowners, by a majority of 101 to 19. Thus a balanced solution of rights and responsibilities was enacted, but by the exercise of power rather than agreement by consensus.

Yet while the eventual outcome appeared to present one side with victory, the Scottish legislation was based on the principles developed by the Forum and balanced the new rights with the reciprocal responsibilities placed on both recreation users and land managers.

Assessment of Participation in Decision-making

It is worth considering how the Forum operated, which was closer to conventional committee practice than the processes of consensus building set out in earlier chapters. In Figure 10.7, the Forum procedures are compared with the principles of participatory decision-making identified in Chapter 4.

Certain principles were met, such as balanced representation, with roughly equal numbers from the key sectors: land managers, recreation organizations and statutory agencies. The size of the group was kept small to promote effective working (see Forum membership in Figure 10.8). Arguably, given the wish to influence recreational behaviour, ways might have been sought to engage with other interested groups, notably representatives from outdoor education, mountain guides, scouting and guiding, and conservation organizations. Moreover, the membership was selected to deal with the original issue – access to the hills. Once the focus was extended to cover the countryside more generally, the interests of other crucial groups, such as conservation groups or dog walkers, had to be considered (although dog walkers lack a representative organization which might be involved in negotiations).

The Forum operated on the basis of committee conventions rather than explicit ground rules. This places particular emphasis on the style of chairmanship, which varied with successive incumbents. Given the need to meet legislative deadlines, the conventional approach certainly provided leadership. The obligations of representatives were unclear, particularly on crucial matters such as accountability to their constituent organizations. Representatives have to be trusted by and be able to speak authoritatively on behalf of their membership. They need to report back and take soundings of members' views, and on occasion to educate the membership on the implications of the negotiations. Different organizations faced different

INITIATION
The terms of reference were limited to the development of national policy and measures to encourage appropriate behaviour and therefore not dealing with individual disputes. Within that remit, agreement was reached on general principles in *Scotland's Hills and Mountains: A concordat on access* (SNF, 1996a) and subsequently on a right of responsible access to the Scottish countryside, which respected the major interests, together with a detailed code of practice.

INCLUSIVENESS
Representation was deliberately limited to ease decision-making with the exclusion of some key interests, such as outdoor education, guiding and conservation interests. This became more critical when the discussions moved from considering access to the hills to access in the countryside more generally.

Accountability: The Forum operated without formal ground rules so that, for example, the arrangements for representatives reporting back to and obtaining feedback from their constituencies were not clearly defined and varied between member organizations. This applied particularly to the circulation of Forum papers.

Openness of and involvement in decision-making: Forum meetings were not open to the public to facilitate negotiation. The tight legislative timetable proved to be a major constraint in the later stages and meant that some issues remained unresolved. The limited time allowed for comment on legislative amendments precluded consultation within organizations. Forum minutes are on the public record but do not provide a verbatim account of a meeting.

INFORMATION
Papers drafted by the secretariat (SNH) provided the principal source of information for the deliberations of the Forum.

INFLUENCE
Although the Forum's advice was sought by government, via SNH, and Scottish Executive observers attended meetings, the Executive was not committed to accepting Forum recommendations.

Figure 10.7 *The Scottish Access Forum – Assessment of Participation in Decision-making*

problems during the Forum's deliberations. Some organizations worked informally and did undertake wide consultation, but clearly the NFUS did not operate in this way. As a result, their regional committees, who had not been consulted, subsequently rejected the agreement because of the diversity of views within the membership. The advantages of explicit adherence to consensus building principles become clear when the political heat is turned up. Without formal ground rules tying participants to consensus procedures, the temptation to revert to political manoeuvring is very difficult to resist.

Probably the most crucial point that comes from closely examining the whole process was the lack of delegated authority given to the Forum.

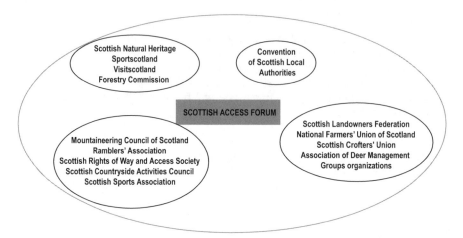

Figure 10.8 *Membership of the Scottish Access Forum*

Although it had spent three years building consensus, the civil servants in the Scottish Executive (following the convention that a minister's position should not be compromised) were not committed to taking the Forum's advice. Thus the Scottish Executive was preparing the legislation while sub-groups of the Forum worked on sections of the code, and the pressure of deadlines curtailed debate. The Forum lost control of the process, and this added to the frustration of its members. The legislative timetable worked against maintaining consensus.

The outcome of the Forum's deliberations was nearer compromise than true consensus. It appears that within the Forum, neither side got all that it wanted. Initially at least, the RA failed to get all it wanted on lowland access, while the NFUS was unable to confine the new access provisions to paths in the hills. The landowners agreed to the establishment of a path network on the understanding that resources would be made available from government to local authorities to manage the network. Although additional funding has been made available to local authorities, it was possible that it could be used for other purposes.

So although agreement was reached, there were important consequences of not following the principles of consensus building, notably concerning the accountability of representatives to the members of their organizations and the lack of commitment in advance of key decision-makers in the Scottish Executive to the agreement. By reverting to type and entering the political lobbies, the outcome depended on the exercise of power.

The process is depicted in two ways. Figure 10.9 traces the attempt at collaborative decision-making from the inception of the Access Forum working on voluntary principles at the behest of the Conservative government at Westminster in 1994. Devolution of responsibility for land reform and access in 1997 to the Scottish Parliament removed the veto power held by the landowners emanating from their representation in the House of Lords.

Aftermath of previous episode
Landowners resist change in status quo while RA
asserts right of access
Balance of power
Power evenly balanced but landowner representation
in the House of Lords gives them a parliamentary veto at Westminster

Latent Phase
Degree of politicization
Both interest groups have strong ideology and are well organized
Understanding of issue
Effects of access on deer stalking are contested
Communication
Little direct communication between groups
Tactics
RA exerts pressure by staging events and lobbying. SLF and NFUS
retain influence by regular lobbying of Scottish Executive

Initiative
Adversarial process is replaced by voluntary participation in negotiations
within Access Forum. National agreement would be subject to local
acceptance by individual landowners

Attempt at participatory decision-making initiation
Focused agenda designed to meet needs of all interests
Inclusiveness
Forum membership balanced and representative but no clear ground rules
to cover accountability of representatives
Forum meets in private, legislative timetable restricts
time for wider consultation
Influence
Agreement reached recognizing rights of access with code covering
responsible behaviour but Scottish Executive not committed
to accepting Forum recommendations

Analysis
A potentially sound decision-making process of negotiation
within representative Forum is disrupted by NFUS reversion to lobbying.
Subsequent changes in draft legislation result in counter lobbying
and parliamentary majority in favour of pro-access legislation
Balance of power
Devolution of responsibility to Scottish Parliament removes veto power
of House of Lords. Political representation in Scottish Parliament
provides majority for legislation

Figure 10.9 *Integrated Analysis of Conflict and Decision-making –
Scottish Access Forum*

The relationship between decision-making and power is further analysed in
Figure 10.10, showing how the landowners were dominant and resisted
change in the form of access legislation, and were unchallenged as long as

authority rested with the parliament in Westminster (south-western quadrant). Negotiations within the Access Forum established a phase of collaboration and an outcome that appeared to satisfy the main interest groups (north-eastern quadrant). Lobbying by the NFUS marked a reversion to adversarial politics, and the draft legislation was an attempt to revert to the status quo (south-eastern quadrant), but this was a temporary outcome. The RA was able to muster support and appeal to the sympathetic majority in the Scottish Parliament, and the final form of legislation symbolized a transfer of power (south-western quadrant). However, the work of the Forum contributed significantly to the final legislation: rights of access are complemented by a code of behaviour (see Figure 10.10).

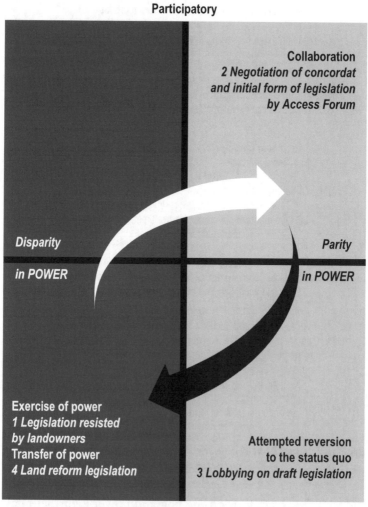

Participatory

Collaboration
2 Negotiation of concordat and initial form of legislation by Access Forum

Disparity

in POWER

Parity

in POWER

Exercise of power
1 Legislation resisted by landowners
Transfer of power
4 Land reform legislation

Attempted reversion to the status quo
3 Lobbying on draft legislation

Non-participatory

Figure 10.10 *Changes in Power and Decision-making – Countryside Access in Scotland*

Key Points from the Case Study

- The account of the history of countryside access in Chapter 2 highlighted certain key factors. These have proved to be just as relevant in the recent history of access legislation in Scotland.
- Certainly, ideological differences between private landowners and recreation groups seeking freedom of public access have been at the heart of the controversy.
- The value of political organization in gaining power and influence has been crucial in contesting those claims. The RA has varied its tactics between being prepared to negotiate, both at Letterewe and nationally, and keeping up the pressure by actively campaigning. The farming and landowning interests have followed similar tactics, negotiating and lobbying effectively.
- Although the outcome in the form of legislation was achieved by a parliamentary majority, the Access Forum in Scotland effectively set the agenda for the legislation.

CONCLUSIONS

The analysis of the case studies in this chapter demonstrates both the importance of power and the development of a form of discourse which allows a just solution to emerge. Whilst some of the criticisms of alternative dispute resolution (ADR) from political scientists can be countered by process design, it is naïve to ignore the realities of power. For example, Amy (1987) saw a very limited role for environmental mediation, arguing that it assumed a pluralistic view of politics in which power was evenly distributed between the interested parties, or that some of the many sources of power were available to the weaker parties. The case studies analysed in this chapter lend support to the argument that changing the form of decision-making to one that is more participatory does not necessarily lead to a just outcome. Furthermore, the neutral third party can only play a limited role in altering the balance of power. Within a representative democracy, the way to alter that balance profoundly, to move from disparity to parity, is by political activity. That is the contribution of political advocacy, a necessary but not always popular role. Many environmental activists – such as Rachel Carson (1962) and Marian Shoard (1980) – have followed the tradition of dissent, albeit for different reasons, and shunned popularity in favour of principle. The essential role of the uncompromising activist can be recognized in the activities of the FEN regarding the Northern Maine Woods.

In both cases presented in this chapter, the centre ground developed a consensus and appeared to lose the battle, yet won the war. Both cases lend further support to the argument that consensus building is a long-term process which takes years, rather than an instant solution dependent on applying the latest technique. In the Northern Maine Woods, the negotiations instigated by Governor King attempted to devise a long-term solution in the heat of a political debate. That the negotiations were successful in reaching an agreement says a lot for the calibre and commitment of those involved. That they failed to get popular support says as much about the failings of adversarial politics as the minor flaws in their process. Yet over the longer term, most of the elements of the Forest Compact are in the process of implementation. But that has only happened because of the shift in power brought about by the environmental activists.

The Scottish case has many parallels. Time has shown that the work of the Access Forum has been far more influential than seemed likely at the height of the political debate on access legislation. In effect, the Forum set the agenda with a vital agreement in principle, which won the support of the landowning organizations. Whilst their membership may have had misgivings, given the political reality of the changes of power following devolution and the political commitment of the majority parties, access legislation was inevitable. The outcome may have been portrayed as a victory for recreation interests, but the final form of the legislation, which balanced rights and responsibilities, was the brainchild of the Forum.

There is no reason why consensus building should be conceived as naïve, although all too many of its advocates appear to be so ideologically driven as to gloss over its weaknesses. Consensus building will never replace the political process, but it can play a vital complementary role. It is an analogous role to that developing in the justice system, whereby the results of mediation are ratified by the courts. What is then required is commitment to implementation.

In both of these case studies the state, in the form of government agencies, played a facilitative role, unlike the case studies presented in Chapter 9. In Maine, the State Forest Service took no active part in the Compact negotiations but its forest inventories and other research contributed valuable information. In Scotland, the CCS and its successor SNH convened meetings of the Access Forum. Similarly, collaboration within the North Oxford County Coalition (NOCC) described in Chapter 6 was instigated by government agencies, the federal Environment Protection Agency (EPA) and the state Department of Environmental Protection (DEP) working in concert.

The difference between the two cases is in the commitment of the ultimate decision-makers. The Maine state governor instigated the Forest Compact negotiations and was committed to backing any subsequent legislation. In the case of the Access Forum, the whole-hearted commitment of the Scottish Executive civil servants to be bound by the outcome of a consensus process was lacking. Sadly, this example appears to be representative, and it stems in part from government's lack of a full appreciation of the principles of consensus building and a lack of proficiency in its skills. This insistence on controlling decision-making is further explored in Chapter 11.

Part 4
The Case for Reform

Chapter 11

Conclusions on Removing the Barriers

It is sobering that 30 years on [from Sherry Arnstein's seminal paper] we are still finding it difficult to engage with communities. (Bartlett, 2000)

SYNOPSIS

This book set out to examine a series of seemingly simple questions concerning why conflicts occur, often on a recurring pattern; what role they play in the political process; and how individuals and organizations respond to conflict. This chapter will reconsider these questions before drawing conclusions on the institutional changes that would be required in Britain to incorporate the principles of consensus building into environmental decision-making.

HOW AND WHY ENVIRONMENTAL CONFLICTS OCCUR

The opening chapters explored the nature of environmental conflicts and used social theory to identify patterns and consistencies. Arguably, conflict and cooperation can be viewed as two sides of the same coin. Often it is the previous relationships between parties that determine whether they are more likely to resort to conflict rather than cooperation. Personality clashes, adversarial tactics and poor communication epitomize conflicts, while good relationships, a conciliatory approach and regular communication characterize cooperation. At times of conflict, there are profound misunderstandings over the nature of the issue, relevant information is lacking or its interpretation is in contention. Even the prevailing system of decision-making and its ability to deliver a fair outcome may be in dispute. Conflict is rarely an isolated event, but it is more likely to recur in phases, when previous history looms large in the minds of the participants. But at the heart of a conflict there lies intense competition for resources and influence between parties with opposing beliefs about how the world should be. During periods of cooperation these differences are suspended, and even when the nature of the issue is unclear, the strength of the relationship enables the stakeholders to handle uncertainty. This brings us to the issue of how such relationships are established.

THE ROLE OF CONFLICTS IN THE POLITICAL PROCESS

The earlier analysis of conflicts, politics and power demonstrated the marked cultural differences between the worlds of politics and consensus. The familiar rough and tumble of adversarial politics, with its echoes of the theatre or the sports arena, is given legitimacy by the process of election, but actually relies as much on negotiation behind closed doors. There are those who argue for the value of political debate, in which prolonged argument reveals the truth and the stronger argument wins, but then truth has many faces. Consensus building also relies on debate, but starts from a different premise: that the needs of all stakeholders, not just those with the loudest voices, should be met. In this case, justice in the form of a fair outcome depends on some overarching mechanism to overcome the inevitable disparities of power. Thus consensus building assumes either a balance of power or a willingness on the part of the powerful to respect other interests and treat them, for the current purposes at least, as equals. These are conditions that are somewhat easier to fulfil in the world of personal relationships than in the world of politics. Hence the increasing use of mediation in handling family and neighbourhood disputes compared to environmental conflicts.

The relationship between the distribution of power and the type of decision-making is crucial in determining whether the outcome of an environmental dispute will be unjust and unstable, with the potential for further conflict, or will reach an equitable and stable state of resolution. Disparities in power between the parties allow the powerful to exercise or consolidate their power, and they will be assisted by an adversarial system of decision-making. But the resulting injustices mean that eventually, opposing groups will emerge with the potential for radical change by the transfer of power. Yet the political struggle may take a different turn if the conflict approaches stalemate, so that neither side can gain victory. At this point, the prospect of negotiating becomes more attractive, and there is an opportunity to change the system of decision-making. If this is taken, it becomes possible to collaborate. Resolution of the conflict depends on the balance of power being maintained.

Standing back from the fray, conflict can therefore be viewed positively as a means of adjusting to social change, providing there is both 'flexibility' (Coser, 1956) in the form of decision-making and a means of balancing power. Politics, as 'the art of peaceful conflict' in Campbell's (2004) terms, provides a process of adjustment. This sequence of events – of conflict moving to resolution via political struggle – provides a necessary safety valve in a democratic society. This positive role of conflict was illustrated by the case study of the Northern Maine Woods (Chapter 10), in which the political activism of outsiders reduced the influence of the forest industry and shifted the centre of the debate about the environmental sustainability of current forest practices. Meanwhile, negotiations between moderate insiders established a working relationship and developed the framework for a longer-term solution, as set out in the Forest Compact. This illustrated that within a representative democracy, the way to alter the balance of power is by political advocacy, a necessary but not always popular role.

USING CONSENSUS BUILDING TO PREVENT OR RESOLVE CONFLICT

The argument has been developed that consensus building is a generic process that can be used to prevent or resolve conflict, as long as its application is tailored to the specific situation and follows a set of key principles of process design. Following the argument that prevention is better than cure, this resumé of the potential contribution of consensus building starts with an assessment of ways of achieving more effective public participation.

A lack of trust on the part of both decision-making agencies and the communities they serve emerged as the major theme throughout Chapters 7 and 8 on participation and partnership. Indeed, powerful decision-makers may be just as ambivalent about working in partnership with other organizations as they have been about more general public involvement in decision-making. Initially it seemed that the problem could be solved solely by devising a participation strategy and selecting the most appropriate techniques at various stages of the process. Whilst this approach is intrinsically sound and preferable to improvisation, the problems of community disillusion with consultation (defined as a tokenistic rather than a fully participatory process) are not entirely technical. The problem of the lack of commitment on the part of decision-makers, which leads to community apathy and mistrust, is basically political and hinges on their use of power.

The responsibilities of office, combined with conflicting mandates, political pressures to deliver and the limited accountability of government agencies, tend to make the agencies reluctant to negotiate with local communities or enter into genuine partnerships. Thus it seems that organizational culture tends to view participation and mediation as threatening, with the risk of a loss of control. What might have seemed to be an obvious approach – participation to prevent conflict – proves from the wider literature to be intrinsically difficult, as it requires decision-makers to have the confidence to delegate responsibility and suspend power differentials. The literature on this topic, dating from the 1970s, makes salutary reading as little appears to have changed over the years.

Whether a partnership has influence and progresses towards its targets depends largely on the degree of commitment of the decision-making bodies and the personal contributions of committed individuals. The Texel case study illustrated the reluctance or inability of local political decision-makers to enter into long-term commitments. In part, this stems from the short-term nature of politics and the constraints of the electoral cycle. Commitments entered into by one party may not be recognized by its successors.

Conflict Prevention by Participatory Planning

The analysis of the four case studies of partnerships in Chapter 8 can be used to identify the key factors which need to be applied to ensure that public participation follows consensus building principles. These have been set out following the framework developed in Chapter 4 to assess whether a process of decision-making is truly participatory, using the criteria of initiation, inclusiveness, information and influence.

Initiation
- Using public participation to reach agreement on the purpose of a partnership and developing a strategy to address public concerns (Morecambe Bay Partnership).
- Gaining local credibility by carrying out projects of value to the local community within the first year of a newly formed partnership (Upper Deeside Access Trust – UDAT).

Inclusiveness
- Gaining and maintaining continuing support from a broad range of organizations and individuals by following a policy of open governance, using a range of consultations, working parties, workshops and annual conferences or meetings (Morecambe Bay Partnership and UDAT).
- Continuing debate after an initial visioning exercise within a range of local fora, and ensuring that all stakeholders have the opportunity to contribute to practical projects on sustainability (Texel 2030 and the Foundation for Sustainable Texel).

Information
- Circulating information widely during the early consultations, continuing with regular newsletters on topical themes (Morecambe Bay Partnership, UDAT and Pentland Hills Regional Park – PHRP).

Influence
- Maintaining staff continuity and the long-term involvement of team players among the agency representatives ensures that the partnership works and gains continuing community support (Morecambe Bay Partnership and UDAT).
- Delegating clear responsibility to a project team with the resources, project staff and experienced supervision to undertake work which is beyond the capability of local landowners (UDAT).

- Relating the ideas generated in the participatory workshops to the current policies of sponsoring local authorities to maintain their political commitment (PHRP).

Consensus Building to Resolve Conflict

The proposition that negotiation only becomes feasible when political struggle has produced a situation of stalemate was illustrated by various case studies. In effect, the case study of the North Oxford County Coalition (NOCC) in Chapter 6 illustrated this method of getting from conflict to resolution: negotiation proved to be the only way out of the crisis facing the environmental regulation agencies. Certainly, their intervention counter-balanced the power of the local pulp mill. External interventions were also crucial to the collaborative management of the Skomer Marine Nature Reserve and in the Rhine Delta (Chapter 9). The latter case also provides examples of cooperation, both since the designation of the Oosterschelde as a national park and in the development of strategies for the Veerse Meer, with the effect of resolving earlier conflicts and securing multiple use goals. The initiation of mediated negotiations to resolve conflict was seen to be dependent partly on pressure on the disputing parties to reach settlement, and partly on the presence of an influential insider who is aware of the potential benefits of mediation. This precondition and the following features of successful consensus building applied to the NOCC and the Peak District Access Consultative Group (PDACG).

Initiation
- Responding to a current conflict by recognizing the opportunity to negotiate and realizing the value of mediation.
- Providing the resources to engage an impartial third party to undertake an initial assessment of the feasibility of mediated negotiations and likelihood of their success.

Inclusiveness
- Ensuring that an impartial conflict assessment is undertaken to identify the stakeholders and their underlying concerns, and set out the basic structure of possible negotiations for ratification by the stakeholders.
- Ensuring that all stakeholders voluntarily participate (either directly or through representation) in mediated negotiations in which the interests of all parties are respected and their legal rights are not prejudiced.
- Building conditions of trust by requiring that negotiations are conducted according to agreed ground rules which ensure clarity of purpose, confidentiality, equal access to information and mutual respect.

Information
- Obtaining relevant information on the issues underlying the dispute and an objective interpretation of the risks to stakeholders involved.

Influence

• Obtaining a firm commitment in advance from the ultimate decision-makers that they will act on the outcome of the negotiations.[1]

REMOVING THE BARRIERS: THE WIDER APPLICATION OF ENVIRONMENTAL CONSENSUS BUILDING IN SCOTLAND

The previous sections have provided general prescriptions for the wider use of consensus building. This section recognizes that any analysis of the opportunities for institutional reform has to be set in a specific context. It therefore takes the current situation in Scotland as a case study for potential change, whilst recognizing that many of these suggestions could be applied elsewhere.

An earlier assessment of environmental disputes in Scotland was based on an analysis of a monthly news digest (*Scottish Environmental News* – SCENES) over the three years 1996–1998 (Sidaway, 1999a). It identified the types and approximate incidence of disputes which fell into two main categories:

1   developments that fell within the statutory remit of the development control and planning system; and
2   a large range of other issues, including the procedures used for public land acquisition, land management, compensation payments for conservation areas such as sites of special scientific interest (SSSIs), access for recreation, afforestation and the felling of woodlands, species protection, coastal fisheries and fish farming, shipwrecks and pollution.

The general limitations of decision-making were as follows:

• Dispute resolution procedures are less well developed for certain issues that fall outwith the scope of the statutory planning system.
• Polarization easily occurs, resulting in a situation of conflict in which few organizations remain sufficiently neutral to play a mediating role.
• Certain organizations have conflicting roles, e.g., they perform both regulatory and policy-making functions.
• Partnerships of organizations that might play conciliatory or mediating roles are not formally structured to follow consensus building procedures or necessarily equipped with such expertise.
• Discussion about local developments is often confounded by interlocking debates about national policy, suggesting that improvements could be made to processes of policy development (Sidaway, 1999a).

Opportunities Within the Planning and Development Control System

There is significant government interest in Scotland in the potential cost savings from bringing mediation into the planning process for industrial and residential development.[2] The existing process is shown in a simplified form in the following diagram, in which the potential opportunities for improving public participation or using mediation are shown in italics (see Figure 11.1). Potentially, mediation could be used in the preparation of a draft plan (*Stage One, opportunity B*) or in individual cases (*Stage Two, opportunity D*) to attempt to curtail the lengthy processes of appeals and public inquiries. However, it would be more effective to reduce the risk of conflict at an earlier stage by supplementing formal consultation processes with more effective public participation in the preparation of statutory plans when policy decisions are made on which areas may be developed (*Stage One, opportunity A*). It would be to the advantage of developers if they were to undertake a participatory exercise with local stakeholders before a site application is submitted to the local planning authority (*Stage Two, opportunity C*), thereby reducing or even eliminating objections to their proposals.

The British planning process is very oriented to the interests of the developer, with no right of appeal for other stakeholders if an individual application is approved by the local planning authority. In fact, there are moves to change the legislation in Scotland to introduce a 'third party right of appeal', which exists in Ireland and in some states of Australia. Whilst developers argue that this would generate more objections and slow down what they see as a cumbersome planning process, advocates of this reform argue that it would provide an incentive for developers to secure the early participation of other stakeholders and minimize the potential for conflict in the later stages. It has also been suggested that developers should be legally obliged to undertake an effective participation process on individual applications, as it is in the developer's interests to agree both the process and proposals with the community when putting forward an application.

This example demonstrates that consensus building would not replace the official process of decision-making, but that it can play a vital complementary role. It is an analogous role to that developing in the justice system, whereby the results of mediation are ratified by the courts. In the opportunities identified in Figure 11.1, the responsibility for the final decision on a plan would still rest with the local authority or perhaps the Scottish Executive. For planning applications, the final decision would still be taken by the local planning authority or by the Scottish Executive, when the decision is subject to appeal.

There would need to be a clear separation of roles within the local authority. As the planning department is responsible for planning policy and advising its committee on individual cases, it cannot also play an impartial role between the developer and objectors. This has to be undertaken by an

---

STAGE ONE

STRUCTURE (REGIONAL) AND LOCAL PLANS
are prepared by local planning authorities (elected councils)
which receive representations from interested parties
during the course of a period of formal consultation
A. Opportunity to secure more effective public participation

Substantive comments on the draft plan may be the subject of a
public inquiry (hearing) before a planning reporter (i.e., an arbitrator)
B. Opportunity for mediation prior to hearing

Final version of plan is approved by the Scottish Executive

STAGE TWO

DETAILED PROPOSALS
Individual planning applications need to conform to local plans
Developers will discuss the suitability of proposals with planning officials
C. Opportunity to secure more effective public participation

Developers submit applications
There is a limited opportunity for other stakeholders to submit objections
The decision is made by elected councillors based on advice from planning officials
If approved, other stakeholders have no right of appeal

If rejected, developer has right of appeal
Application may be modified and resubmitted
D. Opportunities for mediation prior to hearing
Public inquiry (hearing before planning reporter)

Decision by Scottish Executive

Figure 11.1 *The Planning and Development Process in Scotland*

independent facilitator or mediator. The appointment of independent
facilitators and mediators should be administered by the Chief Executive's
Department of the local authority, or the next tier of government which is
responsible for appeals – in Scotland, the Chief Reporter's Office.

Disputes Outwith the Planning System

In general, the principles of early public involvement in the planning stages or
negotiations between key stakeholders are valid, but it is not clear how such
procedures can be initiated over this wide range of decisions. Indeed, the
earlier case studies demonstrated that government agencies were more likely
to act in a partisan way within an adversarial system of politics. In many cases,
conflict was triggered by government agencies striving to develop and
implement an aspect of public policy within their mandates. The situation is

further complicated where environmental agencies perform both regulatory and promotional functions, as in the case of Scottish National Heritage (SNH), where its dual functions are not as clearly delineated as, say, the enterprise and authority functions of the Forestry Commission. Such roles need to be clearly separated.

However, government agencies can also play a facilitative role. In Maine, the State Forest Service took no active part in the compact negotiations, but its forest inventories and other research contributed valuable information. In Scotland, the Countryside Commission for Scotland (CCS) and its successor SNH convened meetings of the Access Forum, which collaboratively developed a broadly supported policy for countryside access. Similarly, collaboration within the NOCC was instigated by two government agencies, the federal Environment Protection Agency (EPA) and the state Department of Environmental Protection (DEP), working in concert. This last case also shows how environmental regulators may encourage participatory decision-making without compromising their statutory duties. The US EPA provides an example of a regulatory agency which has also pioneered the use of alternative dispute resolution (ADR) methods.

Consensus building principles are just as relevant to partnerships and inter-agency working as they are to the relationships between agencies and communities. It has been argued that the failure to find solutions to the multiple problems of the British uplands is as likely to stem from institutional politics as from further technical specification of either problems or solutions (Sidaway, 2002). The failure to develop integrated policies is due not to the obstinacy of individuals but rather the sectoral nature of government, in which departments and agencies are engaged in a struggle for survival. This struggle to maintain autonomy is typified by demarcation disputes, the failure to delegate executive authority to partnerships, unrelated initiatives by different agencies and unconnected levels of decision-making. Underpinning this is a system of accountability which rewards performance based on readily quantifiable and narrowly focused short-term criteria, rather than the development of longer-term relationships with external bodies, partly because they are intrinsically difficult to assess.

OPPORTUNITIES FOR INSTITUTIONAL REFORM

If joined-up government is to become more than fashionable rhetoric, changes to these reward systems are needed which benefit cooperation. If this cannot be achieved, then it would be as well to jettison the rhetoric of integration and to concentrate on clarifying objectives and setting realistic limits to intended cooperation. If the aspiration to achieve integration is genuine, then political direction has to instigate a cultural shift. The move beyond power-brokering within committees to genuine consensus will not be easy to accomplish. It will entail an unfamiliar degree of openness in decision-making, and carefully designed strategies to ensure that interests are represented on their own terms and respected in the ensuing dialogue.

There is also a need to develop more transparent methods of debating and developing public policy. Here, the principle of delegating authority and allowing representative bodies to influence decision-making certainly holds true. The case studies provide a telling contrast between the Maine Forest Compact negotiations and the Scottish Access Forum. In the Maine case, the state governor instigated the Forest Compact negotiations and was committed to backing any subsequent legislation. But the civil servants in the Scottish Executive were not committed to take the Forum's advice, although it had spent three years building consensus, as they followed the convention that the minister's position should not be compromised. Sadly, this appears to be the rule in Scotland and it stems in part from government lacking a full appreciation of the opportunities offered by consensus building principles. Reform should begin at the highest level, in this case the Scottish Parliament, by examining the feasibility of legislation requiring consensus building options to be considered as the first option rather than the last resort, perhaps on the lines of the US Alternative Disputes Resolution Act of 1996. In essence, this act requires federal agencies to adopt a policy of applying ADR instead of litigation whenever possible, to designate a senior official as its dispute resolution specialist, who ensures that the agency complies with the act, and to provide regular training for all officials involved in implementing this policy.

Comparable legislation would require Scottish agencies to appoint mediation and public participation specialists, and that the operation of the act might be overseen by a department of environmental justice within the Scottish Executive. There is no doubt that this would be a marked change in policy towards developing the facilitative role within government, and it would go some way to remedying an institutional inadequacy: the absence of an effective conflict resolution mechanism in British environmental planning which can steer disputes towards equitable negotiation.

Developing Institutional Capacity

It is important to emphasize the distinctions between decision-makers gaining greater awareness of the value of consensus building, their acquisition of 'in-house' skills, and the potential conflicts of interest between the roles they may perform. The initiation stages of both participation and mediation exercises crucially require commitment at a senior level in decision-making agencies. Senior executives may in turn be influenced by an internal advocate, as was illustrated in many of the case studies. An ADR or participation specialist with credibility in the organization can play this vital intermediary role, which is similar to that of a company lawyer or research manager who is well versed in legal or research processes and has the skills and experience to contract appropriate external professionals, but does not act as a practitioner. Crucial tasks, such as the impartial assessment of whether mediated negotiation is feasible or the design of participation strategies, require the application of external professional skills. They cannot be done 'in-house' because of the potential conflict of interest with executive responsibility, and because they will not be perceived as impartial by other stakeholders. Crucial requirements in developing the capacity for consensus building are summarized below.

Initiation
- Higher levels of awareness of the general potential of consensus building.
- Gaining access to professional expertise, and being prepared to seek and accept impartial advice on when consensus building is feasible and how specific participatory processes should be designed in collaboration with stakeholders.

Inclusiveness
- Greater willingness to work in partnership with those with influence in other organizations and the wider interested public.

Information
- Willingness to share information and learn from others.
- Responding constructively to stakeholder contributions and providing feedback, particularly by setting out the rationale for the acceptance or rejection of suggested options.

Influence
- Having the confidence to delegate or be influenced by stakeholders without compromising executive responsibilities.
- Recognizing that consistency, continuity of ideas (and preferably personnel), mutual respect, honesty, integrity and, above all, time are needed to build trust with partners.

However, identifying the responsibilities and process at appropriate stages of decision-making is only one aspect of implementation of environmental consensus building. There also needs to be development of a range of training programmes to increase the number of suitably qualified mediators and facilitators, as well as awareness training for decision-makers. This is difficult enough in the field of environmental mediation in Britain, where there is little specialist training and few opportunities to practise, although the recognized standards for the family and community mediation services provide a basis for quality control. The Scottish Mediation Network, which covers all aspects of mediation and has been funded to develop emergent sectors, including environment and planning, provides a framework for professional development. What is needed is a counterpart organization for public participation.[3]

While the move to develop ADR in Britain is principally driven by the cost of litigation, decision-makers will also need reassurance that ADR works from well documented case studies, ideally of work undertaken by respected peer agencies. Thus there is a further need to evaluate and document case studies which demonstrate good practice that could be more widely adopted in Britain.

Allowing Time for Consensus to Develop

Consensus building is not easy to apply in practice, being both unusual in an adversarial culture and time-consuming. Certainly those consensus processes that have affected real change work over timescales measured in years rather than months. The NOCC negotiation spanned seven years and transformed community attitudes in the process. It has taken a similar period for the main elements of the Forest Compact for the Northern Maine Woods to be implemented. But this has only happened because of the mutual understanding built up over the years within a policy community of influential individuals from the forest industry and the environmental organizations. Similarly, the work of the Access Forum in Scotland over many years has proved to be far more influential than seemed likely at the height of the political debate on access legislation. Even the participatory exercises in Texel and the PHRP, which have had less obvious outcomes, have proved to be influential over the longer term. If these seem to be lengthy processes, consider the alternatives. The development of major projects puts these time periods into perspective. Constructing a motorway can take at least 20 years when the three years of actual construction are preceded by 17 years of contested planning, as in the case of M3 bypassing Winchester (Bryant, 1996).

FINAL REFLECTIONS

To return to the beginning, the early analysis of case studies identified two themes which ran through to the closing analysis, namely: the political nature of conflict, and a general public distrust of officialdom learnt from bitter experience. Both themes reflect the centrality of power and decision-making to any study of environmental conflicts. Many of the subsequent case studies confirmed the view that changing decision-making to make it more participatory does not of itself produce fair and just outcomes, unless there is parity in power amongst the stakeholders. But the route to balancing power is though political activism and not within the remit of a third party neutral. So the most important messages from this book are that there should be complementary processes of participation, politics and negotiation, and that conflict is not necessarily the problem but often part of the solution.

Similarly the government agencies who have erected barriers to participation and mediation cannot be dismissed as the problem, but have to be part of the solution. The task is to find effective ways to engage the agencies in participation, to encourage them to change their cultures, and to persuade their political masters to change the remits, resources and timescales on which they operate. These are all political questions and provide the keys to such agencies embarking on the long-term process of building trust with communities. If resisting participation is in itself a political act on the part of decision-makers, it follows that there is a politics of conflict resolution and prevention, and that initiatives to change the system of decision-making will require a degree of political activity to gain the necessary political support to change the decision-making culture.

In the preface, I predicted that the most crucial readers of this book would be the decision-makers, because of the issues of power, control and public involvement in decision-making, or the lack of it. If anything changes it will be because of changes of hearts and minds on the parts of decision-makers. My message to them is: Be more confident in yourselves. Trust people, and delegate power to them, and they will trust you. Be less preoccupied with outcomes and performance indicators, and be more concerned about processes and relationships. Allow others the time needed to reach consensus.

Notes

PREFACE

1   In this book the terms 'dispute' and 'conflict' have been used synonymously.

CHAPTER 2 Introduction to the Principal Case Studies

1   Ten other individuals and organizations representing a wide range of interests have not been included in this analysis.
2   The following analysis is based on a study which explored whether attitudes to the regional park had been modified since designation (Sidaway, 1991a). The information provided in written representations was supplemented by interviews with most of the individuals or organizations that had made representations at both stages.

CHAPTER 3 Using Social Theory to Explain Conflicts

1   Coser (1956) analyses Talcott Parsons' use of the medical analogy, and terms like 'tension', 'strain', 'endemic', and 'deviant behaviour' within a 'sick society'. He prefers to draw an analogy with adjustments in the Earth's crust, and to use the terminology of tectonics – like 'earth tremor' and 'earthquake' – to register the intensity of conflicts.
2   An informal coalition of conservation and access organizations has ensured that motor sports have largely been considered 'inappropriate' to the quiet enjoyment of the countryside in Britain and have effectively been denied access, with the exception of limited categories of rights of way (see Elson et al, 1986; Harrison, 1991).

CHAPTER 4 Alternative Dispute Resolution – The Contribution of Negotiation and Consensus Building

1   The reader should recognize that this figure has been simplified to illustrate the essential differences in process. A more comprehensive listing would cover some 30 procedures. Assessments of the full range of such variations is found in Acland,

1995; Barach Bush, 1995; Colosi, 1993; and Palmer and Roberts, 1998, etc.
2   Again, there are problems of terminology. SPIDR (1997) lists 23 different terms, including consensus building, for what it prefers to call 'collaborative agreement seeking processes'.
3   Details of how to conduct negotiations are not given here, but are to be found in standard texts, such as Fisher et al, 1997, and Susskind, Levy and Thomas-Larmer, 2000.

CHAPTER 5 Mediation and Its Contribution to Resolving Environmental Disputes

1   As with the choice of mediator, any technical expert brought in to assist should be acceptable to the group as a whole.
2   Typically, of approximately 15,000 administrative decisions taken each year by a district administrator in the US Federal Highway Administration, 60–70 may be determined at a higher level on appeal, and one or two of these might become major conflicts which might be eligible for ADR (Kussey, 1992).
3   Zondervan (2002) provides a more recent review of community mediation in the USA.
4   The author was engaged by the Board to conduct the initial assessment on the basis of his previous research on these issues in the Peak District, so he was therefore known to most of the contending parties. He subsequently mediated meetings of the PDACG.

CHAPTER 6 'Clearing the Air' – The North Oxford County Coalition

1   The quotations in this chapter are taken from interviews with the author obtained in 2001. The respondents gave permission for the interviews to be tape-recorded and were given the opportunity to comment on the chapter in draft.
2   Following the distinctions made in Chapter 4, I have referred to the CBI team members as 'mediators', and one of the tasks they undertook was the facilitation of meetings. The respondents that I interviewed referred to them as 'facilitators'.
3   In fact, the resources devoted to monitoring air quality by the DEP over the years were as significant as those expended on the NOCC exercise. Continuing monitoring has shown a significant reduction in chlorine and dioxin emissions following the installation of new pulp processing equipment (Maine DEP, 2001; Doering, 2001, personal communication).

CHAPTER 7 Public Participation in Decision-making and Partnerships

1   In this book, the terms 'public participation' and 'public involvement' are taken to be synonymous and used inter-changeably, as in much of the literature.
2   Alternative dispute tresolution (ADR) is discussed in Chapter 4.

CHAPTER 8 Building Trust – Crucial Lessons in Participation and Partnership

1 The board of VVV Texel consists of representatives from the ferry operator, the tourism accommodation sector, the retailing sector and the municipality.
2 Participatory appraisal (PA) uses group animation to facilitate information gathering and sharing, analysis and action. Its purpose is to get development practitioners, government officials and local people to work together (World Bank, 1996).
3 The term 'open meeting' was used to avoid expectations that the format of a conventional public meeting, with all its disadvantages, would be followed (see Chapter 7, p138, and Figure 7.8).
4 During the course of the event, several participants commented to the author, who was acting as lead facilitator, that it would not have been possible to reach that degree of consensus two or three years previously.

CHAPTER 9 Organizations, Power and Conflict

1 This account of events at Skomer is based on Sidaway, 1988 and subsequent re-analysis in Sidaway, 1996.
2 The research on which this study is based was undertaken intermittently by the author over the period 1991–2002. The original study of the Oosterschelde was undertaken in 1991 and was extended to include the other phases of the Delta scheme in 1992 (Sidaway and van der Voet, 1993). Later, the material was re-analysed (Sidaway, 1996), and a number of interviews was conducted by the author in 2001 and 2003 to investigate national park designation in the Oosterschelde.
3 For a full account of the Delta scheme, see Ministry of Transport and Public Works, 1989.
4 The government departments represented on the Steering Group of the Oosterschelde were: the Ministry of Agriculture, Nature Management and Fisheries; the Ministry of Finance; the Ministry of Housing, Physical Planning and Environment; the Ministry of Traffic and Public Works; and the Ministry of Economic Affairs.
5 Staatsbosbeheer (SBB) is the state forest service, which is also responsible for managing nature reserves, while Natuurmonumenten performs a similar role in the non-governmental sector.

CHAPTER 10 Consensus and the Political Process

1 For example, Hattersley (1998) is in fact arguing against compromising ideological principles within coalition government.
2 This case study is based on research undertaken by the author in Maine between 1998 and 2002, partly funded by the Carnegie Trust for the Universities of Scotland.
3 This case study concentrates on the original Access Forum concerned with public access to private land, established in 1994, rather than the Access Forum

for Inland Water established in approximately 1999, which is largely concerned
with management issues.
4   This account of the Forum is based on documentary evidence and presentations
made in February 2002 to a module on participation in policy and planning for
MSc students at the University of Edinburgh organized by the author.
5   The responsibilities of the public, land managers and public bodies were set out
in the 36-page *Draft Scottish Access Code* published by the Scottish Executive
in 2001.

CHAPTER 11 Conclusions on Removing the Barriers

1   As noted earlier, a firm commitment to act on the recommendations of the
PDACG was not obtained.
2   At the time of writing (October 2004), the environment and planning initiative
group of the Scottish Mediation Network (chaired by the author) is promoting
a project to assess the needs for mediation in a pilot area and how those might
be met.
3   At time of writing (October 2004), there are plans to form a British network
affiliated to IAP2.

References

Acland, A F (1995) *Resolving Disputes Without Going to Court: A consumer guide to alternative dispute resolution*, Century Business Books, London

Amy, D (1987) *The Politics of Environmental Mediation*, Columbia University Press, New York

Anderson, P (1990) *Moorland Recreation and Wildlife in the Peak District: Summary*, Peak Park Joint Planning Board, Bakewell

Anon (1989) Explanatory text to the Ramsar Designation for the Oosterschelde

Anon (2000) 'Nuclear installations inspectorate report on Sellafield', *The Guardian*, 19 February

Anon (2003)'Nine month ban on emissions imposed by UK Environmental Secretary after criticism at EU ministerial summit and Greenpeace claims of traces in Scottish farmed salmon', *Herald*, Glasgow, 24 June

Arnstein, S (1969) 'A ladder of participation', *Journal of the American Institute of Planners*, vol 39, 216–224

Auerbach, J (1983) *Justice Without Law? Resolving disputes without lawyers*, Oxford University Press, Oxford.

Augsburger, D W (1992) *Conflict Mediation Across Cultures: Pathways and patterns*, Westminster/John Knox Press, Louisville, KY

Avruch, K and Black, P W (1993) 'Conflict resolution in intercultural settings: Problems and prospects', in Sandole, D J D and van der Merwe, H (eds), *Conflict Resolution Theory and Practice: Integration and application*, Manchester University Press, Manchester

Barach Bush, R A (1995) 'Dispute resolution – the domestic arena: A survey of methods, applications and critical issues', in Vasquez, J A, Johnson, J T, Jaffe, S and Stamato, L (eds), *Beyond Confrontation: Learning conflict resolution in the post-Cold War era*, University of Michigan Press, Ann Arbor, MI, 9–37

Barr, A (2003) 'Participative planning and evaluation skills', in Banks, S, Butcher, H, Henderson, P and Robertson, J (eds), *Managing Community Practice*, The Policy Press, Bristol

Barry, M and Sidaway, R (1999) 'Empowerment through partnership: The relevance of theories of participation to social work practice', in Shera, W and Wells, L (eds), *Empowerment Practice in Social Work: Developing richer conceptual foundations*, Canadian Scholars' Press, Toronto

Bartlett, D (2000) 'The world is run by those who turn up – more ideas on public participation', *ECOS*, vol 21, no 2, 37–42

Baumgartner, T, Burns, T R and De Ville, P (1978) 'Conflict resolution and conflict development: The theory of game transformation with an application to the lip factory conflict', in Kriesberg, L (ed), *Research in Social Movements, Conflicts and Change*, vol 1, 105–142, JAI Press Inc., Greenwich, CT

Bell, A G (1985) *Report of a public inquiry into objections lodged against the Pentland Hills Regional Park Designation Order 1984*, Scottish Office, Edinburgh

Bellman, H (1992) Interview with author, Madison, WI

Birkhoff, J E (2002) *Evaluation and Research*, Association for Conflict Resolution, www.acresolution.org

Bleakley, S (1994) 'Coastal conflicts: Past mistakes, future direction? An analysis of two conservation initiatives: Loch Sween proposed marine nature reserve and Morecambe Bay – a consultative strategy', unpublished MSc dissertation, University of Edinburgh

Bleakley, S (2003) Interview with author, Kendal

Bleakley, S (2004) Personal communication

Bolman, L G and Deal, T E (1992) 'What makes a team work?', *Organizational Dynamics*, vol 21, no 2, 34–44

Bos, V I (2004) Presentation to students of Wageningen University during study tour of Texel, 27–28 March

Bosma, N J (1992) 'We bouwen geen communicatiebruggen; Storm in de Voordelta: conflict tussen recreatie en natuur', *Recreatie and Toerisme*, vol 2 no 5, pp16–17

Boucher, N (1989) 'Whose woods these are', *Wilderness*, fall, 36

Boulding, K (1990) *Three Faces of Power*, Sage Publications, Newbury Park

Boulton, A (1990) 'New strategies for the Northern Forest: A look at the Northern Forest Land Study', *Forest Watch*, July, 22–25

BOW-Bulletin (1992) *Ontwikkelingen rond de Voordelta; chronologisch overzicht*, Bulletin Nr.4, Breed Overleg Waterrecreatie, Bunnik

British Sub-Aqua Club (1986) Proposed Skomer Marine Reserve, Letter to Director Wales, Nature Conservancy Council, 1 September

British Sub-Aqua Club (1987) Proposed Skomer Marine Nature Reserve: Letter to Secretary of State for Wales, 15 January

Brown, B (1993) 'Public organizations and policies in conflict: Notes on theory and practice', in Sandole, D J D and van der Merwe, H (eds), *Conflict Resolution Theory and Practice: Integration and application*, Manchester University Press, Manchester and New York

Brown, H J and Marriott, A L (1993) *ADR Principles and Practice*, Sweet and Maxwell, London

Bryant, B (1996) *Twyford Down: Roads, campaigning and environmental law*, E and F N Spon, London

Buckles, D (ed) (1999) *Cultivating Peace: Conflict and collaboration in natural resource management*, International Development Research Centre and World Bank Institute, Washington, DC

Bullimore, B (1987) *Skomer Proposed Marine Nature Reserve: Report of the Nature Conservancy Council Liaison Officer for the period 5 May–20 September 1987*, Nature Conservancy Council, Aberystwyth

Burt, T P, Thompson, D B A and Warburton, J (eds) (2002) *The British Uplands: Dynamics of change*, Joint Nature Conservation Committee Report No 319, JNCC, Peterborough

Burton, J W (1972) *World Society*, Cambridge University Press, Cambridge and New York

Burton, J W (1995) 'Conflict provention as a political system', in Vasques, J A, Johnson, J T, Jaffe, S and Stamato, L (eds), *Beyond Confrontation: Learning conflict resolution in the post-Cold War era*, University of Michigan Press, Ann Arbor, MI

Burton, T L (1976) *Making Man's Environment: Leisure*, Van Nostrand Reinhold Ltd, Toronto

Callander, R (1987) *A Pattern of Landownership in Scotland*, Haughend Publications, Finzean

Campbell, B (2004) 'An infantile disorder', *The Guardian*, 26 July

Canadian Correctional Service (1997) *Consultation: A framework document*, CCS, Ottawa

Canadian Round Tables (1993) *Building Consensus for a Sustainable Future: Guiding principles*, CRT, Ottawa

Carpenter, S and Kennedy, W J D (1988) *Managing Public Disputes: A practical guide to handling conflict and reaching agreements*, Jossey-Bass, San Francisco, CA

Carson, R (1962) *Silent Spring*, Houghton Mifflin, Boston, MA

CCS (Countryside Commission for Scotland) (1987) *Nineteenth Report 1 January 1986 to 31 December 1986*, CCS, Battleby

CCS (Countryside Commission for Scotland) (1988) *Twentieth Report 1 January 1987 to 31 December 1987*, CCS, Battleby

CCS (Countryside Commission for Scotland) (1989) *Twenty First Annual Report 1 January 1988 to 31 December 1988*, CCS, Battleby

Centre for Leisure Research (1986) *Access to the Countryside for Recreation and Sport*, Countryside Commission and Sports Council, Cheltenham and London

Chester, A (2003) Interview with author, Kendal

Chevalier, J M and Buckles, D (1999) 'Conflict management: A heterocultural perspective', in Buckles, D (ed), *Cultivating Peace: Conflict and collaboration in natural resource management*, International Development Research Centre and World Bank Institute, Washington, DC

Chornenki, G (1997) 'Mediating commercial disputes: Exchanging "power over" for "power with"', in Macfarlane, J (ed), *Rethinking Disputes: The mediation alternative*, Cavendish Publishing, London

Clark, G, Darrall, J, Grove-White, R, McNaughten, P and Urry, J (1994) *Leisure Landscapes – Leisure, Culture and the English Countryside: Challenges and conflicts*, Centre for the Study of Environmental Change, Lancaster University, Lancaster

Cleaver, F (2001) 'Institutions, agency and the limitations of participatory approaches to development', in Cooke, B and Kothari, U (eds), *Participation: The new tyranny?*, Zed Books, London and New York

Cole, J (1992) 'The curse of Selsdon man', *New Statesman and Society*, 13 November, 9

Coleman, A M (2001) 'Strategies for visitor management in the Cairngorms: An examination of two approaches', unpublished MSc dissertation, University of Edinburgh

Colosi, T R (1993) *On and Off the Record: Colosi on negotiation*, Kendall Hunt Publishing Company, Dubuque, IA

Connor, D M (1997) *Public Participation: A manual*, Development Press, Victoria, BC

Cooke, B and Kothari, U (eds) (2001) *Participation: The new tyranny?*, Zed Books, London and New York

Cornelius, H and Faire, S (1989) *Everyone Can Win: How to resolve conflict*, Simon and Schuster, Sydney

Coser, L A (1956) *The Function of Social Conflict*, The Free Press, New York

Coser, L A (1967) *Continuities in the Study of Social Conflict*, The Free Press, New York

Countryside Council for Wales (1993) *Skomer Marine Nature Reserve: Agreed management policy*, CCW, Aberystwyth

Cramb, A (1996) *Who Owns Scotland Now? The use and abuse of private land*, Mainstream, Edinburgh

Creighton, J L (1978) 'Why conduct public involvement programs for regulatory functions?', in Creighton, J L, Delli Priscoli, J and Ballentine, T (eds), *Public Involvement in Corps Regulatory Programs: Training manual*, Institute for Water Resources, Washington, DC

Creighton, J L (1992) *Involving Citizens in Community Decision Making: A guidebook*, Program for Community Problem Solving, Washington, DC

Creighton, J L, Delli Priscoli, J and Dunning, M (eds) (1983) *Public Involvement Techniques: A reader of ten years experience at the Institute for Water Resources*, IWR Research Report 82-R1, US Army Corps of Engineers, Fort Belvoir, VA

Crumley, J (1991) 'Fighting the green corner', *The Scotsman*, 21 October

Delli Priscoli, J (1980) 'Developing public involvement evaluations: A federal agency perspective', paper given at Washington, DC, 4 February

Delli Priscoli, J (1983) 'Why the federal and regional interest in public involvement in water resources development?, in Creighton, J L, Delli Priscoli, J and Dunning, M (eds) *Public Involvement Techniques: A reader of ten years experience at the Institute for Water Resources*, IWR Research Report 82-R1, US Army Corps of Engineers, Fort Belvoir, VA

De Marchi, B and Ravetz, J R (2001) *Participatory Approaches to Environmental Policy: Environmental valuation in Europe*, Policy Research Brief No 10, Cambridge Research for the Environment for European Commission DG XII, Cambridge, www.landecon.cam.ac.uk/eve/

Department of Environment, Transport and the Regions (1997) *Involving Communities on Urban and Rural Regeneration: A guide for practitioners*, DETR, London

Department of the Environment (1992) *Coastal Zone Protection and Planning: The government's response to the Second Report from the House of Commons Environment Select Committee*, HMSO, London

Deutsch, M (1973) *The Resolution of Conflict: Constructive and destructive processes*, Yale University Press, New Haven, CT and London

Doering, E (2001) Interview with author, Augusta, ME

Doornbos, M, Saith, A and White, B (2000) 'Forests: Nature, people, power', *Development and Change*, special issue, vol 31, no 1

Dower, J (1945) *National Parks in England and Wales*, HMSO, London

Dros, C H (2004) Presentation to students of Wageningen University during study tour of Texel, 27–28 March

Druckman, D (1993) 'An analytical research agenda for conflict resolution', in Sandole, D J D and van der Merwe, H (eds), *Conflict Resolution Theory and Practice: Integration and application*, Manchester University Press, Manchester and New York

Duim, V R van der and Caalders, J (2004) 'The margins of Texel', *Journal of Sustainable Tourism*, vol 12, no 5, 367–387

Duim, V R van der and Lengkeek, J (2004) 'All pervading island tourism: The case of Texel, the Netherlands', in Boissevain, J and Selwyn, T (eds), *Tourism on the Foreshore: Society, economics and politics on the coast*, Amsterdam University Press, Amsterdam

Duim, V R van der, Caalders, J, Cordero, A, Duynen Montijn, L van and Ritsma, N (2001) *Developing Sustainable Tourism: The case of Manuel Antonio and Texel*, Wageningen University, Flasco and Buiten Consultancy, Wageningen/San Jose/Utrecht

Duke, J (1979) *Conflict and Power in Social Life*, Brigham Young University Press, Provo, UT

Eelman, N (2004) Presentation to students of Wageningen University during study tour of Texel, 27–28 March

Elson, M J, Buller, H and Stanley, P (1986) *Providing for Motorsports: From image to reality*, Sports Council Study 28, The Sports Council, London

English Nature (1993a) *Estuary Management Plans: A co-ordinator's guide*, English Nature, Peterborough

English Nature (1993b) *Strategy for the Sustainable Use of England's Estuaries*, English Nature, Peterborough

Environment Council (1995) 'Memorandum to the House of Commons Environment Committee', *Session 1994–5 Fourth Report: The environmental impact of leisure activities*, Vol 3, Appendices, HMSO, London

Environmental Resources Management/Sidaway, R (1997) *The Glen Muick, Lochnager and Ballater Area Study: Recommendations for a visitor strategy*, Final report to the Lochnagar Advisory Committee, ERM, Edinburgh

Ertel, D (1991) 'How to design a conflict management procedure that fits your dispute', *Sloan Management Review*, vol 32, no 4

Fagan, G (1997) *New Ideas in Rural Development No 3: Involving rural communities – the CADISPA approach*, The Scottish Office Central Research Unit, Edinburgh

Fisher, R J (1990) 'Needs theory, social identity and an eclectic model of conflict', in Burton, J (ed), *Conflict: Human needs theory*, St Martin's Press, New York

Fisher, R, Ury, W and Patton, B (1997) *Getting to Yes: Negotiating agreement without giving in*, Arrow Business Books, London

Forester, J (1989) 'Planning in the face of conflict: Negotiation and mediation strategies in local land use regulation', *Journal of the American Planning Association*, vol 53, no 3, 303–314

Francis, P (2001) 'Participatory development at the World Bank: The primacy of process', in Cooke, B and Kothari, U (eds), *Participation: The new tyranny?*, Zed Books, London and New York

Friedmann, J (1987) *Planning in the Public Domain: From knowledge to action*, Princeton University Press, Princeton, New Jersey

Friends of the Pentlands Society (2004) *Information Leaflet*, Friends of the Pentlands, Edinburgh

Glasbergen, P (ed) (1991) *Integrale beleidsplanning voor de grote wateren*, SDU Uit geverij, 's-Gravenhage

Grabrovaz, M (1995) *Review of Estuary Projects*, English Nature, Peterborough

Grant, W (1978) *Insider Groups, Outsider Groups and Interest Group Strategies in Britain*, Working Paper No 19, University of Warwick, Warwick

Gray, J (2001) 'Wars of want', *The Guardian*, 21 August

Gubbay, S (1990) *A Future for the Coast*, WWF/MCS, Ross on Wye

Hailey, J (2001) 'Beyond the formulaic: Process and practice in South Asian NGOs', in Cooke, B and Kothari, U (eds), *Participation: The new tyranny?*, Zed Books, London and New York

Handy, C B (1985) *Understanding Organisations*, third edition, Penguin, London

Hansard (House of Lords) (1981) *Wildlife and Countryside Bill, 13 July 1981*, HMSO, London, 924–938

Harrison, C (1991) *Countryside Recreation in a Changing Society*, The TMS Partnership Ltd, London

Hattersley, R (1998) 'Out vile consensus', *New Statesman*, 30 January, 30–31

Henkel, H and Stirrat, R (2001) 'Participation as spiritual duty: Empowerment and secular subjection', in Cooke, B and Kothari, U (eds), *Participation: The new tyranny?*, Zed Books, London and New York

Hildyard, N, Hedge, P, Wolverkamp, P and Reddy, S (2001) 'Participation and power: Joint forest management in India', in Cooke, B and Kothari, U (eds), *Participation: The new tyranny?*, Zed Books, London and New York

Hill, H (1980) *Freedom to Roam: The struggle for access to Britain's moors and mountains*, Moorland Publishing, Ashbourne

Hilton, V and Sidaway, R (2000) *Local Opinions and Ideas for the Future of the Pentland Hills Regional Park*, unpublished report to Pentland Hills Regional Park

Hippisley Cox, R (1973) *The Green Roads of England*, Garnstone Press, London

Hobhouse, A (1947) *Report of the National Parks Committee (England and Wales)*, HMSO, London

Holt, A (1995) 'The origins and early days of the Ramblers' Association', essay presented to the 60th anniversary meeting of the National Council of the Ramblers' Association, 8–9 April, Warwick University

Holt, A (1998) *Managing Conflict over Access to Open Country: A case study of the Peak District National Park*, The Ramblers' Association, London

Hopkins, H (1986) *The Long Affray: The poaching wars in Britain*, Papermac, London

House of Commons Environment Committee (1992) *Second Report, Coastal Zone Protection and Planning*, Volume 1 Report, House of Commons Paper 17-1, HMSO, London

House of Commons Environment Committee (1995) *The Environmental Impact of Leisure Activities*, Session 1994–5 Fourth Report, Volume 1, HMSO, London

Hunter, R L C (1987) *The Law of Arbitration in Scotland*, T and T Clark Ltd, Edinburgh

IAP2 (International Association for Public Participation) (2003) 'The IAP2 Public Participation Toolbox', website, www.iap2.org

Innes, J (1999) 'Evaluating consensus building', in Susskind, L, McKearnan, S and Thomas-Larmer, J (eds), *The Consensus Building Handbook: A comprehensive guide to reaching agreement*, Sage, Thousand Oaks, CA

ITAD Ltd, BMT Cordah Ltd (2002) *Assessment of the Effectiveness of Local Coastal Zone Management Partnerships as a Delivery Mechanism for Integrated Coastal Zone Management*, Scottish Executive, Edinburgh

Joad, C E M (1946) *The Untutored Townsman's Invasion of the Country*, quoted in Holt, A (1995)

Jordan, A G and Richardson, J J (1987) *British Politics and the Policy Process*, Allen and Unwin, London

Jordan, G and Maloney, W A (1997) *The Protest Business? Mobilizing campaign groups*, Manchester University Press, Manchester

Kolb, D M and Babbitt, E F (1995) 'Mediation practice on the home front: Implications for global conflict resolution', in Vasques, J A, Johnson, J T, Jaffe, S and Stamato, L (eds), *Beyond Confrontation: Learning conflict resolution in the post-Cold War era*, University of Michigan Press, Ann Arbor, MI

Kuiper, J (2004) Presentation to students of Wageningen University during study tour of Texel, 27–28 March

Kussey, E (1992) Interview with author, Washington, DC

Lach, D and Hixson, P (1996) 'Developing indicators to measure values and costs of public involvement activities', *Interact: The journal of public participation*, vol 2, no 1, 51–67

Liebmann, M (ed) (2000) *Mediation in Context*, Jessica Kingsley Publishers, London and Philadelphia

Lengkeek and Velden, K van der (2000) *Leefbaarheidsonderzoek Texel: een verkenning van leefbaarheidaspecten in relatie met toeristische ontwikkeling op Texel*, Wetenschapswinkel, publicatienummer 173, Wageningen, NL

Lesnick, M (1992) Interview with author, Keystone, CO

Liddle, A M and Gelsthorpe, L R (1994) *Crime Prevention and Inter-agency Co-operation*, HMSO, London

Lineberry, W P (ed) (1989) *Assessing Participatory Development: Rhetoric versus reality*, Westview Press, Boulder, CO

Lockley, R M (1947) *Letters from Skokholm*, J M Dent & Sons Ltd, London

Lothian Regional Council (1989) *Pentland Hills Regional Park: Subject local plan 1989–94*, Lothian Regional Council, Edinburgh

Lothian Regional Council (1995) *The Essential Character of the Hills: Descriptive survey of the landscape, wildlife and recreational character of the Regional Park*, Lothian Regional Council Planning Department, Edinburgh

Lowe, P (1994) 'Drawing the threads together', *Communities and the Countryside: Proceedings of the National Countryside Recreation Conference*, Countryside Recreation Network, University of Wales, Cardiff

Lowe, P and Goyder, J (1983) *Environmental Groups in Politics*, George Allen and Unwin, London

McCool, S F (1986) 'Experiencing management for quality: Implementing the limits of acceptable change', paper presented at conference on Science in the National Parks, July 13–19, Fort Collins, CO

McCormick, J (1991) *British Politics and the Environment*, Earthscan, London

McEwan, J (1977) *Who Owns Scotland?*, Polygon, Edinburgh

McGhee, J (1993) 'The open war', *Evening News*, Edinburgh, 5 March, 10

Mack, R W and Snyder, R C (1957) 'The analysis of social conflict: Towards an overview and synthesis', *Journal of Conflict Resolution*, vol 1, 212–248

Mackie, D (2004) Personal communication

McMahon, J (1998) *An Ecological Reserves System Inventory: Potential ecological reserves on Maine's existing public and private conservation lands*, report prepared for the Maine Forest Biodiversity Project, Maine State Planning Office, Augusta, ME

McOwan, R (1993) 'Open season', *Scotland on Sunday*, January 31

Madigan, D, McMahon, G, Susskind, L and Rolley, S (1990) *New Approaches to Resolving Local Public Disputes*, National Institute for Dispute Resolution, Washington, DC

Maine Department of Environmental Protection (2001) *Report on the Special Study of Air Quality in the West Paris, Maine Area*, Maine DEP, Bureau of Air Quality, Augusta, ME

Marks, J B, Johnson, E and Szanton, P L (1984) *Dispute Resolution in America: Processes in evolution*, National Institute for Dispute Resolution, Washington, DC

Mather, A (1996) *East Grampians and Lochnagar Visitor Survey 1995: Overview*, Scottish Natural Heritage, Aberdeen

Mediation UK (1995) *Training Manual in Community Mediation Skills*, Mediation UK, Bristol

Milliken, R (1990) 'Nudging owards equilibrium', *Habitat*, vol 7, no 3, 47–48

Ministry of Transport and Public Works (1989) *The Delta Project: Preserving the Environment and Securing Zeeland against Flooding*, Ministry of Transport and Public Works, 's-Gravenhage

Moore, C W (1986) *The Mediation Process: Practical strategies for resolving conflict*, Jossey-Bass, San Francisco, CA

Moore, C W (1996) *The Mediation Process: Practical Strategies for Resolving Conflict*, Second Edition, Jossey-Bass, San Francisco, CA

Moore, L (1998) *Beyond Basics: Facilitation challenges*, IAP2 Training Session, Tempe, AZ

Morecambe Bay Partnership (1996) *Morecambe Bay Strategy*, Morecambe Bay Partnership, Grange over Sands

Morecambe Bay Partnership (2001) *Baywatch Newsletter 5*, May

Morecambe Bay Partnership (2003) 'Who we are, what we do', www.morecambebay.org

Mosse, D (2001) 'People's knowledge, participation and patronage, operations and representation in rural development', in Cooke, B and Kothari, U (eds), *Participation: The new tyranny?*, Zed Books, London and New York

Murray, J S (1989) 'Designing a disputing system for central city and its schools', in Goldberg, S B, Brett, J M and Ury, W M (eds), *Dispute Systems Design: A special section of* Negotiation Journal, October, 365–372

Mutch, W (1977) 'The expansion of Turnhouse, Edinburgh Airport', in Sewell, W R D and Coppock, J T (eds), *Public Participation in Planning*, John Wiley, London

Natural Resources Council of Maine (2001) 'Sustainable forestry advocacy in Maine: Recent history and lessons learned', unpublished report to the Ittleson Foundation, NRCM, Augusta, ME

Nature Conservancy Council (1986) *Skomer Proposed Marine Nature Reserve: Consultative paper*, supplement, NCC, Peterborough

Newberger, E H (1975) 'A physician's perspective on the interdisciplinary management of child abuse and neglect', in Ebling, N and Hill, D (eds), *Child Abuse Intervention and Treatment*, Publishing Sciences Group, Acton, MA

Ozawa, C P and Susskind, L (1985) 'Mediating science-intensive policy disputes', *Journal of Policy Analysis and Management*, vol 5, no 1, 23–39

Palmer, M and Roberts, S (1998) *Dispute Processes: ADR and the primary forms of decision making*, Butterworth, London

Peak District Access Consultative Group (1994) *Report of the Peak District Access Consultative Group to the Peak Park Joint Planning Board*, PPJPB, Bakewell

Peak Park Joint Planning Board (1992) *Strategy for Access to Open Country: A balanced approach*, PPJPB, Bakewell

Peak Park Joint Planning Board (1995) Memorandum by the Peak Park Joint Planning Board, in House of Commons Environment Committee, *The Environmental Impact of Leisure Activities*, Session 1994–5 Fourth Report, Volume II, Minutes of Evidence, London, HMSO, pp70–91

Pentland Hills Regional Park (1999) *Integrated Management Strategy: Consultancy brief*, PHRP, Edinburgh

Pentland Hills Regional Park (2000) *Caring for the Hills: Integrated management strategy 2000–2005*, PHRP, Edinburgh

Pentland Hills Regional Park (2003) *Report for 2002–2003*, PHRP, Edinburgh

Pentland Hills Technical Group (1972) *Pentland Hills: Conservation and recreation*, Midlothian County Council, Edinburgh

Philipsen, J (2004) 'The Texel 2030 Project', presentation to students at Wageningen University, 29 March

Philipsen, J, Duim, V R van der and Sidaway, R (2003) 'Anticipating the future of Texel: Use and usefulness of prospective scenarios', unpublished paper, Wageningen University, Wageningen

Pondy, L R (1972) 'Organisational conflict: Concepts and models', in Thomas, J M and Bennis, W G (eds), *The Management of Conflict and Change*, Penguin Books, London

Pross, A P (1993) 'Canadian pressure groups: Talking chameleons', in Richardson, J J (ed), *Pressure Groups*, Oxford University Press, Oxford

Provincie Zeeland (1988) *Zeeland in Facts and Figures*, Provincie Zeeland, Middelburg

Pruitt, D G (1995) 'The psychology of social conflict and its relevance to international conflict', in Vasques, J A, Johnson, J T, Jaffe, S and Stamato, L (eds), *Beyond Confrontation: Learning conflict resolution in the post-Cold War era*, University of Michigan Press, Ann Arbor, MI

Ragan, J F (1983) 'Constraints on effective public participation', in Creighton, J, Delli Priscoli, J and Dunning, M (eds) *Public Involvement Techniques: A reader of ten years experience at the Institute for Water Resources*, IWR Research Report 82-R1, US Army Corps of Engineers, Fort Belvoir, VA

Raiffa, H (2002) 'Analyzing conflicts for diagnostic consultation and assessment', in *Environmental Conflict Resolution: The state of the field and its contribution to environmental decision making*, US Institute for Environmental Conflict Resolution and the Udall Center for Studies in Public Policy at the University of Arizona, Tucson, AZ

Ramblers' Association (2001a) 'Way ahead: Saving our paths', *The Rambler*, no 7, 10

Ramblers' Association (2001b) 'Freedom to roam', special supplement to *The Rambler*, no 7, Spring

Ramblers' Association (2004) *Walk: Magazine of the Ramblers' Association*, no 4

Ramirez, R (1999) 'Stakeholder analysis and conflict management', in Buckles, D (ed), *Cultivating Peace: Conflict and collaboration in natural resource management*, International Development Research Centre and World Bank Institute, Washington, DC

Reidel, C (2000) 'The political process of the Northern Forest Lands Study', in Klyza, C M and Trombulak, S C (eds), *The Future of the Northern Forest*, Middlebury College Press, Hanover, NH

Richardson, J J (ed) (1993) *Pressure Groups*, Oxford University Press, Oxford

Roberts, S (1979) *Order and Dispute*, Penguin, Harmondsworth

Rolde, N (2001) *The Interrupted Forest: A history of Maine's wildlands*, Tilbury House, Gardiner, Maine

Roscoe, G A and Weiss, J (1999) *Empowering Communities to Address Environmental Health: The Northern Oxford County Coalition – lessons learned*, US Environment Protection Agency, Boston, MA

Rothwell, P and Housden, S (1990) *Turning the Tide*, Royal Society for the Protection of Birds, Sandy

Rowley, C and Lewis, L (2003) *Thinking on the Edge*, Living Earth and Morecambe Bay Partnership, Kendal

Sandole, D J D (1993) 'Paradigms, theories and metaphors in conflict and conflict resolution: Coherence or confusion?', in Sandole, D J D and van der Merwe, H (eds), *Conflict Resolution Theory and Practice: Integration and application*, Manchester University Press, Manchester

Schatzow, S (1977) 'The influence of the public on federal environmental decision-making in Canada', in Sewell, W R D and Coppock, J T (eds), *Public Participation in Planning*, John Wiley, London

Schwietzer, M, Carnes, S A and Pelle, E B (1999) 'Evaluating public participation efforts', *Improving the Practice*, first quarter, 1–6

Scimecca, J A (1993) 'Theory and alternative dispute resolution: A contradiction in terms?', in Sandole, D J D and van der Merwe, H (eds), *Conflict Resolution Theory and Practice: Integration and application*, Manchester University Press, Manchester

Scott, P (1992) *Countryside Access in Europe*, Scottish Natural Heritage, Edinburgh

Scottish Executive (2001) *Draft Scottish Access Code*, Scottish Executive, Edinburgh

Senecah, S L and Sobel, G B (1998) *Environmental Mediation: Ethical issues for practitioners to ponder*, Presentation to International Association for Public Participation, Phoenix, AZ, 7 October

Sewell, W R D and Coppock, J T (1977) 'A perspective on public participation in planning', in Sewell, W R D and Coppock, J T (eds), *Public Participation in Planning*, John Wiley, London

Shoard, M (1980) *The Theft of the Countryside*, Temple Smith, London

Shoard, M (1999) *A Right to Roam*, Oxford University Press, Oxford

Sidaway, R (1979) 'Long distance routes in England and Wales – their history and pointers for future research', in Burch, W R (ed) *Long Distance Trails: The Appalachian Trail as a guide to future research and management needs*, School of Forestry and Environmental Studies, Yale University, New Haven, CT, pp11–27

Sidaway, R (1988) *Sport, Recreation and Nature Conservation*, Sports Council Study 32, The Sports Council and the Countryside Commission, London

Sidaway, R (1991a) 'Attitudes to the designation of the Pentland Hills Regional Park', unpublished report to Countryside Commission for Scotland

Sidaway, R (1991b) *Good Conservation Practice for Sport and Recreation*, Sports Council Study 37, Sports Council, London

Sidaway, R (1992) 'Outdoor recreation and conservation in Britain, USA and the Netherlands', paper presented at the Fourth Symposium on Society and Natural Resources, Madison, WI, May

Sidaway, R (1996) 'Outdoor recreation and nature conservation: Conflicts and their resolution', unpublished PhD thesis, University of Edinburgh

Sidaway, R (1998a) 'Access management by local consensus', *Rights of Way Law Review*, 13 January, 7–12

Sidaway, R (1998b) *Good Practice in Rural Development No 5: Consensus building*, Scottish National Rural Partnership, The Scottish Office, Edinburgh, www.scotland.gov.uk/cru/documents/gpg5-00.asp

Sidaway, R (1999a) 'A consensus clinic for rural development in Scotland', unpublished report to Rural Forum, Perth

Sidaway, R (1999b) 'Pentland Hills Regional Park: Integrated management strategy', submission to the regional park manager, Pentland Hills

Sidaway, R (2000) *Caring for the Hills: A consultation draft management strategy*, Pentland Hills Regional Park, Edinburgh

Sidaway, R (2002) 'Integrated management in the uplands: Is it possible to reach consensus?', in Burt, T P, Thompson, D B A and Warburton, J (eds), *The British Uplands: Dynamics of change*, Joint Nature Conservation Committee, Peterborough

Sidaway, R and van der Voet, H (1993) *Getting on Speaking Terms: Resolving conflicts between recreation and nature in coastal zone areas of the Netherlands, literature study and case study analysis*, Woerkgroep Recreatie Report No 26, Landbouwuniversiteit, Wageningen

Skomer Marine Reserve Steering Committee (1976) *Skomer Marine Reserve Management Plan*, The Committee, Haverfordwest

Slaikeu, K A (1989) 'Systems in the health care industry', in Goldberg, S B, Brett, J M and Ury, W M (eds), *Dispute Systems Design: A special section of* Negotiation Journal, October, 395–400

Slee, B and Snowdon, P (1997) *Good Practice in Rural Development No. 1: Effective partnership working*, Scottish Office Central Research Unit, Edinburgh

SLF and MCofS (Scottish Landowners' Federation and the Mountaineering Council of Scotland) (1984) *Access for Mountaineers and Hillwalkers*, SLF and MCofS, Edinburgh

SNH (Scottish Natural Heritage) (1992) *Enjoying the Countryside: A Consultation Paper on Access to the Countryside for Enjoyment and Understanding*, SNH, Edinburgh

SNH (Scottish Natural Heritage) (1994) *Enjoying the Countryside: A programme for action*, SNH, Edinburgh

SNH (Scottish Natural Heritage) (1996a) *Scotland's Hills and Mountains: A concordat on access*, SNH, Edinburgh

SNH (Scottish Natural Heritage) (1996b) *Care for the Hills: Guidance on the careful use of Scotland's hills and mountains for open-air recreation*, SNH, Edinburgh

Sobel, G (2002) 'Analyzing conflicts for diagnostic consultation and assessment', in *Environmental Conflict Resolution: The state of the field and its contribution to environmental decision making*, US Institute for Environmental Conflict Resolution and the Udall Center for Studies in Public Policy at the University of Arizona, Tucson, AZ

Sparrow, C (2003) 'Stunning breakthrough on "van Hoogstraten" footpath', *The Rambler*, Spring, 8–9

SPIDR (Society of Professionals in Dispute Resolution) (1997) *Best Practices for Government Agencies: Guidelines for using collaborative agreement-seeking processes*, SPIDR, Washington, DC

Steel, T (1965) *The Life and Death of St Kilda*, National Trust for Scotland, Edinburgh

Stephenson, T (1989) *Forbidden Land: The struggle for access to mountain and moorland*, Manchester University Press, Manchester

Stewart, G (1996) 'Standing ground', *The Scotsman*, November 7, 15

Stuurgroep Oosterschelde (1992) *Evaluatie Beleidsplan Oosterschelde*, Stuurgroep Oosterschelde, Middleburg, Netherlands

Susskind, L (1981) 'Citizen participation and consensus building in land use planning: A case study', in De Neufvile, J (ed), *The Land Use Policy Debate in the United States*, Plenum Press, New York

Susskind, L and Cruikshank, J (1987) *Breaking the Impasse: Consensual approaches to resolving public disputes*, Basic Books, New York

Susskind, L, Carpenter, S and McKearnan, S (1999) *The Consensus Building Handbook: A comprehensive guide to techniques and strategies*, Sage, Thousand Oaks, CA

Susskind, L, Levy, P F and Thomas-Larmer, J (2000) *Negotiating Environmental Agreements*, Island Press, Washington, DC

Symonds, H H (1933) *Walking in the Lake District*, W & R Chambers, London and Edinburgh

Talbot, A R (1983) *Settling Things: Six case studies in environmental mediation*, The Conservation Foundation and the Ford Foundation, Washington, DC

Taylor, H (2001) 'Insights into participation from critical management and labour process perspectives', in Cooke, B and Kothari, U (eds), *Participation: The new tyranny?*, Zed Books, London and New York

Tempel, R van der (2004) Presentation to students of Wageningen University during study tour of Texel, 27–28 March

Ter Haar, E (1979) 'Het beslissingproces' (The decision-making process), in van der Perk, J C and van der Voet, J L M (eds), *Stedelijke Recreatie (Urban Recreation)*, WIRO-rapport 7, Lelystad

Thompson, J M (1977) 'The London motorway plan', in Sewell, W R D and Coppock, J T (eds), *Public Participation in Planning*, John Wiley, London

Thurlings, J M G (1962) 'The dynamic function of conflict', lecture delivered to the Netherlands Sociological Society, 26 April

Tice, T (1990) Interview with author, Seattle, WA

Tonkin, E (2002) 'Analyzing conflicts for diagnostic consultation and assessment', in *Environmental Conflict Resolution: The state of the field and its contribution to environmental decision making*, US Institute for Environmental Conflict Resolution and the Udall Center for Studies in Public Policy at the University of Arizona, Tucson, AZ

Upper Deeside Access Trust (1999) *First Annual Report 1998–99*, UDAT, Tarland

Upper Deeside Access Trust (2002) *Fourth Annual Report 2001–2002*, UDAT, Tarland

Upper Deeside Access Trust (2003) *Fifth Annual Report 2002–2003*, UDAT, Tarland

Ury, W L, Brett, J M and Goldberg, S B (1988) *Getting Disputes Resolved: Designing systems to cut the costs of conflict*, Jossey-Bass, San Francisco, CA

Van Amstel, A R, Herngreen, G F W, Meyer, C S, Schoorl-Groen, E F and van de Veen, H E (1988) *Vijf visies op natuurbehoud en natuurontwikkeling; knelpunten en perspectieven van deze visies in het licht van de huidige maatschappelijke ontwikkelingen*, Publicatie RMNO, No 30, Rijswijk

Van Doorn, J A A (1966) 'Conflict in formal organisations', in de Reuck, A and Knight, J (eds), *Conflict in Society*, Churchill, London

Van Hoogstraten, N (1998) quoted in 'Sayings of the week', *The Observer*, 6 December

Van Til, J and Van Til, S B (1970) 'Citizen participation in social policy: The end of the cycle', *Social Problems*, 17, 313–323

Vidal, J (1998) 'A glorious summer for discontent', *The Guardian*, August 15, 11

Wack, P (1985) 'Scenarios: Shooting the rapids. How medium-term analysis illuminated the power of scenarios for Shell management', *Harvard Business Review*, vol 44, no 6, 139–150.

Walker, G B and Daniels, S E (1996) 'The Clinton administration, the Northwest Forest Conference and managing conflict: When talk and structure collide', *Society and Natural Resources*, vol 9, 77–91

Warburton, D (1997) *Participatory Action in the Countryside: A literature review*, Countryside Commission, Cheltenham

Warburton, D (1998) 'Participation in conservation: Grasping the nettle', *ECOS*, vol 19, no 2, 2–11

Watson, A (1991) *Critique of report 'Moorland Recreation and Wildlife in the Peak District' by Penny Anderson*, The Ramblers' Association, London

Weber, M (1948) *The Theory of Social and Economic Organisation*, The Free Press, Glencoe, IL

Weekly, M (1961) *A Memoir of Thomas Berwick Written by Himself*, Cresset Press, London

Widditsch, A (1983) 'Recommendations for effective public participation', in Creighton, J, Delli Priscoli, J and Dunning, M (eds), *Public Involvement Techniques: A reader of ten years experience at the Institute for Water Resources*, IWR Research Report 82-R1, US Army Corps of Engineers, Fort Belvoir, VA

Wightman, A (1996) *Who Owns Scotland?*, Canongate, Edinburgh

Wilcox, D (1994) *The Guide to Effective Participation*, Partnership Books, Brighton

Wilcox, D and Mackie, D (2003) 'Participation: How can we make it work?', presentation given at the Practical Approaches to Participation Workshop, Macaulay Institute, Aberdeen, 29–30 October

Williams, M. (2003) 'Why doesn't the government respond to the public?', *Participation Quarterly*, fall, 5–7

Wordsworth, W (1835) *Guide Through the District of the Lakes*, fifth edition (1970), Oxford University Press, London

World Bank (1996) *The World Bank Participation Sourcebook*, World Bank, Washington, DC, www.worldbank.org/wbi/sourcebook/sbpdf.htm

Young, M (1991) *An Inside Job: Policing and police culture in Britain*, Clarendon Press, Oxford

Young, S C (1993) *The Politics of the Environment*, Baseline Books, Manchester

Zondervan, D B (2002) 'Community mediation in the USA: Current developments', in Liebmann, M (ed), *Mediation in Context*, Jessica Kingsley Publishers, London and Philadelphia

Index

Page numbers in *italic* refer to Figures and Boxes.
Page numbers in **bold** denote glossary definitions.